ESSENCE OF BUDDHISM

ESSENCE OF BUDDHISM

Introduction and Edited by :

Dr. Vijay Kumar Mathur

BHARATIYA KALA PRAKASHAN
DELHI (INDIA)

First Edition : 2001

Published by **C.P. Gautam**
BHARATIYA KALA PRAKASHAN
3421-A, IInd Floor, Narang Colony, Tri Nagar,
Delhi-110035. Phone : 7153083

ISBN : 81-86050-72-8

Laser Type Setting by
A-ONEGRAPHICS
X-4, Gali-2, Brahmapuri, Delhi-110053
Phone : 218 3470

Print at
Santosh Offset, Delhi

CONTENTS

PREFACE

The present work is a compendium of articles on Buddhism by scholars and intellectuals. It presents a comprehensive view of all aspects of Buddhism. The personality of Buddha embodying deep conpassionate nature has enchanted me all the time. My interest in Buddhism was further aroused in 1997 when National Museum, New Delhi sent the holy relics of Lord Buddha to Thailand for exposition and I was fortunate to be deputed to escort the relics from Thailand to India. I was thrilled when I held the casket containing relics in my both hands and this was beyond my imagination. During my month long stay at Puttomonthan temple at Bangkok, I came into contact with a large number of intellectuals and *Bhikṣus* and our talk centered round the various aspects of Buddhism such as cultivation of moral values, on self—restraint and contentment, on truthfulness and benevolence and Masters great message of love and sympathy for all beings. This actuated me to take up this work. I have incorporated the essence of discussions that I had with them. My grateful thanks to my father Dr. N.L. Mathur whose constant guidance made it possible for me to give the work its present form. My special thanks are also due to Dr. Daljeet Keeper (Painting), National Museum for encouraging me to complete the work.

My thanks are also due to C.P. Gautam of Bharatitya Kala Prakashan for having completed the work so nicely and in such a short time.

Delhi, 4.7.2001

Dr. V.K. Mathur

ABBREVIATIONS

Aṅg. N.	Aṅguttara-Nikāya
Ann. Mus. Guimet	Annales du Musée Guimet
Āpast.	Aphorisms on the Sacred Law of the Hindus
Arch. Surv.	Archaeological Survey
Avad. Kalp.	Avadāna-Kalpalatā
Avad. Śat.	Avadāna-Śataka
Aṣṭ. P. Pāram.	Aṣṭasāhasrika-Prajñā-Pāramitā
Bhadrak.	Extracts from the Bhadrakalpāvadāna
Bibl. Ind.	Bibliotheva Indica
Badhiv.	Mahā-Bodhi-Vaṃsa
Brahma-S.	Vedāntadarśana with the Commentary of Śaṅkara and the Tīkā of Govindānanda
Buddhac.	The Buddha Carita of Aśvaghoṣa
Buddhav.	Buddhavaṃsa
Bull. Rel. de l'Inde	Bulletin des Religions de l'Inde
Cariyā-P.	Cariyā-Piṭaka
Corp. Inscr.	Corpur Inscriptionum Indicaerum
Dharma-S.	Dharma-Saṃgraha
Dhātuk. P.	Dhātukathā Prakaraṇa and its Commentary
Dhp.	Dhammapada

Dh. Saṅgaṇi	Dhamma-Saṅgaṇi
Dīgha-N.	Dīgha-Nikāya
Dīpav.	Dīpavaṁsa
Divy.	Divyavadāna
DMG.	Zeitschrift der Deutschen Morgenlādischen Gesellschaft
Ep. Ind.	Epigraphia Indica
Gautama Dh.	Gautama Dharmaśāstram
GGA.	Göttinger Gelehrte Anzeigen
Ind. Ant.	India Antiquary
Inscr. in Ceylon	Ancient Inscriptions in Ceylon
JA.	Journal Asiatique
JASB.	Journal of the Asiatic Society of Bengal
Jāt.	The Jātaka together with its commentary
Jāt. Mālā	Jātaka-Mālā
JBB. RAS.	Journal of the Bombay Branch of the Royal Asiatic Society
JPTS.	Journal of the Pali Text Society
JRAS.	Journal of the Royal Asiatic Society of Great Britain and Ireland
Kār. V.	Kāraṇḍa-Vyūha.
Kathāv. P.A.	Kathāvatthu-ppakaraṇa-Aṭṭhakathā
Lal.V.	Lalita-Vistara
Mahāv.	Mahāvaṃsa
Majjh. N.	Majjhima-Nikāya
Manu.	Manu-Saṃhitā

Mhv.	Le Mahāvastu
Mil. P.	Milinda-Pañho
MV.	Mahāvagga
Par. Dīp.	Paramattha Dīpanī
Peta-V.	Peta-Vatthu
Pugg. P.	Puggala-Paññatti
Rec.	A Record of Biddhist Kingdoms
Rev. Hist. Re.	Revue de l'Histoire des Religions
Saddh. Paṇḍ.	Saddharma-Puṇḍarīka
Saddh.S.	Saddamma-Saṃgaha
Sam. Pās.	Samanta-Pāsādikā
Saṃy. N.	Saṃyutta-Nilkāya
Sarvad. Saṅg.	Sarvadarśana Saṅgrahaa
Sāsanav.	Sāsanavamsa and Sāsanavaṃsa
SBE.	Sacred Book of the East
S. Nip.	Sutta-Nipāta
Sum. Vil.	Sumaṅgala-Vilāsinī
S. Vibh.	Sutta-Vibhaṅga
Tār.	Tāranātha's Gesehichte des Buddhismus in indien, aus dem Tibetischen übersetzt von
Therag.	Theragāthā
Therīg.	Therīgāthā
Ud.	Udāna
Versl. Meded. K. Akad.	Verslagen en Mededelingen der Koninklijke Akademie
Vim. V.	Vimāna-Vatthu
Vis. M.	Visuddhi-Magga

Voy.	Voyages des Pélerins Buddhistes
Vyu.	Mahāvyutpatti
Yājñav.	Yājñavalkya-Dharmaśāstram
Yoga-S.	Pātañjala-darśanam

INTRODUCTION

Buddhism, one of the dominant religions of the world, was founded by Buddha or Gautama Siddhartha. He was born in 563 B.C. in the Lumbini gardens at a short distance from Kapilavastu. He was the son of the Sakya chief of Kashatriya caste who ruled in Kapilavastu. From his childhood, he showed signs of contemplative mind and deep compassionate nature. At the age of sixteen, the king married him to a beautiful and gentle princess Yasodhara by name and surrounded him with the choicest material of luxury. One day he met in turn an old man, a sick person and a corpse. His eyes were then opened and he began to realise that the world was a place of sorrow and toil, cruelty and disease. Distressed, he decided to renounce his worldly life in order to find a path out from the misery and suffering of life and to attain a state of assurance and peace. Just then a son was born to him and he called him Rahula. On full moon night of May, in his twenty-ninth year, he stole out of his palace, leaving his wife and his new born son. Mounting his favourite horse Kanthaka, he rode out in quest of truth. This is called the 'Great Renunciation'. For some time, he lived at Gaya and tried to find salvation by practising penances and austerities but to no purpose. After prolonged meditation, he found illumination while sitting under a pipal tree at Bodh Gaya. Hastening to Varanasi, he gave his first sermon in Deer Park and this is commemorated as 'the setting in motion the wheel of law'. The rest of his life was spent in spreading the knowledge of his doctrines. At the age of eighty, in the town of Kusinagara he passed away. After death, his body was cremated and the ashes were distributed among his followers and enshrined in stupas-dome shaped burial mounds-in various parts of the country.

Buddha emerged as the greatest religious teacher of the world. His teaching served as a model for the disciples to immitate and follow. He did not proclaim himself a savior who will take upon himself the sins of those who follow him. Buddha's dignified bearing, high intellectual endowments, his penetrating glance, his oratorial power, the firmness of his convictions, his gentleness, kindness and liberality, and the attractiveness of his character all testify to his greatness. In him united truest princely qualities with the intelligence of sage and the passionate devotion of one who had spiritual revelation. Though born of an aristocratic and ruling class, Buddha lived the life of an ordinary man, discarding the narrow distinction of caste, rank and wealth. He never professed to be anything more than a man. His teaching was perfect and based all his reasoning on the fact of man's existence, and developed his practical philosophy by the observation and minute study of human nature. His aim was to rescue mankind from the fetters of passion and to convince them of an ideal higher than mere worldly good.

Buddha had two distinct characters. In the first and earliest character, he was the typical *yogi,* the great teacher who gained power by self-suppression and by the conquest of the passions. In his second, he was the great friend of the common people, advocating universal equality, brotherhood and universal compassion for all forms of animal life. While delivering his first sermon at the deer park at Sarnath which he gave to his five disciples, Buddha had no idea of teaching any philosophical system, his main purpose being to impart to the people at large the art of living, free from sorrows and delusions of all kinds. He gave the essential doctrines of the pure religion divested from extraneous elements. He accepted the world as he found it and addressed himself, in the most earnest manner, to the task of elucidating the causes of man's unhappiness and pointing out the practical means of attaining the blissfulness of *Nirvāṇa* or deliverance from sorrow.

According to Buddha, the world is full of miseries, sufferings and sorrows. 'Birth is suffering, old age is suffering, disease is suffering, death is suffering, association with the unpleasant is suffering, separation from the pleasant is suffering and not to get what one wants is suffering'. The term suffering included all evil and dissatisfaction. The second great truth is that the cause of misery is Trishna, the grasping desire to live for self enjoyment. Sensations *(Vedana)* begotten by the surrounding world, create the illusion of a separate self. The illusory self manifests its activity in things for selfish enjoyment which entangles man in pain and suffering. The third great truth is that emancipation from misery *(duhkha nirodho)* is possible by abandoning selfish craving. When all selfish cravings are destroyed, there is necessarily an end of suffering. The fourth great truth is that the Noble Eightfold Path is the means by which man can get rid of all selfish cravings and attain perfect freedom from suffering. That is right beliefs, right aspirations, right speech, right conduct, right mode of livehood, right effort, right mindedness, and right rapture.

Under right views, Buddha gave prominence to a stern examination of all views and ideas. We are, as we think and if we reflect wrongly, we act wrongly. To remove wrong views, right knowledge is necessary. Right aspiration, is a product of right views. Since base cravings are to be expelled, other desires are to be encouraged, like love of service to others, desires to do and seek justice, and the like. It will thus be seen, that Buddha never taught an annihilation of all desires, but merely the necessity for a change of desire. In other words, giving up the idea of the separateness of the individuality of the ego, one has to work for the good of the whole world. In the Vajradhvaja Sutta, Buddha has stated "I must bear the burden of all creatures". This is in full accord, with the theory of *Sanyasa* where a man gives up worldly life, not because he is afraid of it, but because, his love is so all absorbing that it can not be limited to one family.

Right aspirations produce right speech, right conduct and right mode of livelihood. Right speech is defined by Buddha as "to abstain from falsehood, to abstain from harsh language, and to abstain from frivolous talk". Right action is unselfish action, and not mere ceremonialism. Buddhism insists on purity of motives, and humility in life. Right conduct leads to right modes of livelihood. Right effort is necessary, because Buddha could not tolerate, sentimental intentions, and slovenly or half hearted applications. One has to inhibit the bad instincts, and to encourage the good ones in him. Right effort is associated with right thinking. All these produce the right rapture or the goal of life. Buddha avoided the extreme nature of Brahmanism, based on pleasure loving and that of Jainism based on self-mortification. In fact, Buddha teachings were based on pure and disciplined way of life in which stress was laid on morality.

Buddha formulated in so many words the existence of the theory of *karma*. When a persecuted disciple came to him, he consoled him, with the words "suffer it be so, oh *Arhat*, you are now feeling results of your *karma,* that might have cost you centuries of suffering in purgatory." In the Milinda Panha, Nagasena says "It is through a difference in their Karma, that men are not all alike. But some are long lived, some short lived, some healthy, and some sickly, some handsome and some ugly, some powerful and some weak, some rich and some poor, some of high degree, and some of low degree, some wise and some foolish". The theory of *Karma,* is much older than Buddhism, though, it was in Buddhistic philosophy only, that it got formulated for the first time, with some precision and logical definiteness. Our past produces our present, and our present, conditioned by our actions, has got the capacity to lay out the pattern of our own future existence.

A very subtle theory about the process of death and rebirth, or as it is technically called *Patisandhi* is well brought out in Buddhaghosha's Visuddhi Magga, from which the following extract is taken :—'For when in any existence, one arrives at the gate of death, either in the natural course of things or through violence; and when by a concourse of intolerable, death dealing pains, all the members, both great and small, are loosened and wrenched apart in every joint and ligament; and the body, like a green palm-leaf exposed to the sun dries up by degrees; and the eyesight and other senses fail, and the power of feeling and the power of thinking and vitality are making the last stand in heart then consciousness residing in that last refuge, the heart continues to exist by virture of *karma* otherwise called the predisposition. This *karma,* however, still retains something of what it depends on, and consists of such former deeds as were weighty, much practised, and are now close at hand; or else, this *karma* creates a reflection of itself, or the new mode of life now entered upon, and it is with this as its object, that consciousness exists.

Now, while conciousness still subsists, in as much as desire and ignorance have not been abandoned, and the end of the evil of the object is hidden by that ignorance, desire inclines the conciousness to the object; and the *karma* that sprang up along with the conciousness, imples it towards the object. The consciousness being in its series, this inclination towards the objects by desire and impelled towards it by *karma* like a man who swings himself over a ditch by means of a rope hanging from a tree on the higher bank, quits its first resting place, and continues to subsist in dependence on objects of sense and other things and either does or does not alight on another resting place created by *Karma.* Here the former consciousness from its passing out of existence, is called rebirth. But it is to be understood, that this latter consciousness did not come to the present existence from the previous one, and also that it is only to causes contained in the old existence namely *karma* or predisposition, to inclination....that its present appearance is due. *Karma* thus does not affect the liberated soul, or the *Arhat.* It produces results, only when an action is based on craving or desire. Hence, even the liberated man, has to work hard ceaselessly, for the good of the world, since the result of the *Karma,* will not affect him. This is the theory of *Karma* and Buddhism being a practical religion, shows just enough that is necessary for man, to order his conduct and actions, on correct lines and does not attempt to speculate further.

Buddha originally did not found any new religion. Later, he organized a monastic order called the *Sangha* to carry his teachings to the different corners of the country. In the beginnig, this *Sangha* was open to men only, but later on, the Master hesitatingly admitted even women into the order. In course of time a new set of rules was evolved for the Buddhists and thus eventually Budhism became a separate religion. Buddha during his life time did not write any treatise containing his teachings. When he died, his followers called a general council *(Saṇgiti)* of the Masters chief disciples at

Rajagriha to compile the teachings of the Lord. Five hundred monks led by Mahakashyapa then gathered at the Satapanni cave near Rajagriha. The council was held under the auspices of king Ajatsatru. Buddha's teachings were collected and compiled in three books called Tripitaka or three baskets. These are Vinaya Pitaka, Sutta Pitaka, and Abhidamma Pitaka. These are all in Pali language. The Vinaya Pitaka contains the rules relating to the monastic system. The Sutta Pitaka contains the stories and parables as told by the Buddha. The Abhidamma Pitaka deals with higher matters of religion, the philosophical aspect of Buddhism. A century after the passing away of the Master, the second Buddhist council was held. It was convened at Vaisali, during the reign of Kalasoka, a descendant of Ajatsatru. Some of the monks wanted relaxation in monastic life and in about 376 B.C., a representative meeting of the monks was held at Vaisali. Ten points were raised which contained proposals of relaxing the monastic discipline. The third Buddhist council was called by Asoka, the great Mauryan emperor, probably in 240 B.C. It met at Pataliputra and was presided over by Tissa Moggaliputa, the most learned monk of his time. The main achievement of this council was that internal difference of the monks were patched up and great stress was laid on purity and service. The fourth Buddhist Council was called by Kanishka at Kundalvana in Kashmir. It was prsided over by Asvaghosha and Vasumitra. By this time the Buddhist Sangha had been divided into two definite sects, the Mahāyāna and the Hīnayāna. The council failed to bridge the gulf between the two. Mahayanism believed in the divinity of the Buddha, in efficacy of prayer, faith and devotion. Instead of being looked upon as a great teacher to be revered and followed, the Buddha was deified and worshipped as a living savior. Boddhisattva, the future Buddha and the embodiment of compassion also became the object of worship. It infused a new life in the old Buddhism. The Hīnayāna, however stuck to the primitive form and was unprogressive.

The ultimate aim of the scheme of training laid down by the Buddha is the attainment of Nirvāṇa. It corresponds to what in other religions is called salvation. In the Upanisads it is spoken of as *Moksha*. It consists in the destruction or cessation of craving *(Tanha)* and other defilements of the mind, followed by the positive experience of a state of unalloyed bliss. An *arhat* can attain it during his life-time and there is no rebirth for him after the death of his present body. Some writers have wrongly drawn the conclusion that there is complete annihilation of the individual after the attainment of *nirvāṇa.* According to Dr. Rhys Davids, *nirvāṇa* is a state of blissful repose experienced by an *arhat,* before his total annihilation aftrer death. That this view is wrong is proved by a number of considerations. In one of the discourses, Gautama Buddha says, "a monk whose mind is thus released cannot be followed and tracked out even by the gods, including Indra, Brahman and Prajapati, so that they could say, 'there rests the consciousness of a released person and why ? Even in this actual life, monks, I say, that the released person is not to be thoroughly known. Though I thus say and thus preach, some ascetics and Brahmanas assume wrongly, baselessly, falsely and groundlessly, saying that the ascetic Gautama is a nihilist and preaches the annihilation, destruciton and non-existence of an existent being. This is what I am not and do not affirm." What Buddha measns to say is that after release or *nirvāṇa,* the *arhat* no longer retains his separate individuality which may be pointed out as distinct entity. He is merged completely in the ultimate reality whatever it may be. It is akin to the Upanisadic doctrine that the individual soul after attainment of *mokṣa,* is reabsorbed in the universal self as a wave is merged again in the ocean from which it takes its rise. Though the separate individuality is lost, it does not for that reason become non-existent. This would become further apparent from the following dialogue, which took place between king Prasenjit of Kosala and the renowned nun Khema, some time after the death of Gautma Buddha.

"Venerable lady" asked the king, "does the Exalted one exist after death?"

"The Exalted one, O great king, did not declare, that he exists after death."

"Then does it means that the Exalted one does not exist after death."

"The Exalted one did not declare either, that the Perfect one did not exist after death."

As this answer puzzled the king, the venerable Khema, in order to make her meaning clear, said that just as the water of the ocean is vast and immeasurable, deep and unfathomable, and cannot be measured by human measuring vessels, similarly the Perfect one has gone to a state which is profound and immeasurable like the ocean. Such being the case, no positive statement can be made about the perfect one. "The deep nature of the Tathagata cannot be fathomed, even as the sands of the Ganga or the water-drops in the ocean cannot be reckoned."

It is also worth knowing, that just as in the Upaniṣadas, a distinction is made between final release *(mokṣa)* and attainment of heaven, the Buddha similarly speaks to his followers of the difference between the permanently blissful condition of *nirvāṇa* and the temporary though happy sojourn in the various formless heavens *(Arupa Loka).* As in the

Upanisads, so in Buddshism, *nirvāṇa* is far superior to the felicity of mere heavenly existence. There is very little to doubt that the conception of *nirvāṇa* is very much akin to the conception of *mokṣa* as contained in the Upanisads.

Nirvāṇa is a positive state of consciousness ,though it is indescribable in logical categories. Referring to the various stages of spiritual realization, Anurudhha, a disciple of the Buddha, says in one of the dialogues in Majjhima Nikāya that he and his fellow disciples have attained the highest state of knowledge and insight beyond which they could not think of any other higher or more excellent state of realization. On hearing this, the Buddha expressed satisfaction at the spiritual achievement of his disciples. *nirvāṇa* is thus the highest wisdom, insight and blissfulness. Speaking of this experience in one of the dialogues, the Buddha says, "There is, O monks, a stage in which there is neither earth nor water, neither fire nor air, neither infinity of space nor infinity of consciousness, neither nothings nor non-perception, neither this world nor that world, neither sun nor moon." This idea is further made clear in the following words. "In that stage there is neither coming nor going, nor staying nor passing away, neither is this world nor that caught between them. It is indeed the end of sorrow," The idea meant to be conveyed by this enigmatic mode of speech is that the experience of *nirvāṇa* lies in quite a different dimension, and so it is not possible to describe it in the ordinary terms.

An ordinary person has to pass though a large number of births and deaths before he qualifies himself for *nirvāṇa* or final release. It is only in the case of an *arhat* who has attained *nirvāṇic* conciousness, that a question is oftern asked in Buddhist works whether after death an *arhat* would be completely annihilated or he would continue to exist in some form. The Buddha's point of view like that of the Upanisads is that after, the attainment of *nirvāṇa* the saint does not cease to exists, but becomes unfathomable and immeasurable like the ocean, because now he has become one with the deep ocean and partakes of its vastness and unfathomableness.

At a very early stage, Buddha enjoined upon his disciples the task of preaching the noble doctrine for the benefit of all people. "Go ye forth, O Bhiksus, for the gain of the many, for the welfare of the many, in compassion for the world, proclaim the glorious doctrine, preach ye a life of holiness, perfect and pure." Such was the command of the Buddha, and his loyal Bhiksus went in all directions, carrying the message of the Master to the doors of the common people. Thus from the very inception Buddhism was a missionary religion. Buddhism had a great pan-human appeal. It was this spirit of human brotherhood, which helped it to spread through out the country, and even among the invading foreigners. Most of them were absorbed into Buddhism. This, in turn, led to the rapid spread of Buddhism through out Central Asia.

The spread of Buddhism within the county as well as in foreign land was greatly helped by two mighty kings of India, Asoka and Kanishka, one after the other. Asoka sent religioius missions to a number of countries, the most important mission being the one which he deputed to Ceylon under the leadership of his son, Mahendra, in the 3th century B.C. Later on, Buddhism spread to Burma, Siam and other countries of South East Asia. The form of Buddhism, which was introduced into these countries, was to formulate a negative system, and hence, the *Madhyamikas* are sometimes also called *'sarva vainasikas'* or nihilists.

It is now generally accepted, that the four schools of Buddhistic thought, shaped themselves, roughly into their present form, sometimes after the period of Kanishka.

Kanishka held a council of Kashmir, where a great commentary on the Ahidharma, called the Vibhashika, was written, and people who accepted this commentary called Vibhasika, came to be known as Vaibhashikas. The original *Vibhasha*, in Sanskrit is now lost, though there are Chinese translations of it.

The exact period, when these great schools of thought, came to be established is not known but from the evidence available, it would appear, that round about the 1st or 2nd century A.D. these assumed the present form they now hold. The Vaibhashikas, came into prominence about three centuries after the time of Buddha, and the *Sautrantikas* about a century later. Asanga, the founder of Yogachara schools, is generally attributed to the 3rd century A.D., while Acharya Nagarjuna, the founder of Madhyamika schools, also flourished round about the same age, on the Nagarjunakonda. It is thus clear, that speculative thinking in Buddhism, developed sometime during the beginning of the Christian era, and its origin may perhaps be traced to one or two centuries earlier also.

Buddhism was from the first, both ethic and religion, for the Founder, having a great mystical experience, believed that by way of moral living, man can arrive at transcendental rapture. Men are of various temperaments and abilities; to each he adapted his teaching. To those ready for the heights of mysticism he offered The Eightfold Path-which begins in right ideas, and goes on to ecstatic and rapt contemplation. To others he offered a way of part-time devotion:to morality of a simple kind, and to the occasional keeping of holy days and mild asceticism.

What the new teacher had to say was already in germ in the Upanishads. He insisted that the man of pure life, was on the road to salvation from rebirth. He held out the promise of rebirth in a heavenly world to the good house-holder, who could not detach himself from the duties of his station. He offered to all moral ideals suited to their attainments and position. *Tṛṣṇā*-Desire-was the great enemy, and detachment being the spirit in which it would be overcome. But he might more of Ahimsa, and allowed no animals sacrifices, and he laid great emphasis on compassion, karuṇā, and on love.

To his own Kashtriyas he says 'Be kind : oppress none. All love their lives.'

To priests he says, 'Better is the life of morality than many sacrifices. He is the true Brahmin who leads a pure life.'

To the ascetic he says, 'Better than matted hair and ashes are truth and discipline.'

He condemns austerity, and to all alike he offers a sane Middle Path, and preaches it in the vernacular and in homely parables.

It was only from the 4th century onwards that the new religion began to spread amongst the Chinese people. The period from 618 to 907 A.D. was the period of its greatest popularity in China. The success of Buddhism was largely due to the efforts of Kumara Jiva in the 4th and 5th centuries A.D.

Tibet came into contact with Buddhism in the 7th century, through the marriage of its king Srong-Tasn-Gampo with two Chinese princesses of Buddhist faith. A number of scholars went from India to Tibet and translated many Buddhist works into Tibetan. A new wave of Buddhism spread to Tibet across the Himalayan barrier. By the 9th to 10th centuries, the whole of Tibet was converted to Buddhism. In 372 A.D., Buddhism reached Korea from China. From China it was intoduced to Japan in 552 A.D.

Buddhism has got four great schools of thought viz.,

The Vaibhashika, the Sauatrantika, the Yogachara, and the Madhyamika systems of thought. Buddha himself, was a practical path finder, who insisted upon the rigorous use of logic and reasoning, in trying to explain metaphysical phenomenon he never preached blind faith to his followers, but always insisted, that, they should give close consideratoin to all the aspects, that were presented before them, and arrive at a correct conclusion of their own. Moreover, Buddha himself was enigmatic, about certain basic factors of philosophy, like the existence or non-existence of the soul, or the permanence of the world etc.

During the life time of Buddha, all these difference and schisms, did not sprout forth, since Buddha's towering personality, so over-whelmed all his disciples, that they did not attempt to differentiate between his teachings. But sometimes after the demise of Buddha, at a period of time, when the disciples were no longer intimate with the adóring personality of the master, these smaller and minor points of difference of opinion, came to be exaggerated, and different thinkers, laid down their own lines of thought, with the result that several schools of thought sprung up in Buddhism itself.

At the first great council in Vaishali itself, there were doctrinal disputes, which led to the great meeting called 'Mahasangha' of the seceders, who later split themselves into eight different schools of thought. Thus, at the time of the Vaishali council itself, the Theravadins or the orthodox ascetics of Buddhism, and the Mahsanghikas or the seceders, differed about doctrinal points. While the Mahāsaṅghikas or the seceders, developed eight different councils,, the Theravadins also spilt up into a number of councils, do not refer to all these sub-sects, but Buddhism, and Buddhist systems of thought, are associated only with four great schools, of which two belong to the Hīnayāna, or the older sect, and the two to the Mahāyāna or the newer sect.

The Hīnayāna schools are the Vaibhashikas and the Sautrantikas, according to whom, everything exists, only in space and time, and there is a self-existent universe. The Mahāyāna schools are the Yogacharas and the Madhyamikas. The Yogacharas hold, that, mental thinking is creative, and is the ultimate principle. The conflagration, in a world, is to be extinguished by the water of Truth. Face life as it is, sorrowful, transient, and you will no longer crave for it. Of the doctrine of Causality is the keynote of the Buddhist metaphysics, the doctrine of *Anatta* is the unique thing in its psychology. And both doctrines are applied with an ethical purpose . He seeks to get rid of the 'ego' of egoism. The self is unreal because it is a compound. Analyse it and you will see that it is a stream of consciousness made up of elements of sensation, of cognition, of volition; and you will realize that there is no 'soul' in the ordinary sense of separate entity or substance.

Out of the seeming pessimism of this philosophy of transiency, emerges a sane optimism, as is beginning to be recognized by Western writers only today. Buddhism insists on *dukkha,* sorrows, inorder that it may show men the way to *sukha,* happiness : 'One thing only do I teach, O monks-sorrow and the uprooting of sorrow.' Over against the world of birth and death, of *Samsara,* it sets the unchanging calm of *Nibbana,* Nirvāṇa beyond joy and sorrow. All religions, as William James has pointed out, are alike in having as their basis (1) an uneasiness, and (2) its solution. Gautama has his own solution to offer. He is a physician; and having diagnosed the disease he goes on te prescribe for its cure.

The secret of his success is, in a word, his love. He left a group of men and women, filled with devotion to his person and faith in his teaching. His magnetism had such, that men were converted in many cases long before their reasons could be satisfied, and such was his insight into human hearts, that we find him adapting his method, with so sure a touch, as to win the title 'Physician'. They found in him one who was intensely interested in them, never impatient. The poor sweeper Sunita, who had seen him moving serene and majestic amongst kings and nobles, adored the courtesy with which he smiled as he greeted him, and to the humblest he gave his best, sometimes discerning beneath rags and sores a mind ready "as a clean spotless robe for the dye." And only waiting for the right word to be numbered among the saints. Men respected the fearless teacher, who redefined so many of their religious and social catchwords, and who set up a new religious democracy, in which worth rather than birth was the standard, and in which liberty was sanely tempered and controlled by law.

The introducation of Tantric modes of worship was a potent cause of the degradation of Buddhism. The Tantric worship has some good features, but there is, also in Tantraism, an element which had a most debasing influence on immature minds. It would not be wrong to suggest that the total harm wrought by the debasing Tantric practices in, on the whole, greater than any good might have accrued from the Tantric modes of worship.

Under the influence of Tantraism, the Bodhisattva came to be represented as accompained by female deities. The great Bodhi-Sattva Avalokitesvara had Tara as the female counter-part and the bliss of *nirvāṇa* came to be associated with the union of the female deity with the Buddha or the Bodhi Sattva, and so the idea gained, ground, that a similar bliss can be obtained in this world by performing certain religious rites in which sex-union played an important part. Giving vent to passion was regarded as a method for overcoming passion. So, in this period, we find the Bhiksus leading, on the whole, not very reputable lives. They lost their credit with the common people who turned away from the religion of which those *Bhiksus* were the representatives. From the 7th century onwards Buddhism in Bihar and western Bengal had come very much under the spell of Trantric Hinduism.

Buddhism was not an institutional religion in the accepted sense of the word. The Buddha brought about radical reforms in religious conception, but he did not bring about any marked change in the social and religious customs of the people. He exhorted the people to lead pure lives, but other-wise they followed, without any interference, the social customs to which they had been born. The lay-followers of Buddha revered him as a great teacher, but they were practically Hindus in their social and religious observances. Their birth, death, marriage and other ceremonies continued to be performed as before. All these factors taken together led to the absorption of the erstwhile followers of Buddhism into the bosom of Hinduism. While Buddhism as a distinct creed disappeared from India, all its great points were assimilated by Hinduism. It can therefore be reasonably maintained that Buddhism lives in present-day Hinduism, which is, in many respects, on account of Buddhist influences, different from what it was before the advent of Buddhism.

In India, various factors led to the decline of Buddhism in course of time. Of these factors, fall in the academic and moral standards of the members of the Buddhist Sangha was an important one. They became self-centered and forgot their duty towards the spiritual and moral welfare of the people around them. The objective of social service and altruism, placed before them by the Buddha was completely lost sight of. In course of time even the zeal for personal perfection through spiritual exercises and philosophical studies abated. Formerly the monasteries were great centers of learning, but it seems that about the time when Sankara came into the field i.e. in the 7th and 8th centuries, these Buddhist centers did not turn out great scholars and religious disputants who could hold their own against the attacks of non-Buddhist dialecticians. That was the reason why Sankara and Kumarilla Bhatta could easily vanquish the Buddhists in public discussions. It is said, "in those days, defeats in controversis were serious events in the life of the Indians, bringing about the rise and fall of a religion or a sect or teacher." It is therefore probable, that the vigorous public campaign which Śaṅkara carried on against Buddhism had a great deal to do in undermining its prestige and influence amongst the people, for banishing Buddhism from India.

The final cause which led to its disappearance, from India, was the wholesale destruction of the monasteries and the Buddhist monks brought about by the Muslim conquerors. In 1193, a general of Kutbuddin seized the capital of Bihar with a mere handful of men, and massacred all the monks living in its monasteries. Similarly these conquerors destroyed the religious places of the Buddhists at Sarnath and other places. "Whereas Hinduism was spread over the country. Buddhism was concentrated in the great monasteries, and when these were destroyed, there remained nothing outside them, capable of withstanding either the violence of the Muslims or the assimilating influence of the Brahmans. Hence Buddhism suffered far more from therse invasions than Hinduism."

It is said that Mukunda Deva who ruled Orrisa in the 16th century and was finally defeated by the Mohammadens, was a Buddhist. Barring a few traces which can still be found in some parts of Orissa this great religion of Buddha has now practically become extinct in the land of its origin.

CHAPTER-I

THE LIFE AND TEACHINGS OF THE BUDDHA

—Susant De Alwish

The usefulness of all religions in the world today, and the urgent necessity for the peoples of this world to live a spiritual way of life cannot be over emphasized. We are living in a period of history when the whole of mankind is on the brink of total annihilation, at a time when certain Heads of States are preparing themselves and gearing their countries to a war-footing owing to fear, distrust and hatred of other countries. If we are to create the atmosphere of total peace, not merely the absence of war but the conditions under which we can co-exist in the understanding that all 'isms' have the comman objective of the welfare of mankind, we should strive to create the defences of peace in the very minds of these statesmen. The only way by which we can establish these bastions of peace is by spiritual upliftment of ourselves and our leaders which in turn can only be done through religion.

'Of all the teachers in the world the Buddha was one who taught us most to be self-reliant, who freed us not only from the bondages of our fasle values but from dependence on the invisible being or beings called God or Gods. He invited every one into a state of freedom which he called Nirvāṇa. All must attain it one day and that attainment is a complete fulfilment of man,' said Swami Vivekananda speaking about the Buddha.

The late and revered Jawaharlal Nehru in his literary

masterpiece, *The Discovery of India,* has described the Buddha in meditation in his inimitable style :

> "Seated on the lotus flower, calm and impassive, above passion and desire, beyond the storm and strife of the world, so far away he seems, out of reach, unattainable, yet again we look and behind those still unmoving features there is a passion and emotion, strange and more powerful than the passions and emotions we have known. His eyes are closed but some power of the spirit looks out of them and a vital energy fills the frame. The ages roll by, but the Buddha seems not so far away after all; his voice whispers in the ears and tells us not to run away from the struggle but calm-eyed to face it and to see in life even greater opportunities for growth ad advancement."

As I reflect on these two tributes I become humbly aware of the magnitude of the task which I have taken on myself, of presenting to you a glimpse of the life of this great Teacher, which will give you the background to an understanding of the fundamental tenets of the Buddha Dhamma.

In order to have a correct understanding of the life and teachings of the Buddha it is necessary to consider the conditions and the age in which he lived. The Buddha lived in the sixth century B.C., an era of grat intellectual and social activity in different parts of the world. In India in the sphere of religion the Vedas still held great sway and the Brahmanas who were the custodians of this learning had become a hereditary priest-hood. Often these Vedic rites included animal sacrifice of a very cruel and revolting character. On the other hand, there were others who felt that mas's natural attachment to worldly enjoyment and sensual pleasures prevented him from being mighty and powerful.

They therefore, resorted to austerity or self-mortification in its different forms to control the senses. Then there was another group which in their pursuit of the truth and mystery of existence, renounced home and family and engaged in meditaion and self-development in the seclusion of the forest or as wandering mendicants. They did not believe in the extremes of self-mortification.

If one were to describe the situation, 'it was an atmosphere where religion was conjoined with speculative philosophy and where a spirit of broad tolerance which embraced many schools of thought' prevailed. Discussions centred on question such as : Did the world have a beginning in time or was it eternal? Was there a soul apart from the body? What was it like and what happened to it after death? Was there a condition under which one could live and yet not live? It was to men deeply engrossed with such ideas as these that the Buddha preached a new gospel which in its essence was as follows :

'To live mastered by the body, he said, or to live totally neglecting the body is equally wrong. There is a middle way, the way of good life. The good life is to be one's best in thought and word, in will and deed.' This discovery he proclaimed to the world in unequivocal terms. He announced : 'Wide open are the portals if immortality, let those that have faith and courage come and share their faith. Happy is the solitude of him who is full joy, who has learned the truth, who sees the truth. Happy is freedom from malice in this world—self-restraint towards all beings that have life. Happy is freedom from lust in this world, getting beyond all desires, the putting away of that pride which comes from the thought, I am.' This truly is the highest message.

Let us, therefore, now dwell on the life of the Teacher who brought this message into the world. I do not propose to go into the details of the early part of his life as you in India would be very familiar with it. I would summarise it briefly :

The Buddha was born on the full moon day of the month of May in 623 B.C. in Lumbini Park. His father was king Suddhodhana who was the Ruler of the Sakyas, a proud clan of Kshatriyas warriors from the foothills of the Himalayas, with his capital at Kapilavastu. His mother was the lady Maya. She was on her way to her parents' home to give birth to the child when unexpectedly the baby was born under the shade of a flowering Sal Tree.

After his birth the Brahmins who lived as priests, astrologers and soothsayers in the King's court, read the auspicious marks on the child's body and predicted its high destiny. He was named Siddhartha which means the all-prospering one or one whose purpose has been achieved. Seven of the eight Brahmins predicted that the Prince will be a Chakrabarti, a world emperor, or a wise teacher, supremely enlightened one. The one dissentient, Kondanna, said : 'On King, this Prince will one day go in search of truth and become a supremely enlightened Buddha.'

Queen Maha Maya, the mother, died on the seventh day after the birth of the child. The baby was thereafter nursed by his mother's own sister, Prajapathi Gothami. Although the child was brought up amidst all abundance and luxury, the father saw to it that his son received and education required of a prince. He became skilled in many a branch of a knowledge and in the arts of war, easily excelling others. King Suddhodhana was, therefore, naturally proud of him but he had also reason to be concerned. His son was not like other children for he would often be found sitting alone in deep contemplation. It is recorded in the Texts that although one seven years old when he was taken out for the annual ploughing festival with its pomp and pageantry which he watched in the company of his own attendant-women, he forgot his surroundings and entered into a deep state of trance seated cross-legged. This experience provided the strength and hope for the Prince later in his search of supreme enlightenment. King Suddhodhana, in view of what the soothsayers had predicted, took every precaution to prevent his son coming to know the sorrowful aspects of life. He provided him with three palaces for the three seasons with all the earthly joys of life. Everything that could give him knowledge of human misery and death was carefully kept away from his sight. At the age of sixteen he was married to the beautiful Yasodhara whose hand he won in an open contest with the Sakya Princes.

After marriage he expressed a desire to see the outside world. The king agreed but made all arrangements to ensure that wherever he went the streets and houses were decorated and that there was a spirit of gaiety and festivity among the people. At the same time the king made sure that the sick, the aged, the infirm, the blind and the maimed were kept away from his sight. But on one occasion when the Prince went driving with his charioteer Channa from the royal gardens he saw to his amazement what his eyes had never seen before—a man weakened with age and in the last stage of decay. This was the first shock the Prince received.

The second was the sight of a man with mere skin and bones utterly unhappy, smitten with disease, and strength gone from him.

On a third occasion he saw a group of persons bearing on their shoulders the corpse of a dearly beloved kinsman. The Prince began to have a glimpse of the woes of the world. The more he came in contact with the world outside of his palace the more conceived he became that the world was lacking in true happiness. From his charioteer Channa he learnt further that even he, his beloved Princess Yashodhara and his kith and kin, all without exception, were subject to ageing, disease and death.

The next incident that stirred him was a recluse moving with measured steps, calm and serene, one who had renounced his home to live a life of purity, to seek the truth and solve the riddle of life. He turned homewards in deep contemplation nursing the possibility of renunciation but before he reached home he heared that a son had been born to Yasodhara, a fetter to his immediate plans.

As he pondered over all these cruel realities of life, his determination to find a way out hardened. 'There is a getting born and a growing old, a dying and a being re-born. And from the suffering an escape is not known, even as from old age and death. How shall I escape? Surely there must be a way out of this mass of ill; just as there is warmth as opposed to cold, and light as against darkness, there must likewise be happiness as opposed to sorrow.' He was thus overcome by a powerful urge to seek and win the deathless, to strive for deliverance from old age, illness, misery and death—to seek it for himself and for all beings which suffer. Eventually, on the night of the full moon at the youthful age of twenty-nine he called Channa, his charioteer, to his side and riding his favourite horse, Kanthaka, left the palace and city unnoticed during the night to the banks of the river Anoma. Having cut his long hair with his sword and given over his princely clothes and ornaments to Channa, he bade him return and so began a long and tireless quest for knowledge that would lead him to the solution of the mystery of life.

For seven days he lived in solitude as an ascetic on the banks of the river Anoma. He did so because at that time many people in India believed that the way of happiness was by means of purification through asceticism and the more rigorous the asceticism the more thorough the purification. He came on foot to the city of Rajagaha begging his food from door to door. He first revolted against the sight of the mixture of hot and cold food but soon overcame it and took it merely to keep his body alive, to pursue his quest.

In his search for salvation he sought out famous teachers of religion of the time. He first went to Ālāra Kālāma and later on to Uddaka for advice. He acquired all the knowledge these teachers could give him, joining in their religious exercises which took him to the highest concentrative thought but there it ended. He realized that he was still far from his goal. Dissatisfied with anything short of enlightenment he declined their invitation to stay on and proceeded in his wanderings until he reached the thick forest near Uruvela and applied himself in solitude to the severest penances and self-tortures. Soon five other ascetics who admired his fortitude and endurance joined him. They were Kondanna, Bhadiya, Bhappa, Mahanama and Asija. For six long years he subjected himself to rigorous self-mortification to test the belief that purification and final deliverance could only be achieved by such practices. In the Majjima Nikāya it is stated that he lived on leaves and roots, steadily reducing all food. He wore rags from dust heaps; he slept among corpses, or on a bed of thorns. The utter paucity of nourishment left him a physical wreck as he described himself, "like waste, withered leaves became all my limbs". After six years of struggle he came to death's very door but still found himself nowhere near the goal. It became abundantly clear to him from his own experience that self-mortification was not the way to enlightenment but undiscouraged he sought new avenues to reach his goal. He realized that with the body so weakened he could not take the road to enlightenment. He then abandoned self-torture and extremism, taking the minimum of food so as to sustain himself. His five companions were disappointed at this and left him. Having regained his strength he resolved to make a final effort in complete solitude with determination and faith in his own purity and strength.

On the full moon day of the month of May when he was 35 years old he sat down in the evening at the foot of a fig tree with a strong determination, "Let my skin, sinews and bones shiver and wither; let my flesh and blood dry up. I will not step up from this seat until I have attained supreme and absolute insight." As he sat there he went through his final and most strenuous struggle, the struggle against the inclinations and desires of the human heart. Indolence and pride, delusion, love of the world, craving for existence and enjoyment, fame, power, wealth, love of family life and all the delights and joys presented themselves to him in their most seductive forms. But he, cross-legged, sat there in perfect concentration, alert and strenuous and applied himself to the mindfulness on breathing gradually, cleansing his mind of all impurities and desires. He gained the knowledge of recollecting past births, gained the divine eye and beheld the disappearing and re-appearing of being in good stages of existence and in stages of war, each bearing according to his deeds. Then he applied his mind to the acquisition of the knowledge of destruction of the corruptions.

His struggle was crowned with success. He tore asunder the veil of ignorance and sensed the truth thus becoming the Buddha, the awakened one. He realized the truth of universal suffering, the truth of craving being the cause of sorrow, the truth that there is a state where sorrow is completely extinguished and happiness reigns and the truth that there is a way that leads to the conquest of suffering. He had found emancipation. His destiny had at long last been fulfilled.

The wondrous being who became the Buddha was indeed yet a man. In fact, as Buddhist writers have repeatedly pointed out, it is this essential humanity of the Buddha that shines out most perfectly through the canonical records of his life and activities. He lived with the people proving by his personal example that what he had become, they could, every one of them, become themselves and that we are all of us potential Buddhas. According to the teachings of Buddhism, there is in each one of us the germ of the Buddha ideal in different stages of development. It is this humanity that is the most striking thing about the Buddha. For forty-five years till his death at Kusinara at the age of 80 in 553 B.C. on the full moon day of May, his life was one of frequent activity, teaching and preaching, continuously travelling on foot, carrying the message of happiness to all those who would care to hear.

Now I propose to place before you the essence of the Buddha's teachings.

Before we consider the fundamental teachings of Buddhism I should like to invite your attention to the oft-posed question, "Is Buddhism a religion or a philosophy?" Dr. G.P. Malalasekera has very lucidly answered this question. He says,

> Some prefer to call it a religion, others a philosophy. In fact, it is both. In it the most lofty religio-moral doctrines are united with the deepest philosophical truths to form one integrated whole. It enlightens its followers as to the nature of the universe and the laws reigning therein; it discloses to man the essence of his being, shows him his true, higher destiny extending beyond the fleeting earth-life, awakens his slumbering moral forces and

faculties, kindless in him a desire for the good and noble, teaches him to be humane, patient, and unselfish, gives him consolation in sorrow, confidence at the moment of death and declares to him the way that leads to the highest emancipation from unrest, sorrow and suffering to perfect peace, supreme happiness and consummate emancipation. Thus, Buddhism is a religion.

It is likewise a philosophy. It demands of its adherents belief only through a conviction gained and confirmed by one's own investigation and examination and by earnest reflection. Its doctrines are not based on the will of an incomprehensible god, creator, or a super-natural revelation but on the natural constitution of the world and on the laws of life which are open to all to discover for themselves, should they so desire. It does not seek to frighten the evil-doer by threatening him with eternal punishment. It seeks rather to clear up the eye of the erring one, obscured by earthly delusion, so that he may be able to see the truth. It leads the honest struggle on the way to spiritual development and moral self-perfection up to a standpoint where everything transitory lies behind him as unsubstantial appearance and where prejudice, doubt and illusion disappear in the light of knowledge. It is thus a philosophy in the best sense of the word.

He proclaimed for the first time the Dhamma in a discourse called the Dhamma Chakka Pavatanna Sutta (the foundation of the kingdom of righteousness) at Isipatana, the Deer Park near Benaras to the five ascetics who had at one time practised self-mortification with him. This discourse is universally known as the Four Noble Truths and contains the essence of the Buddha's doctrine in a most lucid form. I can do no better than to quote the Four Noble Truths as proclaimed by the Buddha in his first discourse :—

There are two extremes that he who strives for deliverance should avoid. One extreme, the craving for the satisfaction of passions and other pleasures of the senses, is vulgar, base, degrading and worthless. The other extreme exaggerated asceticism and self-mortification, is painful, vain and also worthless. Only the Middle Path which the Tathāgata has found, avoids these two wrong ways and opens the eyes, bestows insight, and leads to wisdom, to deliverance, to enlightenment to Nirvāṇa.

It is the Noble Eightfold Path, namely, right views, right aspiration, right speech, right deeds, right livelihood, right endeavour, right mindfulness, right concentration.

Now this is the Noble Truth of Suffering :—

Birth is suffering, disease is suffering, death is suffering; sorrow, grief, lamentation, pain are suffering; union with unpleasant things is suffering; separation from the beloved is suffering; unsatisfied desire is suffering; in short the whole five groups of clinging are suffering.

Now, this is the Noble Truth of the Cause of Suffering, namely, verily it is this thirst, this craving for existence, and enjoyment, which leads to rebirth; seeking satisfaction now in this way, now in that. It is the craving for the satisfaction of the passions, the craving for existence in this life or hereafter, and the craving for not to be what one dislikes.

Now this is the Noble Truth of the Cessation of Suffering, namely, verily it is the complete destruction, conquering, annihilation of these cravings.

Now this is the Noble Truth of the Path that leads to the Cessation of Suffering : Verily it is this Noble Eightfold Path, namely : right views, right aspiration, right speech, right deeds, right livelihood, right endeavour, right mindfulness, right concentration.

It is fundamentally the teaching of emancipation. Emancipation must needs imply the existence of evil from which men must be freed. Both facts are equally important as he said it : "One thing do I teach and one only—suffering and the extinction of suffering. The two are inseparable. They are complementary."

If you reflect on the substance of his first sermon, you will notice that it does not for instance give any account of the creation of the world. No promise is held out for exemption from pain and evil in return for prayer or ritual or sacrifice nor any favourable intercession by the divine powers. Without proclaiming himself a Saviour, willing and able to take upon himself the sins of mankind, he declares that each man and woman must bear the burden of their own evil actions. He categorically affirms that no God, even can do for any man that work of self-conquest and self-emancipation which in the teaching of the Buddha stands for salvation.

Buddhism, therefore, is neither optimistic nor pessimistic but on the contrary teaches all truth that lies mid-way between them. He perceived the universality of sorrow and did prescribe a cure for this universal sickness of humanity. At the same time he did not expect his followers to be constantly brooding over this fact and lead a miserable and unhappy life. He exhorted them to be always happy and cheerful; for joy is one of the factors of enlightenment. Buddhism is saturated with a spirit of free enquiry and complete tolerance. It is a teaching of the "open mind and the sympathetic heart". The starting point of Buddhism is reasoning or understanding—the Sammaditti. To the seekers if truth the Buddha says : "Do not accept anything on mere hearsay; do not accept anything by mere tradition; do not accept anything on account of mere rumours; do not accept anything by mere supposition; do not accept anything by mere inference; do not accept anything merely because it agrees with your preconceived notions; do not accept anything merely because it seems acceptable; do not accept anything thinking that the ascetic is to be respected by us. But when you know for yourselves these things are involved, these things are blame-worthy, and so on, then indeed do reject them." When a Buddhist worships an image he does not do so expecting worldy favours but pays homage to what it represents. When an understanding Buddhist offers flowers and whilst doing so in a spirit of homage to one whom he respects, he also appreciates the comparison, that like the flower which fades, the body is also subject to decay. Similarly, when he lights a lamp which dispels darkness he thinks of the Dhamma which lights the way to enlightenment. Buddhism appeals more to the intellect than to the emotion. It is concerned more with re-shaping the lives of the devotees than with their numerical strength. It must be said to its credit that throughout its peaceful march of 2,500 years no drop of blood was shed in the name of religion, no monarch wielded the sword to propagate the Dhamma and no conversion was made either by force or by any repulsive methods.

Apart from the four Noble Truth and the Noble Eight-fold Path, the doctrine of the Karma and re-birth is another essential teaching of the Buddha.

I am sure there must have been many an occasion when you would have yourselves asked, why the world is full of inequalities; why is it that one should be inferior and another superior; why should one be born rich and another poor; why it is that some people should be born blind, deaf, deformed, maimed and die young while others are strong and healthy and live to the age of 80 or 100.

These questions, I submit, are satisfactorily answered by Buddhism. This variation has often been attributed to heredity and environment. It cannot be denied that they are partly instrumental but they are not totally responsible for those distinctions and differences that exist among people. Heredity perhaps explains only the similarities but what of the differences. Heredity for instance, cannot give us a satisfatory explanation why one of a noble family should be a criminal or why one in a poor family should turn out to be wealthy and honoured. According to Buddhism, these differences can be explained as due not only to heredity and environment but also to our own Karma or in other words, to our inherited past actions and present deeds. The Buddha himself explained this in reply to an inquiry when he said : "Every living being has Karma as its own, its inheritance, its cause, its kinsman, its refuge. Karma is that which differentiates all living beings into low and high states. Inherent in Karma is the power of producing its due effect, the cause produces the effect, the effect explains the cause; the seed produces the fruit; the fruit explains the seed as both are inter-related." According to Buddhism, there are three factors necessary for the re-birth of a human, i.e. the formation of a foetus in the mother's womb. They are the female ovum, the male's sperm and the Kāmmic energy, Vega. This Kāmmic energy is sent forth by a dying individual at the moment of his death to a new mother's womb ready for conception. "As long as this Kāmmic force exists, there is re-birth, for beings are merely the visible manifestation of this invisible Kāmmic force. In death the organic life ceases but the Kāmmic force which hitherto actuated it has not been destroyed." Birth is, therefore, preceded by death and death is preceded by birth. As a Western writer puts it : "Whether we believe in a past existence or not it forms the only reasonable hypothesis which bridges certain gaps in human knowledge concerning certain facts of every-day life." Psychologists, psychiatrists, medical men and hypnotists have conducted experiments in over 45 cases from fourteen different countries where previous births were recalled and they have been forced to admit the doctrine of re-birth as the only scientific explanation. I refer you to the researches of Dr. E.L. Stevenson and Prof. C.J. Ducasse. I quote the Ven. Nyanatiloka Thero : "What is called the character of man is in reality the sum of the sub-conscious tendencies produced partly by the pre-natal, partly by the present volitional activity of Kamma. These tendencies may during life-time become an inducement to wholesome and unwholesome volitional activities or Kāmma by body, speech or mind." If, however, this thirst for life is fully extinguished then there will be no new re-birth. This doctrine of re-birth should be distinguished from the theory of reincarnation or transmigration because Buddhism denies the existence of an unchanging or eternal soul.

The other essential teaching which I would like to refer to is the Buddha's conception of Nibbāna. This process of birth and death continues *ad infinitum* until this Kāmmic force is transmitted so to say to Nibbāna—the ultimate goal of a Buddhist. Nibbāna is the Pali version of Nirvāṇa. It means the extinction of lust, hatred and ignorance. Nibbāna is not to be found in any place nor is it a sort of haven where a transcendental ego resides. It is a state which is dependent upon the body itself, it is an attainment which is within the reach of all, it is attainable even in present life. As Edwin Arnold attempts describe it : "If any teach Nibbāna is to cease, say unto them they lie; if any teach Nibbāna is to live, say unto such they err."

The way to Nibbāna is a positive way of conduct, a life of extreme physical and intellectual exertion, till one attains that freedom beyond which there is no further. Such a positive code of conduct surely then cannot lead one to a negative state. The tendency, however, is to regard Nibbāna as a negative state because no one could point it out. That Nibbāna is something positive is amply testified by the Buddha's own words : "There is 0 disciples, a state that is not born, not produced, not created, not compounded. Were there not 0 disciples, this state not born, not produced, not created and not compounded, there would be no possible exist for what is born, produced, created and compounded."

From this we can, therefore, conclude that there must exist a sorrowless and deathless Nibbāna which is opposed to the sorrowful and changing Samsara. "Nibbāna is nothing but a state which is to be experienced and it exists not before it is experienced, nor does it exist once one has completed that experience."

As you will readily appreciate, it is not possible for anybody within a short space to lead you into a full and complete understanding of this deep and rich doctrine of the Buddha. What I have attempted is to place before you certain essential teachings as it strikes my mind, to provide you as it were, food for thought for a further study of the Dhamma which you can yourselves read, understand, verify and then accept, as the only way to supreme enlightenment.

CHAPTER-II

BHAKTI AND PŪJĀ IN BUDDHISM

—Dr. S. Dutt

Those who see in *pūjā* only its rites and rituals miss the essence of it, which is the offering of *bhakti* to the Adored.

Bells tinkle; songs sound; lights glitter; incense-smoke floats up from censers; and worshippers foregather with offerings of leaves, flowers and garlands before the image in the sanctuary. But the ritualism is meaningless, and idle accompaniment, unless the *pūjā* is inspired by *bhakti*. It is *bhakti* that lifts it from a mere show to a living, breathing, and meaningful reality.

'Bhakti' is a term of very ancient usage in Indian religious terminology. It has a distinct significance and a variety of nuances which are not covered by its usual English equivalent, 'devotion'. Śāṇḍilya, a late exponent of the *bhakti* cult, explains it as a settled attitude or condition of mind and heart, in which the 'idea of the Lord', rather than His ordainments and teaching, occupies the 'forefront of the mind and heart'. *Bhakti* is known by its 'fruits' they appear in 'reverence and worship paid to the Adored One, the casting out of all unclean thoughts and passions, the celebration of the praise of the Lord, and the wish to continue to live in His service and for His sake alone'. Thus *pūjā,* with pure mind and heart, with *stava* and *stuti,* is, according to Śāṇḍilya, the fruit of *bhakti*. Those who cultivate the state of mind and

heart that *bhakti* implies desire no gain for themselves, but only the bliss of living in the service of the Lord.

In all 'religions of grace', *bhakti* is stressed as a *sine qua non* for the devotee. Such religions are what theologians call 'soteriological'; they posit a Saviour to whom is left to grant the fruits of a man's work and endeavour and the ultimate salvation they conceive in different terms of definition. They replace volitional selfeffort on the devotee's part by complete self-surrender, as Śrī Kṛṣṇa enjoins in the *Gītā* : 'Give ye up all *dharmas* and take refuge in Me alone. From all sins will I deliver thee.' This doctrine of self-surrender to, and taking refuge in, the Lord is very ancient in our country. In the Bhāgavata cult, which originated long before the rise of Buddhism, and Jainism and which is expounded in the *Gītā*, it is the central and cardinal doctrine. In fact, in all the religions of India, it is a more or less pervasive element, rather than a definite or fixed-worded creed.

One of the most significant chapters in India's religious history is the growth and evolution of *bhakti* in Buddhism. Buddhism in the beginning was not a 'religion of grace'. In the oldest canon of Buddhism—the Pāli canon of the Theravāda school—the religion is described as a 'way' (*magga)*; at its end is set the goal of *nibbāna;* and the approach to it is by stages of spiritual advancement by the devotee's own effort. It is described most fully in the manual entitled *Visuddhi-magga (The Path of Purity)* by Buddhaghoṣa, who was the finest flower of Theravāda learning. He ignores completely the efficiency of prayer, propitiation, and the associated acts of worship and *bhakti* offering.

Yet, even in primitive Buddhism, *bhakti* is seen in the germ. The Buddha, who is conceived in it as the Satthā (instructor), has also the appellation Bhagava (Sanskrit,

Bhagavān); and in the ordination ceremony of a monk, the initiate has to chant the formula of 'taking refuge'—in the Buddha, the Dhamma, and the Saṅgha. We find later on the worship of the Lord's body-relics and the mound *(stūpa)* that enshrined them recommended in the canon. There are some poetic anthologies in the canon in which we see that the worship of the *stūpa* and other symbols of the Lord has already developed in the religion. The *śaraṇāgama* ('taking refuge') has ripened from a formula of ordination into a credo.

Yet the early canon of Buddhism insists on faith *(śraddhā),* which is confidence in the truth of the religion, while *bhakti* is a term of rare occurrence in it, and has none of the nuances appertaining to it in Indian religious terminology.

When we pass on to the later phases of Buddhism, we are struck by the resurgence of the *bhakti* element in the religion. *Bhakti* legends abound, of which an outstanding one is the legend of Upagupta and Māra in the *Divyāvadāna.* It is a legend which shows how *bhakti* has encroached on the system of spiritual advancement and attainment by self-effort alone without the aid of divine grace.

Upagupta was a monk who lived in a monastery on a hill-top bear Mathurā. So great was the power of his saintliness that even Māra (the mythical antagonist of the Buddha) was converted by him, and came under the spell of his personality. Māra is described in the legend as a great magician. When he was converted by Upagupta, he asked the master how he should proceed in the new life. Upagupta was an apostle of *bhakti*, and he instructed Māra that all he had to do was to cultivate *bhakti*, for 'even a little of it yields the fruit of *nirvāṇa*'. Then a great longing came over this apostle of *bhakti* to see the Lord in a physical semblance, and at his behest, Māra took on, by his magic the semblance of the Buddha himself. Before that illusory image, the monk fell in prostration, and when Māra, startled by the act, asked him its meaning, he was told by Upagupta that 'he had worshipped the Imperishable in the perishable, just as men do when they worship images of clay'. The legend dates before the invention of the Buddha image in Buddhism and makes manifest the urge that was gathering strength behind it.

Bhakti in Buddhism was articulated at first in symbol worship : it was offered to the *stūpa* or to the representation of the urn in which the Buddha's body-relics were collected after his cremation at Kushinara; to the wheel of Dhamma or the Bodhi tree; to his foot-prints or umbrella. But the image, for which Upagupta had longed and for want of which he had to satisfy his longing with an illusory semblance, appears afterwards; and one of the earliest Buddha images is seen along with the worshipped symbols in Mathurā sculpture in a fragment, which the archaeologists assign to the first century, B.C. or A.D. The figure is that of a Mahāpuruṣa (superman), with the Physiognomical marks of a superman upon it—sign of lotus on palm, wheel on the sole, long ear-lobes, etc. This superman Buddha appears a number of times in Mathurā sculpture.

Ancient Buddha images were of two schools of sculpture, of Gandhāra and of Mathurā. Among experts in iconography, there is a dispute or long-standing whether the Buddha images was first invented at Mathurā or in Gandhāra, and as to what might have been the urge and motive behind the invention.

Gandhāra had come, round the start of the Christian era, under Greek influence from Bactria; the Gandhāra artist imbibed from it the anthropomorphism of Graeco-Roman mythology and so presented the image of the Buddha as an

'Indian Apollo'. The Greek influence at the time did not extend so far east as Mathurā. The priority in respect of the Buddha image between Gandhāra and Mathurā is not settled yet; the influence of the Gandhāra art-modes certainly extended to Mathurā in later times. But, if it was at Mathurā that the first Buddha images were made, there must have been behind them the pure urge of *bhakti* and the desire long cherished by worshippers for something more immediately evocative of *bhakti* than a mere symbol with which the mind has to associate the idea of the Lord by a conscious effort.

In any case, image-worship and symbol-worship existed, and still exist, side by side in Buddhism.

Early in the Christian era, the Mahāyāna form of Buddhism evolved. It largely replaced the old cult in which the place of *bhakti* was restricted by a new cult in which it had the largest scope. For the Mahāyānist devotee, it was a prime requisite for the spiritual journey. No monastery, therefore, of the early Christian centuries was complete without a shrine in which a miniature *stūpa* was installed for ritual worship, or a sancturay to hold the Buddha image. In a later age (A.D. 300-500), which the historians call the Gupta age of ancient India, independent temples were built to house large-sized Buddha images, often of finest sculpture. At Nālandā (in Bihar), the seat of the ancient 'Nālandā University', one may see the ruins of some of the grandest Buddha temples of this age. They form an extensive row parallel to the row of monasteries, where the university functioned.

Bhakti offering to the Lord through prayer and the chanting of hymns and the rituals of *pūjā* developed, as we have seen, in primitive Hīnayāna Buddhism, too, in the later phases of its development. But the rituals of *pūjā* were not so elaborate as in the Mahāyāna. They consisted only in placing flowers, incense, paint, and garlands. But the

Mahāyānist worship of the Buddha image was more elaborate on its ritualistic side.

Śāntideva was a saint and a Mahāyānist *ācārya* of the eighth century A.D. His poem in Sanskrit, entitled *Bodhicaryāvatāra,* is the sublimest canticle in the literature of Mahāyāna Buddhism. In this great poem, the strain of *bhakti* rises to its highest pitch, and side by side, the rites of *pūjā* and their significance are insisted on. The notes themselves are practically the same as performed in Hindu image-worship—bathing the image with scented water, accompaniment of vocal and instrumental music, offerings of flowers, food and clothes (*i.e. naivedya* as in Hindu worship), swinging of lighted censers and burning incense, etc. Buddhist *pūjā* and Hindu *pūjā* seem to have been similar on their ritualistic side; only the images represented deities of the Mahāyāna pantheon; and a time came when several of them (e.g. Tārā) found place in the Hindu pantheon too.

The hypothesis that it was through the upsurge of *bhakti* in Buddhism and the institution of the rite of *pūjā* that a *rapprochement* came about, between the sixth and senenth centuries, between Bddhism and Hinduism, which had been separate religions so far, is not wholly groundless, *Bhakti* and *pūjā* made a large common ground between the two. He whom the Buddhists adored and ceremonially worshipped in their temples and monasteries was admitted into the Hindu pantheon as an *avatāra*, and the Purāṇas confirmed it.

The great temple of *Bṛhadīśvara* at Tanjore, in South India, is one of the oldest of Dravidian temples, dedicated to Śiva. It was built during the reign of the Cola king Rāja-Rāja (A.D. 985-1018). Here on one side of the main *gopuram* (temple gateway), a seated Buddha image is seen installed; and in a broad belt of sculpture girdling the main sanctuary, a Buddha figure is set among Hindu figures from mythology, under the Bodhi-tree, stylized almost out of recognition. In later Sanskrit poetry, the Buddha is celebrated as the ninth *avatāra* of Viṣṇu or Keśava, for instance, in the Kashmiri poet Kṣemendra's *Daśāvatāra-carita* (c. A.D. 1065) and the Bengali poet Jayadeva's *Gīta-Govinda* (twelfth century). But the psychological groundwork for the final acceptance of the Buddha in the Hindu patheon had been set a few centuries earlier—in the reigns of ancient Gupta emperors (A.D. 300-500), some of whom, styling themselves in their coins as *parama-bhāgavatas* (devout followers of the Bhāgavata cult), were at the same time builders of Buddha temples and patrons of Buddhist monk-communities.

Thus, well over a millennium ago, the linkage took place between Hinduism and Buddhism, and it was possible through the spirit of *bhakti* and *pūjā* supervening in the latter. Doctrines divide, but *bhakti* and *pūjā* bring rival faiths together.

CHAPTER-III

BUDDHA'S ANSWERS TO GREAT QUESTIONS OF LIFE

—Swami Budhananda

Life is a remorseless school house. Here we are required to learn our lessons, and learn well, before we can get out and be free.

People are not normally very sentimenal about death but they are sentimental about life. Why ? Beacuse by living, they think, they can enjoy, whereas by dying they are out of luck. So long as we don't see that death is the obverse of life, so long shall we have to learn in the school house of life.

There are two ways of learning : one with tears and the other without tears. When we learn through trial and error, through receiving knocks and shocks, we learn with tears. When we imbibe the wisdom of the sages and follow the precepts of Godmen and saints, we learn without tears.

We are free to choose our ways, but learn our lessons we must before we can get out of the bondage and be free.

Life brings before us many questions Some are basic and some are trivial. The basic questions concern all of us all our life. The trivial questions have relevance only in the particular contexts of individual lives.

The basic questions are indeed the great questions of life. The quality and movement of our life towards freedom all depend on whether or not we have found answers to these basic questions of life. For getting answers to these questions it is not necessary to depend only on our own intelligence and experience. For these answers we can draw from the wisdom of the ages.

One of the wisest men of the world was the Buddha. He answered many of the basic questions of life which at first sight may not always appear to be great. But when we understand the relevance of these questions in reference to our ultimate destiny, which is the attainment of freedom, then they will be found to be great questions indeed. On a certain day when the Buddha dwelt at Jetavana, the garden of Anathapindaka, a lay disciple, a deva or celestial being in the guise of a Brahmin, came to the Buddha and asked him twenty one questions. The questions were asked in five groups of four, and finally one single question. Buddha answered them in a group of four. His answers were like crisp aphorisms, in the minimum number of words. And much wisdom is compressed in the aphoristic answers Buddha gave to those questions.

The Brahmin asked :

What is the sharpest sword?
What is the deadliest poison?
What is the fiercest fire?
What is the darkest night?

The Buddha replied :

A word spoken in wrath is the sharpest sword.
Covetousness is the deadliest poison.
Passion is the fiercest fire.
Ignorance is the darkest night.

In trying to understand these aphoristic replies we have to constantly remember that Buddha's wisdom has only one term of reference and that is Nirvāṇa or attainment of illumination or freedom, which is the cessation of all miseries of life.

The Buddha himself said of his own teachings : 'As the great ocean has only one taste, the taste of salt, so my doctrine has only one flavour, the flavour of emancipation.'

Hence Buddha's answers to these questions have to be understood in reference to the requirements of emancipation. When we know for certain that the attainment of freedom is the ultimate objective of human life, then it becomes natural for us to take that alone as wisdom which leads to emancipation. Buddha had no other criterion of judging issues except from the standpoint of what will and what will not lead to emancipation or cessation of miseries of life.

Buddha's answers to the Brahmin's questions have to be understood from this standpoint alone. Otherwise his answers cannot be understood.

The Brahmin asked : What is the sharpest sword ?

The Buddha replied : A word spoken in wrath is the sharpest sword.

An ordinary sword wounds only the victim who is struck by the sword. But words spoken in wrath, which is the sharpest sword, wounds more the striker than the struck. Anger is temporary insanity. What is uttered in anger rebounds on the speaker with much greater vehemence than when they are released, and cuts the speaker of angry words to the quick. Angry words can cut to pieces bonds of friendship and our own images built by laborious efforts. Many other evil consequences may issue from angry words. At the root of many misfortunes in this world, many tragedies, there are words spoken in wrath.

There in the Dhammapada, the Buddhist scripture, which carries mostly Buddha's words, you read :

Let one be watchful of speech-irritation.

Let him practise restraint of speech. Having abandoned the sins of speech let him practise virtue with his speech.

The Dhammapada syas elsewhere :

Who controls his rising anger as a rolling chariot—him I call the real charioteer. The others only hold the reins.

One should control angry words and practise speaking only good words.

The Brahmin asked : What is the deadliest poision?

The Buddha replied : Covetousness is the deadliest poison.

Buddha's main search was how mankind could be saved from inevitable sufferings of life. Through his independent search for the root-cause of all human suffering Buddha came to the conclusion that it was 'tañhā' or desire.

Desire poisons the limpid springs of life. The purpose of all spiritual disciplines is to minimize and ultimately destroy all desires, and thus become free through desirelessness.

Covetousness, instead of taking a man toward desirelessness, strengthens his existing desires and multiplies them. Hence it is the deadliest poison.

The Brahmin aslked : What is the fiercest fire ?

The Buddha replied : Passion is the fiercest fire.

If our house catches fire we can run away and save ourselves. But passion is such a fierce fire that it overtakes us wherever we may run. It may burn down the work of our entire life. Even a learned man, who knows many things, but does not know how to subdue his passion, will come to grief. His whole life may become like a scorched earth. Śrī Kṛṣṇa therefore says in the Gītā in an imperative mood : 'Conquer first this powerful enemy, the passion,which is diffcult to be subdued.'

Passion is the fiercest fire because it burns to ashes all possibilites of emancipation.

The Brahmin asked : What is the darkest night ?

The Buddha replied : Ignorance is the darkest night.

In the darkest night, if you don't have a torch with you, you cannot find your way. You do not know where you are going. You are not sure whether the next step will land you in a ditch or throw you into a thorny bush.

Such is the case with the wayfarer of life who is ignorant. Even in daylight the ignorant may does not know how to choose a right course of action. He takes the apparent as reality, the impure as pure; he takes the wrong as right. He sees everything in a wrong perspective. His thoughts being rooted in ignorance. His actions are all wrong. From such actions alone miseries of his life multiply, bondages increase. Therefore, one should carefully and with great patience remove one's ignorance and come out of the darkest night into the glow of the golden morning of knowledge.

The next group of four questions were :

Who gains the greatest benefit ?

Who loses most ?

Which armour is invulnerable?

What is the best weapon?

The Buddha replied :

He is the greatest gainer who gives to others.

He loses most who receives from others without giving a compensation.

Patience is an invulnerable armour.

Wisdom is the best weapon.

In answer to the question : 'Who gains the greatest

benefit?', the Buddha replied : He is the greatest gainer who gives to others.

It is a very ancient spiritual concept that the greatest gainer is he who gives the utmost. Ordinarily we think that those who receive are the gainers. But in the spiritual realm, a different law of returns is always operative.

Indicating this the Buddha says in another place : 'Charity is rich in returns; charity is the greatest wealth for though it scatters, it brings no repentance.'

Anāthapiṇḍaka, a lay disciple of the Buddha, a very charitable person and a supporter of orphans, intended to found a *vihar* where the Brotherhood could practise spiritual disciplines.

When Buddha saw that unselfish charity was the moving cause of his offer, Buddha accepted the gift for the Brotherhood. In accepting this offering Buddha said :

The charitable man is loved by all, his friendiship is prized highly; in death his heart is at rest and full of joy, for he suffers not from repentance; he receives the opening flower of his reward and the fruit that ripens from it.

Further said the Buddha, some very precious words, in the same sermon.

Hard it is to understand : by giving away our food, we get more strength, by bestowing clothing on others, we gain more beauty; by founding abodes of purity and truth, we acquire great treasures.

The Brahmin asked : Who loses most?

The Buddha replied : He loses most who receives from others without giving a compensation.

It is a spiritual fact that he gains most who gives to others; it should be clear that he who only takes but does not give to others should lose the most.

Swami Vivekananda says :

There is no higher virtue than charity. The lowest man is he whose hands draw in, in receiving; and he is the highest man whose hands goes out in giving. The hand was made to give always. Give the last bit of bread you have, even if you are starving. You will be free in a moment if you starve yourself to death by giving to another. Immediately you will become perfect, you will become God.

The Brahmin asked : Which armour is invulnerable?

The Buddha replied : Patience is an invulnerable armour.

One who has this armour will have no irrevocable defeat. His ultimate victory is certain. If only we know how to be patient there is no such thing as failure in the world. What looks like failure is only suspended success due to want of patience.

In the Dhammapada, it is said, 'Paatience is the austerity supreme.' Austerities are intended for the attainment of illumination. Patience is said to be supreme austerity because, granted patience, attainment of illumination is inevitable. And practice of all other austerities also depends on patience.

There is a Hebrew saying : 'Let us run with patience the race that is set before us.'

Saddled on patience we are sure to win any race.

In the Koran there is this exhortation : 'O ye who believe! Seek help with patience and with prayer; for God is with the patient.'

The devotee who is patient in resignation and keeps laying at God's door through all seasons, will surely see Him. One day the door will be flung open and he will be in the Great Presence.

The Brahmin asked : What is the best weapon?

The Buddha replied : Wisdom is the best weapon.

'The wise man', as Confucius says, 'is informed in what is right.'

Right thinking, understanding and action are the preoccupations of the wise man. He is occupied in search of truth and not merely in making a living. He lives in this world cautiously and handles the world cautiously. He understands his limitations and is always anxious for self-improvement, and eager to learn. The wise man is not irritated when troubles arise. He keeps his balance under all situations. The wise man dose not seek to defeat others but is anxious to be of service to others.

Wisdom is said to be the best weapon not beacuse it helps to defeat our enemy but because it helps us to have no enemy at all. Man always stands self defeated. Wisdom is the best weapon because it vanquishes within us those causes which cause our defeats in the world.

Wisdom is the best weapon, because it helps us to know the Truth. And knowing the truth we become invincible. 'Know the Turth, and the Truth shall make thee free.'

Then the Brahmin asked the Buddha :

Who is the most dangerous thief ?

What is the most precious treasure ?

Who is the most successful in taking away by violence not only on earth, but also in heaven ?

What is the securest treasure-trove ?

The Buddha replied :

Evil thought is the most dangerous thief.

Virtue is the most precious treasure.

The soul can take away by violence not only on earth, but also in heaven.

Immortality is the securest treasuretrove.

The Brahmin asked : Who is the most dangerous thief.

The Buddha replied : Evil thought is the most dangerous thief.

An ordinary thief may rob you of your precious belongings but he cannot rob you of your character. He cannot rob you of your power of discrimination and bring about spiritual ruination.

But evil thought can rob of your character, your power of discrimination and even of the chances of your spiritual progress.

Moreover evil thought will eventually lead to evil actions. Evil actions will bear poisonous fruits. And those fruits will have to be reaped by the evil-doer.

Evil thought is therefore the most dangerous thief and also the worst enemy of man.

The Brahmin asked : What's the most precious treasure?

The Buddha replied : Virtue is the most precious treasure.

Virtue is the most precious treasure because if we have all the wealth of the world but no virtue, in course of time, everything will become like ash in our mouth. Those who seek to prosper in sinful ways, eventually come to grief. Even if they may avoid the judgment of society, they cannot avoid the judgment of the law of *karma* which comes upon them as effect following the cause, as 'the wheel of a cart following the feet of the ox,' as Buddha says.

Virtue alone is our all-times all-place un-failing upholder, friend and supporter. When a man forsakes virtue there is nothing which can save him. When a man stands by virtue there is nothing which can destroy him.

You may aspire to have pleasure, wealth, wisdom or salvation, the four great values of life. Only those who seek them through the medium of virtue succeed in their aspiration.

Therefore Manu the great law-giver of the Hindus, says : 'You must slowly build up *Dharma* (virtue) even as ants the ant-hill.'

The Brahmin asked : who is the most successful in taking away by violence not only on earth, but also in heaven?

The Buddha replied : The soul can take away by violence not only on earth but also in heaven.

The meaning of this statement which is somewhat obscure appears to be that the soul survives everything else on earth and beyond.

The next questions was : 'What is the securest treasure-trove?'

The answer Buddha gives to this question makes his answer to the previous question a little more clear. He says, referring to the soul, 'And immortality is its treasure-trove.'

Being immortal, the soul is indestructible.

In the next group of four questions, the Brahmin asked:

What is attractive ?

What is disgusting ?

What is the most horrible pain ?

What is the greatest enjoyment ?

To which the Buddha replied :

Good is attractive.

Evil is disgusting.

A bad conscience is the most tormenting pain.

Deliverance is the highest Bliss.

The Brahmin asked : What is attractive ?

The Buddha answered : Good is attractive.

Generally speaking there are two classes of people in the world : the deluded and the awakened. Those who are awakened inwardly they find beauty in purity and goodness. They feel powerfully attracted to men of God though they may be ill-clad and far from being presentable.

The Brahmin asked : What is disgusting ?

The Buddha replied : Evil is disgusting.

To those who are awakened what is most disgusting is the evil in men. Outwardly a man may be handsome, a woman may be beautiful, but if they lack in purity and goodness they will appear to be most disgusting and most ugly to the awakened.

You may find that you are never tired of looking at a picture of Chirst of Buddha or Sri Ramakrishna but you easily get tired of looking at the pictures of beautiful persons, whose shallowness after a while hits your eyes, as it were.

The Brahmin asked : What is the most horrible pain ?

The Buddha replied : A bad conscience is the most tormenting pain.

It is so because one cannot run away from it. No doctor can cure it; no sedative works on a bad conscience. It pricks you all the time relentlessly. Bad conscience embitters all pleasurable things, turns all honey into gall.

The Brahmin asked : What is the greathest enjoyment ?

The Buddha replied : Deliverance is the height of bliss.

Deliverance is that state of our being in which we transcend all the causes of misery rooted in ignorance. Hence it is the highest bliss. Whatever other enjoyment we may have, they are only a very faint reflection of the bliss of deliverance.

In the follwoing group of four questions the Brahmin asked the Buddha :

What causes ruin in the world ?

What breaks off friendship ?

What is the most violent fever ?

Who is the best physician ?

The Buddha replied :

Ignorance causes the ruin in the world. Envy and selfishness break off friendships.

Hatred is the most violent fever.

And Buddha, the Enlightened One is the best physician.

What we call evil—the entire bulk of it—is rooted and nurtured by ingorance.

As Śaṅkarāchārya points out in the *Vivekachudāmaṇi,* from ignorance springs all our bondage. It subjects us to the long train of miseries such as birth, death, disease and decrepitude.

Ignorance is not negation of knowledge alone. It is positive wrong knowledge. It inculcates in us what is called topsy-turvy understanding, by which we take the unreal as the real, and the real as the unreal; true as the untrue and untrue as true; evil as good and good as evil.

When we base all our thoughts and actions on such topsy-turvy understanding, what but ruination can result from it ?

In answer to the question : 'What breaks off freindship,' the Buddha said, 'Envy and selfishness break off friendship.'

The basis of friendship, which is one of the greatest blessings of life, are trust and love. On this basis, friendship develops into understanding of a superior sort and becomes an enduring asset of life. Envy and selfishness eat away trust and love. And when the very basis of frienship is thus eaten away naturally it falls through. Selfishness is not the destroyer of friendship alone. It breaks homes, and business concerns, and charitable institutions.

Swami Vivekanands says :

Selfishness is the devil incarnate in every man. Every bit of self, bit by bit is devil. Take off self by one side and God enters by the other. When the self is got rid of, only God remains. Light and darkness cannot remain together.

In answer to the quesrion : 'What is the most violent fever.'

The Buddha said : 'Hatred is the most violent fever.'

A violent fever unhinges the man suffering from it. In that state a man speaks in delirium and acts like a mad man.

Hatred unhighes a man and destroys his finer sensibilities. Even a learned man, under the spell of hatred, can commit most barbarious acts. What hatred can do to a man is known to those who had the misfotune to see a communal or racial riot, or those who read the accounts of Nazi extermination of the Jews.

No beast can ever behave more nefariously than a man seized by this most violent fever called hatred. And hatred always does more harm to the hating person than to the hated, spiritually speaking. There is nothing like justifiable hatred as there is nothing like acceptable cancer.

Yet the misfortune is, sometimes out of ignorance we even cultivate hatred and inculcate it even in our children in a variety of naive ways; sometimes hatreds are cultivated even on national scales and that through the media of education; sometimes hatred is propagated in the name of religion, in the name of patriotism which leads to mass hysteria.

But those who are thoughtful should understand that to harbour hatred is like kissing a most virulent cobra.

In answer to the question : 'Who is the best physician,' the Buddha replied : 'Buddha, the Enlightened One is the best Physician.'

Kṣemendra, a Samskrit poet, offers salutaions to the Buddha in this manner :

Salutations to Thee, the perfect physician of the sufferings of the world, whose mind is completely filled with overwhelming compassion for creatures.

What moved Siddhartha, the Prince, to renounce the world was the anguish he felt for suffering humanity. He wanted to find a cure for the sufferings associated with human life.

He knew that before he himself was whole he could not heal. After enlightenment he used his illumination exactly in the manner a physician uses his knowledge to cure his patients. Buddha is therefore, a physician of the world.

He is the greatest physician of the world beacuse he shows the way to enlightenment, which cures all diseases for ever by cutting the very root of transmigratory existence which is ignorance.

Here the Buddha is not paying a compliment to himself as a person as the best physician, but indicating that on attainment of the state of Buddhahood, the enlightened one becomes the best physician of the world.

It may be said that every God-man or prophet is the best physician of his times and continues to be even after his physical death.

Then the higher being in the guise of the Brahmin said to the Buddha :

Now I have only one doubt to be solved; pray clear it away. What is if fire can neither burn, nor moisture corrode, nor wind crush down, but is able to reform the whole world.

Buddha, the Blessed One, replied :

Blessing ! Neither fire, nor moisture, corrosion nor wind can destroy the blessings of a good deed. And it will reform the whole world.

Stronger than all the destructive forces that are operative in the world is the power of our own good deeds. The blessing of good deeds are indestructible. In the ultimate analysis, man's true and unfailing saviour is his own good deeds. Both individual and collective salvation is possible only through good deeds alone.

The higher being, having heard the words of the Blessed One was full of exceeding joy. Clasping his hands, he bowed down before him in reverence, and disappeared suddenly from the presence of the Buddha.

We may not be able to unravel the mystery as to who was this Deva or higher being. But we all are grateful to him for putting to the Buddha so many questions on our behalf.

The answers which Buddha gave to these questions are aphorisms of wisdom. The more we shall think on them the better we will understand their relevance to our daily life in reference to our salvation.

CHAPTER-IV

LORD BUDDHA'S CONCEPTION OF THE SOUL

—P.S. Naidu

It is generally believed that Buddhism does not subscribe to the doctrine of an immortal Self or Soul. Not only the general cultured public, but also some students of philosophy accept this belief uncritically. But those who have gone deep into the matter are inclined to question the grounds on which it is contended that Lord Buddha taught that the Self is impermanent. Let us survey the entire position and see whither the arguments lead us.

Some knowledge of the intellectual atmosphere of Buddha's time is indispensable in order to answer correctly questions relating to the teachings of the Tathāgata. In the sixth century B.C., when the Master lived and taught, two views of the Self or Soul seem to have been prevalent. One is the exalted view propunded by the Upaniṣads in the Mahā Vākyas, and the other, the lower (and sometimes degraded, view preached by the Brahminical teachers of the day. These teachers circulated fantastic accounts of the Soul, and went to the extent of giving its physical dimensions. Some of them spoke of it as a thin vapour which escaped from the body at the time of death. It is against these views that Lord Buddha protested strongly. On the other hand, the Upaniṣads teach the identity of the Individual Self and Universal Self. In fact there is only one self pervading the Universe. This Self or Para Brahman is indescribable, and nothing can be predicated of it. It can only be experienced by direct, non-mediate Darśana (or in Nirvāṇa). Apart from thes two views, the exalted, pure and noble view of the Self and the degraded materialistic view which was upheld by some teachers, there was another view known as the Atman-View. This represented the soul as existing apart from body and mind, but belonging to the individual in some unique sense. This soul was unaffected by all that happened to the body and mind of the individual. It was a sort of disinterested spectator, of the phenomenal changes occuring in the body and mind. It is this restricted individualised view that Buddha condemned; it is this lower self that he denied. Nowhere does he deny the Universal Self which the Upaniṣads proclaimed. In fact there is enough evidence to show that Buddha accepted the Upaniṣadic view.

Let us state the Master's position from a different angle. Three things seem to have been indicated in the context of the Buddhistic thought, by the term 'self', namely, body, Soul and Spirit. Of these, the last, *spirit,* is identical with the Supreme Brahman of the Upaniṣads, and the Ultimate Reality of Vedanta. It is the transcendental reality which, when attained, destroys all sense of I-ness or ego-feeling and unites all beings. This reality is beyond the reach of reason, and is indescribable in human language. When questioned about this Ultimate truth, Buddha remained silent, but did not deny it. The 'Siṁśupa leaf' incident may be mentioned here. Taking a handful of leaves, lying loose in the Siṁśupa forest, Buddha asked his followers which were the more numerous, the leaves in his hand or those in the forest. The answer is obvious. Buddha wanted his disciples to understand that what he taught bore the same relationship to what he withheld, as the leaves in hid hand to those leaves in the forest. Only that much as was necessary for a holy life on the earth for attaining Nirvāṇa was revealed. The rest was kept back.

The Vacchagotta incident throws further light on the problem. The wandering ascetic Vacchagotta approaches Buddha and asks, 'Now, good Gautama, is there a Self?' Buddha is silent. 'Is there not a Self?' Again the Master is silent. After the departure of the ascetic, Ānanda asks the Lord why he was silent. The Tathāgata's reply is revealing : 'Had I replied in the affirmative to the first question I would be joining hands with the eternalists; had I said "Yes" to the second. I would be an annihilationist. Knowing as you do, Ānanda, my teaching "all things are not Self", could I have said "Yes" to Vacchagotta's first query. An affirmative answer to the second would have thrown the wandering monk into confusion. Hence, I was silent.'

The net outcome of this discussion is that Buddha had an experience of Self similar to that of the great Upaniṣadic seers, and chose to remain silent about it.

Support for this declaration of Buddhistic belief in the presence of the Universal Self behind the individual may be sought from the *Dhammapada, Digha-Nikāya* and *Vinaya Piṭaka*. The relevant texts are given below :

'Let a Bhikku reprove himself by the Self, and examine himself by the Self, so that he will live happily.' (*Dhammapada,* V. 60)

'Self is the Lord of the Self...'

(*Dhammapada,* V. 379)

'I have taken refuge in the Self.'

(Buddha in *Digha-Nikāya,* II.120)

'... make the Self your refuge and your lamp.'

(*Digha-Nikāya,* II.100)

The Self referred to in these texts, we may safely conclude, is Cosmic or Universal Self which pervades the entire Universe.

It is worth-while to note here the conclusions reached by certain scholars who have made a deep critical study of the problem. Christmas Humphrey,[1] writes : 'Nowhere in the scriptures does the Buddha deny the soul, but any attempt to explain such a complex problem to those whose fault was their love of metaphysical detail would have been of no help to them in attaining liberation from the wheel. Hence, beyond denying that those who said, "There is a self", were any more correct than those who said, "There is no self", the Buddha as always on such subjects, maintained a noble silence.'

Edmond Holmes[2] remarks : 'In these and other discourses, Buddha falls into line with the thinkers of the Upaniṣads, who described by a series of negatives what they regarded as the true Ego—the Divine in man. The coincidences between his teaching and theirs are so significant that the only way to account for them is to assume that his faith -the deepest faith of his heart—was in its essence identical with theirs.'

Dr. Radhakrishnan[3] points out that 'Buddha clearly tells us what the self is not, though he does not give any clear account of what it is. It is, however, wrong to think that there is no self at all, according to Buddha'.

Our conclusion is that Buddha denied the existence of the 'ego', but had profound experience of the Soul. He, however, chose to maintain silence about the Soul.

REFERENCES

1. Christmas Humphrey's *Buddhism,* Penguin Books, 1958, p. 86-87.
2. Edmond Holmes, *The Creed of Buddha,* The Bodley Head, London, 1957, p. 171.
3. S. Radhakrishnan, *Indian Philosophy,* George Allen and Unwin, 1923. Vol. I, p. 386.

CHAPTER-V

LORD BUDDHA AND HIS MIDDLE PATH

—V.K. Mathur

The life of Gautama, the Buddha is a beacon that has been shedding light undimmed for two and a half millenniums now, informing, inspiring and illumination people, and will continue to do so till man values more something higher than the things of the mundane world, till man cares even a little for a righteous kind of life, till man loves to live a peaceful life, nay till man exists, For it was a life of sacrifice intensely lived, in which there was no disparity between the things spoken and things done. It was a life which knew no fear, made no distinction between the high and the low.

Buddha did not lay much stress on the abstruse metaphysical side of philosophy. Perhaps, he thought he should give a practical demonstration of a good life for ages to come than dwell on mere speculation. This trend of his thought is discernible in his reply to the question regarding the existence of the soul. He asks : 'Will you, if you find a man pierced with an arrow, first try to investigate by what hunter it was shot, of what poison it was tipped and so on indefinitely or relieve the sufferer of his miseries by extracting the arrow out and applying soothing balms to the wound?' 'Man' he seems to say, 'is burning in the miseries of this world, show him the path out of it and leave alone all other dry discussions.' His life, therefore, as a most rational one appeals to one and all, starting with the unbelievers, the agnostics and the atheists up to the trustful and the religious. Whatever doctrinal differences, may there have been or still be between his followres and those of other faiths, it cannot be denied that his life has still a charm which thrills people, moves them to the core of their very being. It almost resembles a lyrical song taking you along its current of melodies, now making you see into the depths of despair at his struggle, now lifting you up, on to the crest of joy at his enlightenment, now moving you to tears at the readiness of the Blessed One to sacrifice his life to save that of a lamb, and again making you stand in awe at the sternness in his desire of maintaining the purity of his creed, free of all miracle-mongering.

What pity and compassion must have flowed in those veins, what intense sufferings should have been felt in that heart to be move so! Here we find the ununderstandable Upaniṣadic saying, (*sarvaṁ khalvidaṁ brahma*) "all this is verily Brahman," being literally lived and that not as a practice, but spontaneously as a result of the realization of the Unity of Being.

II

Now let us make a brief survey of his life, a detailed one being beyond our scope at present. Most of the accounts of Buddha's life that we get is from *Lalitavistara* and such other Pali Canons.

The Buddha is the name by which Siddhartha, the Gautama, was known after his enlightenment. He was born in the year 563 B.C. to the provincial king Suddhodana and his queen Maya, of Kapilavasthu, a township in the plains near the foot-hills of Nepal. Foretold, that his son when grown to manhood would either become a powerful king or moved by the woes of the world turn a religious leader, king Suddhodana in order to avoid the latter tradegy, as he considered it, brought up his son away from the three woes of the world : disease, old age and death. When Siddhartha grew into manhood, the father desiring to bind him securely to wealth and kingdom, had him married to a girl of his choice, named Yasodhara, beautiful and loving and virtuous. They had a lovely child who was named Rahula. Suddhodana was now feeling a little secure as he thought the responsibility of the family and love for his wife and child would hold Siddhartha back.

The wheel of time rolled on. Meanwhile, destiny seemed to have been laughing in its sleeves when the king was endeavouring, vainly, to entangle Siddhartha in the world. Siddhartha, now, desirous to know his people set forth from his palace in his chariot. And as if Providence was lying in wait, just for this moment, to strike and strike hard to shock into rude awakingness Siddhartha's consciousness, which was till then kept in the dark about the real state of affairs of the world. He came across the very three phenomena which the king had all the time kept away from his son. He saw on his way an old man, bent double, made feeble by ravages of time, dragging his burden of the body with great effort. He learnt from his charioteer that was the way of all mankind, that this same old man was once a joyous, sportive youth but that time had worked its way and reduced him to that state. Then he saw a palsied man, with some fingers of his hands missing, lying on the road side writhing in pain. To Siddhartha's feelings inquiry regarding the man Channa, the Charioteer, explained that the man was stricken with disease. Disease he said comes to human beings in several forms but none knew how. Then Siddhartha came face to face with a dead body being carried on the hearse. To Siddhartha's enquiring glance Channa said that was the end of all human beings; that those who were born had to die one day. Each of these sights had thrown Siddhartha into deeper and deer contemplation. He was sad. Was there no way out of these triple woes? thought he. As if to show him the way he next met a Saṁnyāsin, serence and self-possessed and dignified, carrying a beggar's bowl. Siddhartha was impressed and asked Channa who that person might be who could be so calm, and learnt that it was a monk who had 'abandoned all longings and led a life of austerity and lived without passion or envy and begged his daily food'. Siddhartha mused within himself, "will, that seems to be the course of life set for me"; "to become religious has ever been praised by the wise and this shall be my refuge and the refuge of others and shall yield the fruit of life, and immortality!"

He drove back to the palace brooding, unheedful of anything, and when the palace was plunged in the calmness of the night his resolve was made. Bidding farewell to his sleeping wife and child Siddhartha rode forth followed by Channa till he had covered a great distance and then putting off his royal robes and jewels, sent Channa back to the palace and himself went into homelessness. He had then reached the age of twenty-nine.

His first encounter after this great renunciation was with the king of Magadha, Bimbisara. Siddhartha who had gone on his begging ground into the city of Rajagriha had attracted attention of the people. When the king came to know of it he went to the place where Siddhartha was and impressed by the beauty of his person and nobility of his bearing, offered to bestow upon him the whole kingdom. Siddhartha refused to have anything to do with the wordly empire but promised the king to teach him his way when he had found it.

From here he proceeded to the hermitage of Ālāra Kālāma, a renowned teacher of the time, and became his disciple and learnt the art of meditation from him. But not satisfied with the metaphysical part of his teachings he retired to a forest and practised austerities, of fasting and mortification, for years until his body was like a withered branch. At the end of six years he considered the state of his mind sitting under a Jambu tree. Mortification had weakened his body and yet he was not in sight of enlightenment. He thought of abandoning the path of fasting and went and bathed in a river but he was so weak that he could not rise from the stream. With great effort he struggled out but on the way to his abode he fell down in a swoon. His companions, the five monks, thought he was dead. But he revived and then he resolved to beg his food, that his health and strength may be restored. Seeing that Siddhartha had broken his fast without attaining enlightenment the monks left him. Now, the daughter of the village headman of Uruvela where Siddhartha was practising his austerities had desires that the great Śākya Muni would design to receive food from her. So on the day he was to attain enlightenment she had a pre-vision. She, therefore, carreid a bowl of thickened milk cooked with rice and offered it to the Great One. Siddhartha took the bowl, went to the river, took his bath and having partaken of the food and refreshed his limbs made the greatest resolve : 'Let my body dry up, my skin and my nerves and my bones waste away, yet this body will not move from this seat until I have attained Supreme Enlightenment, which is difficult of attainment even after aeaons.'[1] Various were the temptations that came to him at that time, yet he overcame them all and as the dawn approached Siddhartha attained to Superme Enlightenment, became the Buddha.

It is said that the Blessed One remained in that state for 49 days enjoying the bliss of emancipation. On the forty-ninth day two merchants who were passing by his majestic figure full of peace and were moved to make an offering of food to the Blessed One. The Buddha accepted their offering and pointed out to them the way of salvation and they became his first lay disciples.

Now the Buddha deeply pondered whether he should teach what he had realized. For he thought the worldlings will not understand the truth because their happiness was in bodily enjoyment. Yet he felt an inner urge that the Truth so dearly earned should not be lost. And then he remembered his five disciples and coming to know that they were living at Isipatana near Banaras he wended his way there. The monks saw their former master approach but resolved not to show him any respect, as he had broken his vow of fasting. But as the Blessed One approached them they involuntarily rose from their seats in spite of their resolution, bowed down to him and offered him a seat and he taught them. That was his first sermon. To them he taught the ineffectiveness of useless austerities and exhorted them to follow the middle path which he had discovered.

By now he had already a good number of monks in his retinue. From Banaras he went to Rajagriha, to king Bimbisāra, and received him into fold, and preached his Dharama. From Rajagriha the Buddha made for Kapilavasthu being invited by his father. There he converted the Sākya Princes to his Dharma and received his son Rahula—who taught by his mother Yaśodhara, had claimed his patrimony—into the Order. Much later at Vesali he decided to admit women into the Order at the prayer of Ānanda who had witnessed a group of earnest women, sore of foot due to walking, and laden with dust, had come to beg of the Tathagata to be ordained as nuns.

For forty-five years the Blessed One travelled, preached and taught the way to salvation. He had now 1200 disciples who were monks. He had a great following among the lay men and women too. Now, when he was full of years (he was then eighty) and his mission was fulfilled the Blessed One proceeded to Pāra where he accepted the hospitality of Canda, a smith. But the Buddha was attacked by a fell disease soon after he partook of the meal offered by Canda and was in great pain. Yet, mindful and self-possessed the Buddha bore it without complaint. He then proceeded to Kusinara and halted in a Sālagrove. Growing weary he asked Ananda, his disciple and attendant, to spread his couch between two Sāla trees and lay down on his right side.

And as the last moments drew near lo, a seeker came and wanted to be taught and he approached Ananda. But Ananda refused permission to allow him to go to the Blessed One, Knowing that the Master was weary and was not to be troubled. However, Buddha who overheard their conversation and knowing that the seeker was sincere caused the man to be brought and dissipated all his doubts. Thus did the Buddha teach evey sincere seeker till the last breath of his life. The Blesses One's last exhortation to the Brethren was : "Decay is inherent in all component things. Work out your salvation with diligence."

III

Now we come to the teachings of the Buddha of which we shall discuss here only about the middle path. A lot of confusion has arisen in the interpreting of this path and passage of time has not helped to remove these misunderstandings. Rather people were and are still not in a mood to break the cherished images of thieir own interpretation of these teachings. People are apt to forget that a great spiritual Master's exhortations cannot be construed properly except in the light of his own life. Secondly, we have also to consider the times in which the Master lived and the context in which he spoke the particular words.

We have, as it has come down to us in translation, the Blessed One's teachings on the middle path as follows :

"The Tathāgata," said the Buddha, "does not seek salvation in austerities, but neither does he for that reason indulge in wordiy pleasures, nor live in abundance. The Tathāgata has found the middle path.

"There are two extremes, O monks, which the man who has given up the world ought not to follow—habitual practice, on the one hand, of self indulgence which is unworthy, vain and fit only for the worldly-minded; and the *habitual* practice, on the other hand, of self-mortification, which is painful, useless and unprofitable."

The Buddha continues :

"By suffering, the emaciated devotee produces confusion and sickly thoughts in his mind. Mortification is not conducive even to worldly knowledge; how much less to a triumph over the senses!"

First of all, we have to understand that fasting and mortification of the flesh was considered at that time the way to salvation. If we recollect what has been said earlier we shall find that the Buddha gave his first sermon to his disciples who had deserted him when he took to begging after being faint with fasting and mortification. The impression of the disciples that he had broken his vow by taking food and was no more a Muni but a man of the world was so great that when they saw him after his enlightenment they addressed him as "Brother", as an equal, and not as their Master. This false notion was to be counter-acted. For the Buddha had come as a saviour and he could not but drive out false notions that were prevalent in his time, to save religion from total annihilation. He had to speak the truth and in forceful language too, fitting the occasion that it demanded. Again, mortification was not the goal of man, whereas people of those times saw salvation only in it. Mortifications were, if anything, only the means. Was not then the goal forgotten in vaingloriousness of austerity? That is why the Buddha exhorts how difficult it is to triumph over the senses by mere austerity, which makes man weak and unable to know even the ordinary things of life. Who was a better authority of what is conducive to salvation than the one who had attained enlightenment himsefl? But the Buddha warns, those who may swing to the other extreme, "Sensuality is enervating; the self-indulgent man is slave to his passions, and pleasure seeking is degrading and vulgar". Yet he does not want to leave undefined what he had got to say about his middle path. So he cotinues: "But to satisfy the necessities of life is not evil. To keep the body in good health is a duty, for othewise we shall not be able to trim the lamp of wisdom, and keep our mind strong and clear.

"This is the middle path that keeps aloof from the extremes."[4]

Those who stop with the Tathāgata's instructions regarding austerity and follow not his later injunctions are in a graver danger of losing their foothold on the spiritual path than the others. This is to be remembered by all aspirants. Further, we have to consider the meaning of ever word of his sayings quoted above. There is the work "habitual" qualifying practice of austerities, which we have put in italics, to show that it is not at all against the injunctions of the Buddha to observe fasts and vigils, occasionally without injuring the body. The idea behind the Tathāgatha's instructions is clear and unambiguous and should not be twisted to suit our needs. Lest people should be led away by his denunciation of austerities the Buddha remarks : "Let him be moderate, let him eat and drink according to the needs of the body." The "needs of the body" again may be a dangerous term. For in the present times our needs have a tendency of increasing in a telescopic manner. But our ancient idea was, as Swami Vivekananda puts it, 'with how little can we keep the body trim and not with how much can we be content'.

The *Bhagavad Gītā* too gives an almost identical teaching : "Yoga cannot be practised by one who indulges in eating nor by one who completely abstains from food; neither can it be practised by one given to too much sleep nor by one who wakes up all the time. To one who is moderate in his food and rest, moderate in his physical exertions, moderate in sleep and wakefulness yoga becomes easy of practice and a dispeller of miseries."[5] Of course, this does not mean there is no stage when man can abstain from food. The Buddha, himself, if we have to believe in traditions, was without any food for 49 days after his enlightenment, immersed in the joy of that bliss. In our own times Sri Ramakrishna lived in that state for six months without being aware, of what went on round him, even of his body. Providentially, however, a wandering monk who happened to come to Dakṣiṇeśwar at that time and comprehended the real state through which Sri Ramakrishna was passing, administered food unto him sometimes even by beating Sri Ramakrishna's person to bring his mind down to the normal plane. But these are exceptional cases where illumination had been attained first. Perhaps, the needs of the body are not so exacting in that state as when man is on the normal plane. But for all others who are still aspirants the middle path prescribed by the *Gītā,* reinforced by the Buddha and reiterated by Sri Ramakrishna is the safest guide.

Sri Ramakrishna, when he was told that a certain person

had given up fish and betel leaf, is said to have remarked, 'What has poor betel leaf and fish done? Let him give up lust and gold'. The meanings is, that lust and avarice are the two greatest impediments on the spiriutal path. If one peforms austerities and yet retains longings for enjoyment her or hereafter he will not be able to attain salvation. Let us not jump to any conclusion without understanding the purport of this teaching. Observe how like a hawk Sri Ramakrishna kept his watchful eyes on his disciples. Sri Ramakrishna was very particular even as to what food, and how much of it each of his boy-disciples took, and never failed to reprimand them if it was more than the needs of the body of the particular individual. That is the middle path which the Buddha also taught. Let us remember this always and be not led astray either way.

REFERENCES

1. इहासने शुष्यतु मे शरीरं
   त्वगस्ति मांसं प्रलयञ्च यातु।
   अप्राप्य बोधिं बहु कल्प दुर्लभां
   नैव सनात्कायमतश्चलिष्यति।।

2,3&4. *Gospel of Buddhism* by Paul Carus, pp. 41 and 42. Pub : The Publication Department, Government of India, Delhi.

5. नात्यश्नतस्तु योगोऽस्ति न चैकान्तमनश्नतः।
   न चाति स्वप्नशीलस्य जाग्रतो नैवचार्जुन।।
   युक्ताहार विहारस्य युक्त चेष्टस्य कर्मसु।
   युक्त स्वप्नावबोधस्य योगो भवति दुःखहा।।

   Bhagavad Gitā, VI. 16 & 17.

CHAPTER-VI

LATER BUDDHISM IN INDIA

—Albert Schweitzer

From some words addressed to Ānanda we know anticipated that the truth he preached would endure only 500 years. Then there must be a fresh revelation of redemption.

This prophecy was not fulfilled. Five hundred years after the Buddha's death, that is to say about the beginning of our era, his doctrine was approaching the height of its flowering season. It is true it was no longer quite the same as he preached it, for it had gone on developing.

In later Buddhism there evolved the belief that from time immemorial the truth leading to redemption has been proclaimed by Buddhas. Goutam Buddha of the Śākya race is thus only one among many. In every world period—later Buddhism adopts from the Sāṃkhya system the conception of successive world periods—and every part of the Universe (that is to say, not only on the earth) from time to time Buddhas make their appearance. Goutam Buddha is not the last. Others will follow him.

According to late Buddhist doctrine, all the Buddhas derive from a heavenly, self-created Proto-Buddha (Ādi-Buddha) from whom the Universe also has its origin. Among the eternal Buddhas whose descent is directly traceable from him, Buddha-Amitābha (he of immeasurable light), the protector of the present world, is pre-eminent. His dwelling-place is the world of Paradise, Sukhāvatī. The dogmatics of the late Buddhism made Goutam Buddha also a heavenly being who took on him the form of a man in order to bring knowledge of redemption to the world. In individual writings of the period he was even described, like the Proto-Buddha, as "the self-created Father of the Universe". The later Buddhist doctrine of Buddhas was not developed consistently, but contains many obscurities and contradictions.

So later Buddhism became a religion. And it was not contented with merely sanctioning the adoration of Buddhas, but brought about the revival of the worship of the gods in general, to which Goutam Buddha had denied all importance.

Whilst it thus developed into a popular religion, later Buddhism wandered far from the doctrine of the historical Buddha that deliverance from reincarnation can only be attained by the monastic life and renunciation of the world. It asserted that those who remain in ordinary life also share in redemption, if in faith they venerate the divine Buddha and confidently dedicate themselves to him.

This new teaching, which announced a way of redemption which all can enter and more easily follow, is called the doctrine of the "big vessel" (Mahāyāna). The original doctrine derived from the historical Buddha is described as that of the "small vessel" (Hīnayāna). By this is meant the vessel which conveys men across the stream of re-birth and suffering to the shore of Nirvāṇa.

Mahāyāna-Buddhism also went beyond the teaching of the historical Buddha in that it no longer regarded liberation from reincarnation as the highest goal to be aimed at. The idea of compassion was so strongly developed in it that it became incomprehensible how the Buddha could let man be preoccupied merely with his own redemption and not also with that of the Universe. Therefore it set up as an ideal that the man who has attained deliverance from reincarnation should renounce entrance into Nirvāna in order to appear again and again on earth and strive for the deliverance of all living creatures. On these saints who again and again voluntarily accept human existence, Mahāyāna-Buddhism confers the rank and dignity of Bodhisattvas, that is to say candidates for Buddhahood.

Mahāyāna-Buddhism is a logical development of the original Buddhism.

The Buddha ponders over the idea of compassion. But at the same time he makes man still in quite egoistic fashion think only of his own deliverance from the cycle of transmigration.

Mahāyāna-Buddhism takes account of the fact that the idea of compassion, once it is there, cannot be satisfied with just any kind of part alloted to it, but wants to dominate thought completely and must therefore demur to all egoistic longing for redemption.

With magnificent sincerity Mahāyāna-Buddhism resists the temptation to trace its origins to the Buddha by "cooking" tradition. It does not deny that the Buddha urged men before all things to strive after deliverance from reincarnation, and that he himself talked of entering into Nirvāṇa. But this he did only, the Mahāyāna teachers explain, because his contemporaries would not have been capable of understanding the higher truth that one ought to renounce Nirvāṇa. Therefore we must set the teaching that proceeds from the spirit of his compassion above that which was preached from his lips.

So, according to the Mahāyāna doctrine, Goutam Buddha did not enter into Nirvāṇa at all, but is labouring on and on in heavenly regions for the spreading in the world of the knowledge of redemption. "He pours down the great rain of religion and makes the big drum of religion thunder forth."

Mahāyāna-Buddhism reached its full development in north-east India, probably during the first two centuries of our era. Its sacred writings are not, like those of the older Buddhism, in the Pāli language, but in Sanskrit.

Mahāyāna-Buddhism reached Tibet and China and was there preserved, whilst in India in the course of centuries Buddhism disappeared altogether; consequently we possess a series of important Mahāyāna texts, of which the Sanskrit originals have been lost, in Tibetan and Chinese translations.

The best-known work of Mahāyāna-Buddhism is the *Saddharmapundarīka* (the Lotus of Good Doctrine). It glorifies Goutam Buddha as a divine being enthroned on a mountain surrounded by thousands of gods and Buddhas and Bodhisattvas. This text was probably in existence before A.D. 200. As early as A.D. 223 and again in A.D. 286 it was translated into Chinese.

The *Lalitavistara* ("The Complete Story of the Play", to give it full, "of the Buddha") describes in legendary fashion how the divine Buddha took human form in the Śākya family and gives an account of his work on earth. The oldest portions of the text probably originated before the Christian era.

The *Sukhāvatīvyūha* ("A Complete Description of the Blessed Land") treats of Buddha Amitābha and the Sukhāvatī-Paradise. This work was translated into Chinese as early as between A.D. 147 and 186.

Nāgārjuna (2nd century A.D.?), a member of a Brahmin family, and the learned poet Śāntideva (7th century A.D.) are great teachers of Mahāyāna.

In Mahāyāna-Buddhism, then, the Buddha's idea of compassion reaches its full development. Its followers aim at attaining to the perfection of "the great compassion". How profound is the saying, "As long as living creatures suffer, there is no possibility of joy for those who are full of compassion!" For the first time in the thought of mankind, world-view is dominated by the idea of compassion.

But this mighty compassion could not develop and exercise its full influence in a natural way. Like the original Buddhism, Mahāyāna-Buddhism too is imprisoned in world and life negation. So that like the former it can really only give its approval to non-activity. Like the former too, it cannot attribute any real importance to the help which goes to alleviate material distress. And like the former again, the only effective act of compassion it can recognise is the diffusion of the knowledge that redemption will be won by denial of the will-to-live.

Mahāyāna-Buddhism is concerned for the deliverance of all living creatures. But it is no more able than the Sāṃkhya system and the Buddha to explain how it is possible and ought to come about.

So Mahāyāna compassion has its hands bound in just the same way as were those of the Buddha himself. Fundamentally it is nothing other than the compassion in thought which the Buddha made a duty for his monks, only it is raised beyond all bounds. Therefore it cannot any longer remain contemplative as in the Buddha, but lives to the full in compassionate desires, often in every orgies of compassionate desires.

The Mahāyāna believer prays for all beings, that they may suffer no want, be spared pain and sickness, not be deserted and oppressed, may pass a happy life free from thought of sin, and that from lower forms of existence they may enter into the higher forms which lead to redemption. Long intercessory prayers of this sort are found in the Mahāyāna writings. Because women are reckoned among the lower beings, supplication is made for them that they may be born again as men. In these prayers there is remembrance also of those who dwell in hell in anguish and torment. The "great compassion" applies not only to the creatures that dwell on earth, but to all living things in all worlds.

From Mahāyāna Texts[1]—"In all lands may all the sufferings of living beings come to an end."—"May all living beings in the ten regions of the universe who are weak, sick, reduced in circumstances and unprotected be freed from their trouble."—"May the beaten be freed from blows, may those who are threatened with death be restored to life, and may those who are in tribulation become free from all fear."—"May those who suffer hunger and thirst receive food and drink in abundance."

"May the blind see, the deaf hear, the women with child give birth painlessly."—"May sounds of pain be nowhere heard in the world. And may no single living being experience what is disagreeable."—"May living creatures avoid the low way" (reincarnation).—"May all women constantly be born again as men, as brave heroes and wise scholars."—"May they see the Buddhas in the ten regions of the universe, sitting comfortably in the glorious trees of precious stones on thrones of beryl, and may they hear the sermons they preach."

"May the torment and anguish of those who dwell in hell come to an end."—"May the fear of being devoured by each other quite the animals; may the ghosts be happy."—"I exult over the liberation of living beings from the sufferings of the cycle of reincarnation."

But Mahāyāna compassion does not exhaust itself merely in abstract wishes, but is concerned also with deeds expressed in wishes. The simple natural act of compassion is not taken into account at all. In the Mahāyāna texts there is indeed much talk to the effect that the hungry should be fed, the thirsty given drink, the sick nursed. But one seeks in them in vain for commands actually to give loving aid to alleviate distress. Mahāyāna-Buddhism ultimately only takes into consideration theoretical acts which contribute towards real complete deliverance from suffering existence. The "great compassion" does not allow the Mahāyāna believer, as the Buddha did, to be satisfied with announcing the truth which brings deliverance. It compels him to be willing in thought to give up for the redemption of others the treasure of good works which he has gained, to take upon himself the sufferings of others, to enter in their stead into a lower form of existence and for them to endure the pains of hell. Instead of simply practising compassion, he is occupied with great deeds of heroic self-sacrifice which he wants to accomplish as a Bodhisattva.

From Mahāyāna Texts[2]—"May I lead all living beings into the city of Nirvāṇa."—"May I, for the sake of the good I have accomplished, be a soother of all sufferings of all beings."—"All merit which I have achieved, I here without concern give up for the welfare of all beings."

"I strive not merely for my own redemption. I must lead all these living beings...out of the flood of transmigration. I must take upon myself the whole mass of the suffering of all beings. In so far as I can, I will taste to the full all sufferings in all evil forms of existence as they are arrived at in all parts of the Universe... I am determined to live in every single form of existence for countless millions of periods of the Universe...It is indeed better that I alone suffer than that all living beings should reach the abodes of the evil forms of existence."

"The Bodhisattvas who realise the connection (between themselves and other beings) and have pleasure only in the mitigation of others' sufferings rush into hell like flamingoes into a lotus grove."

St. Paul similarly in exaltation utters the words (Epistle to the Romans, ix. 3) : "I could wish that myself were accursed from Christ for my bretheren, my kinsmen according to the flesh."

In Mahāyāna-Buddhism compassion makes its appearance in such strength that really it ought to revolt against world and life negation and lay claim to the right of helpful activity. But world and life negation stand firm as a rock for later Buddhism, which remains its thrall although it contains in itself even more living instincts to activity than are found in the Buddha himself.

It is because compassion is so strongly developed in Mahāyāna-Buddhism that we see with such perfect clearness how unnatural it becomes through world and life negation. With the Buddha compassion is still in some degree able to pretend it is contented with non-activity. But in Mahāyāna-Buddhism it can no longer do this, but must endeavour to surmount the difficulties of the problem of non-activity by an illusion of imaginary activity.

But how wonderful that there was once a time when there were in the world millions of people so entirely dominated by feelings of compassion!

It is interesting that Mahāyāna-Buddhism undertakes to find a basis for compassion in knowledge. For this it goes back to the denial of the *ego* by the Buddha. If there be no *ego,* he argues, then there is no difference between one *ego* and another. So the foundations of compassion are really laid in the fact that the thinking man must confess to himself that he cannot really define the boundaries between his own *ego* and those of other beings. In the exercise of compassion this truth of there being no distinction between the I and the Thou (Parāmasamatā) is known through the feelings.

From Mahāyāna Texts[3]—"From habit we connect the conception of the self with our own body, which nevertheless has no self, Why does not the idea of the self as referring to others similarly arise also from habit?"—"No man exists whose suffering is really his own. Of whom then can it be said, that it is *his* suffering? All sufferings without distinction are ownerless. Because they are sufferings, therefore we must keep them off. What sense has any limitation in this (that is to say that one keeps off only suffering that one regards as one's own)?"—"If fear and pain are as much hated by my neighbour as by myself, what then distinguishes my self that I should protect it more than I protect him?"

On the ground of identity of the I and the Thou, as it follows from the doctrine of the Brahman, the Upanishads explain all love as self-love. "In truth", says Yājñavalkya to his wife Maitreyī, "the husband is not dear for the husband's sake, but the husband is dear for the sake of the Self", and "Living beings are not dear for the sake of living beings but living beings are dear for the sake of the Self".[4] That is to say, because the same Brahman dwells in others as in ourselves, that which seems to us to be love for others is merely self-love of the Brahman.

So because of the impossibility of distinguishing between the I and the Thou, it is determined in that Upanishad that all love to one's neighbour is only the profoundest self-love. Mahāyāna-Buddhism on the contrary proves from that same impossibility that there can be no self-love, but only love for one's neighbour. These contrary assertions come to the same thing in the long run. By both of them ethics are reduced to nothing by the explanations given. True ethics presume the absolute difference of one's own *ego* and those of others and accentuate it. The difference, however, is not a plain matter of course but an enigma.

But Mahāyāna-Buddhism does not merely make use of the Buddha's theory of knowledge to explain ethics : it also develops it further as such. Those who undertake to do this are probably Brahmanic thinkers. Otherwise we could not well understand how the Buddha's theory of knowledge is made of service to a belief which is the counterpart of the Brahmanic doctrine of Māyā.

In the opinion of the teachers of Mahāyāna the Buddha only conceded some kind of reality to the world of the senses because his pupils would not have been able to grasp the truth that it has none. As a matter of fact, they said, he assumed that the outer world exists only in our consciousness. That he who knows regards what he knows as something different from himself with an independent existence of its own rests on illusion (Māyā). The outer world is a vision of conceptions which we carry within ourselves. The conformity to law which we observe in it is due to the fact that every conception is the result of a previous conception. In meditation and ecstasy man is liberated from the delusion that the world of the senses is real.

As this teaching, in opposition to the view of the Buddha, holds the conscious *ego* to be a spiritual reality, other Mahāyāna teachers, among them the celebrated Nāgārjuna (2nd century A.D.), advance to the assertion that we can assume the existence neither of a material nor of a spiritual reality. They devise the phrase, "All is nothing". According to them, there is neither Being nor non-Being, but merely Nothing which is neither Being nor non-Being. Not only is the outer world which man perceives an illusion, but so also is his belief that he exists and perceives it. This doctrine is called the doctrine of absolute emptiness (Śūnyatā). It gains a footing, and in Mahāyāna-Buddhism actually attains the importance of a dogma.

But what is compassion doing in an unreal world? How can Mahāyāna-Buddhism combine its ethics with its nihilistic doctrine of existence?

This is only possible on the hypothesis of twofold truth. For if our existence and the existence of the Universe are merely the visions of a dream, they nevertheless as such have for us a relative reality. We must behave in a way which corresponds to the imaginated world and our supposed existence in it. As this world seems to us full of suffering, it is our duty to strive to bring the suffering in it to an end. Following the usual course of thought and imagination, man holds to this relative truth, and through a life passed in a compassionate disposition and through faith in the grace of the divine Buddha attains to celestial bliss. The delusion about duties (Kāryamoha) does not matter. It is not merely harmless, but also beneficent.

But in self-submergence man has insight into the highest truth of "emptiness" and through it wins real deliverance from the delusion of existence.

The Buddha—and in this is seen his greatness—avoids having anything to do with a doctrine of two-fold truth. But as a matter of fact it is present with him through it is hidden. Without embarrassment he premises the Self for the purposes of ethics, the Self whose existence he denies in his theory of knowledge. In Mahāyāna-Buddhism what is hidden in the Buddha becomes manifest.

In this impracticable distinction between an ethical, relative truth and an absolute truth which stands above all ethics, late Buddhist thought admits that it cannot acquire ethics from knowledge of the Universe and cannot combine knowledge of the Universe with ethics.

Ceylon, Burma and Siam remain faithful to the older Buddhism.

According to tradition, Buddhism came to Ceylon through Mahendra, the son (or brother) of the famous Buddhist King of North India, Aśoka (272-231 B.C.). The name Aśoka is an abbreviation of Aśoka-Vardhana, which means "Increaser of freedom from care".

At the beginning of his reign Aśoka, like his father, was a protector of the Brahmins. He was probably converted to Buddhism out of repentance for the conquests he had made with fire and sword. His kingdom comprised not only the valleys of the Indus and Ganges, but also large territories lying to the south of these rivers. He declared himself the protector and promoter of Buddhism and sent out Buddhist missionaries in all directions.

Siam received Buddhism from Cambodia. where it is supposed to have begun to be known in the year A.D. 422. It is said to have reached Burma before the 6th century A.D.

The older Buddhism only suffered alteration in Ceylon, Burma and Siam in so far as in these countries to conceded importance also to popular religion and worship.

To celebrate his jubilee in the year 1893, King Chulalongkorn of Siam published a complete edition of the sacred writings of the older Buddhism belonging to the Tripiṭaka (the Three Baskets).[5]

To-day the older Buddhism is found only in Ceylon and Further India. In India proper (Hindustan)—except in Nepal, on the southern slopes of the Himalayas—Buddhism has altogether disappeared. In Nepal, China, Tibet, Korea and Japan it is Mahāyāna-Buddhism and derivatives of it that are found.

How comes it that Buddhim has ceased to exist in its own home-land, Hindustan?

It was not exterminated by persecutions, but gradually lost its adherents because it could not sustain the competition against Brahmanic teaching with its freshly increasing strength, and Hinduism, which became more and more widespread.

Its decline began about A.D. 800. About A.D. 1600 Buddhism—except in Nepal—ceased to exist in India (Hindustan).

The Brahmanic system and Hinduism are superior to Buddhism by virtue of their mysticism. They stand for the elemental idea of the union of the human spirit with the Spirit of the Universe. Thus they possess something simple and living which is lacking in Buddhism.

The denial by Buddhism of the idea of a highest and purest Being and the idea of the soul involves it in complications. It loses its connection with natural imagining and thinking, and its relationship to the natural piety of the Indian.

Buddhism (in common with the Sāmkhya doctrine and Jainism) is only concerned with the idea of deliverance from reincarnation. But this can never attain the significance of a real world-view. It is too narrow for that. The idea on the other hand of the union of the human spirit with the Spirit of the Universe does comprise a world-view. World-view can in some fashion fit into the idea of deliverance from reincarnation, if men's minds are preoccupied with this. But the idea of liberation from reincarnation cannot become a world-view. This is the real ground of the inferiority of Buddhism as compared with the Brahmanic doctrine and Hinduism. Thought cannot desist from seeking a real world-view.

If Buddhism was able to maintain itself for so many centuries in face of Brahmanism and Hindusim, it was because it is the creation of a great mind and because its ethics are superior to theirs. But in measure as the Brahmanic teaching and Hinduism, stimulated by Buddhism, develop ethically—and this is especially the case with Hinduism—their superiority as compared with that faith makes itself felt.

Brahmanism and Hinduism have the futher advantage that they are in natural association with the religion of the people. The original Buddhism declared its independence of that. It is true that later Buddhism resumed relations with it, but it no longer had the same position in relation to it that had Brahmanism and Hinduism.

And it surely contributed also to the decline of Buddhism in India that it rejected the old sacred writings of the Veda, whilst the Brahmins appeal to them from time immemorial and Hinduism reverences them more and more. And this, in the Indian Middle Ages—which began about the same time as in Europe—when the witness of the past was increasingly valued, became fatal for Buddhism. As it is not rooted in popular religion, it cannot lay claim to the sacred writings for its own purposes. The fact that the Buddha was not a reformer, but a revolutionist, brings its own retribution.

Speaking generally, the decay of the influence of Buddhism in India is to be explained by its uncompromising attitude in the question whether the man who is living a married life cannot also have a share in redemption. The Brahmanic and Hindu systems made to world and life affirmation the great concession that they did not merely tolerate marriage, but recognised it as enjoined by the commands of natural law. They asserted that man can attain to a state of blessedness in the existence in which he fulfils the duties of the father of a household. There are even sayings of Brahmanic teachers which assert that it is necessary for his redemption that a man should pass through the stage of being the head of a family.

With the Buddha on the other hand redemption can only be won in an existence entirely consecrated to world and life negation. Owing to the contempt for married life which accompanied this theory, his doctrine was at variance with popular feeling, which by tradition regarded the institution of marriage as sacred. That is why as time went on his radical world and life negation was defeated by the moderate world and life negation of Brahmanism and Hinduism.

It was Islam that gave the death-blow to Indian Buddhism. Between the years 1175 and 1340 Mohammedan conquerors who came from Persia founded their dominion over the greater part of India. Because Buddhism was not backed up by the religion of the people, it could not offer so tough a resistance to the new faith as did the Brahmanic doctrine and Hinduism. In Java also and in Sumatra and other Indian islands it was Islam that supplanted Buddhism; Jainism too, owing to Islam, lost the position it had previously held.

But indeed no complete explanation can be given of how it came about that Buddhism ceased to exist in India, the land of its origin, where for centuries it had exercised such great power over men's minds. So many events in the domain of spiritual history are in the nature of an enigma.

But that Buddhism ceased to exist does not mean that the Buddha had no more significance for India. At the time when the people renounced his radical world and life negation, his ethical ideas had already become common property. His ethical influence continues down to the present day.

Even his radical world and life negation is still in operation. Gandhi's esteem for celibacy may be traced back to the Buddha.

REFERENCES

1. These Quotations are from Professor Moriz Winternitz's *Der Mahāyāna-Buddhismus* (Siebert und Mohr, Tübingen, 1930), pp. 46-47, 53, 61.
2. Quotations from Winternitz's *Der Mahāyāna-Buddhismus*, 1930, pp. 39, 53, 34-35, 59.
3. Quotations from Winternitz's *Der Mahāyāna-Buddhismus*, pp. 58-60, 44.
4. Bṛhad-Āraṇyaka-upaniṣad, 2.4.
5. On these writings, see p. 90.

CHAPTER-VI

BUDDHISM IN CHINA, TIBET AND MONGOLIA

—Albert Schweitzer

According to a tradition which arose at the end of the 2nd century A.D., the Emperor Ming Ti of China (Later Han Dynasty), by reason of a dream in the year A.D. 61, sent a mission to India to fetch to his own country Buddhist teachers, texts and objects used in worship. In reality, knowledge of Buddhism had already reached China before our own era began, by way of nothern India and eastern Turkestan. So it was the later Buddhism of northern India, from which the Mahāyāna doctrine developed, which spread in China.

As early as the middle of the 3rd century A.D. Buddhism had followers all over China and was already beginning to exercise some influence. In time the Mahāyāna system supplanted the earlier form of later Buddhism.

Between the 4th and 11th centuries A.D. numerous Chinese adherents of Buddhism came as pilgrims to India in order to visit the spots where the Master had sojourned and to fetch sacred writings. They usually chose the difficult route which leads through the desert of Central Asia, through the Tarim-Becken (Eastern Turkestan) and over the Himalayas, and more rarely the sea route via Further India. We possess valuable accounts of such pilgrimages by Fah-Hien and (Hsüan Tsang. Fah-Hien's journey lasted from A.D. 399 to 414, that of Hsüan Tsang from A.D. 629 to 645. The latter brought home 657 Buddhist texts.

The majority of the many translations of Buddhist works into Chinese date from the period before A.D. 1000.

The so-called "Sūtra of the 42 Sections", certainly one of the most ancient writings of Chinese Buddhism, is traced back to the two Buddhist missionaries who are supposed to have come to China in the 1st century A.D. with the ambassadors of the Emperor Ming Ti. It offers a short compendium of the later Buddhist teaching put into the mouth of the Buddha. Ethical thoughts have made their way into the foreground. But the Mahāyāna dogma, that there is no reality at all, is also preached.

How was it that Buddhism, with its negation of the world and life, could exercise such a force of attraction on the Chinese who in their simple way are devoted to world and life affirmation?

It certainly and above all was the enthusiastic ethics of Mahāyāna that enlisted their sympathy. From the time of Confucius (Kung-Tse, 551-479 B.C.) and his successors downward they were accustomed to inquiry about ethical duties. In Mahāyāna-Buddhism they now found an ethic which did not dictate to them in dry commandments, like that of Confucius, but was founded on profound reflections about the nature of Being. The grandeur and inwardness of the ethic of compassion fascinated them.

Buddhism, further, met their religious needs, needs for which Taoism had but little to offer, whilst Confucianism completely ignored them.

The great teacher of Taoism was Lao-Tse (born about 550 B.C. or somewhat earlier), the author of the Tao-Te-King. The original meaning of the word Tao is path. In its metaphorical sense it signifies the fundamental principle of what happens in the Universe. The Tao-Te-King in a collection of aphorisms teaches life in harmony with this.

Along with Lao-Tse, Lieh-Tse (about 440-370 B.C.) and Chuang-Tse (about 380-310 B.C.) may also be named as well-known representatives of Taoism.

Taoism—as becomes specially clear from the writings of Lieh-Tse—is a mysticism, stretching far back into prehistoric times, of union with the Primal Force at work in the Universe, a mysticism which originated in magical ideas and ecstatic experiences. Thus it has the same origin and is at bottom of the same nature as the magic mysticism to which the Brahmanic mysticism goes back. Lao-Tse was not, as is so often assumed, the creator of Taoism, but found it already there. Like Lieh-Tse and Chuang-Tse he made it nobler and more profound by developing from its spiritual and ethical truths.

Alongside of the philosophical Taoism developed by these thinkers, the primitive-religious form persists. In this the idea of union with the Primal Force is overgrown with ideas of magic, and to this union is especially ascribed the important feature that by means of it magical power is won. So it comes about that by Taoism we have to understand a grand, mystical, philosophical system and at the same time a primitive religious mysticism in which magical practices play a great part.

China knows no other popular religion than the Taoist. That is why Mahāyāna-Buddhism, which teaches love to Buddha-Amitābha, redemption through his grace and re-birth to a life of bliss in his heavenly Paradise, finds so great a response.

Through Taoism China is in a sense prepared for Buddhism. The Buddhist exercises in self-submergence in order to reach ecstasy are nothing new to the Taoists. They follow similar practices themselves.

Through Taoism Chinese thought is also in a position to enter into friendly relations with the Buddhist world and life negation. Lao-Tse and Chuang-Tse teach that man attains to being in harmony with what happens in the Universe by abstaining from activity—even from activity that ranks as ethical. All action ensuing on human plans, according to them, implies a disturbance of the Universe, which goes on its course in obedience to a mysterious, meaningful, ordered system. So right conduct consists in kindly inactivity.[1]

Lao-Tse and Chuang-Tse, however, do not leave the firm ground of world and life affirmation. They believe all that happens in the Universe as it appears in the world of the senses to be something that is full of meaning. But their doctrine of kindly inactivity has indeed much in common with that of Buddhism, although it rests on quite different hypotheses.

Thus it becomes explicable how that Chinese mind could feel so strongly attracted to Buddhism as to lose its sense of the fundamental difference between the world and life affirmation with which it was familiar and the Buddhist world and life negation, and how it came to exchange its own world and life affirmation for world and life negation. How potent must have been the effects on the Chinese of the fascination of the foreign system of thought when they became enthusiasts for the ideal of monastic life, which was so alien to their natural feeling and their tradition!

During the centuries when such things were happening in China, in Europe the young peoples of the Great Migration (Völkerwanderung) were being led by the world and life negation of Greco-Roman Christianity to doubt their natural world and life affirmation, and were beginning to set a high value on the monastic ideal of life.

The Chinese understood Buddhism, then, as a kind of

Taoism. To express its concepts and ideas, they drew on the vocabulary of Taoism. And Taoism on its side adopted expressions and thoughts from Buddhism.

At the present day Taoism still contains Buddhist elements.

Taoism and Buddhism of the noblest kind are found side by side in the commandments of the Rules of the Order of Taoist monks in China.

From the Commandments for Monks of Present-day Monastic Taoism in China[2]—1st commandment : "Thou shalt kill no living thing, neither damage its life".—2nd commandment : "Thou shalt not eat the flesh and blood of any living thing".—3rd commandment : "Thou shalt drink no strong drink".—4th commandment : "Thou shalt not eat the five bitter herbs".[3]—5th commandment : "Thou shalt not utter flattery nor speak with a double tongue, nor utter untruths".—6th commandment : "Thou shalt not make malicious nor insulting speeches".—7th commandment : "Thou shalt not accept baseless lies as founded on fact, nor unproved lies as things proved".—8th commandment : "Thou shalt not let thine eyes rest secretly on women and girls, and so shalt thou avoid awakening even the slightest of unchaste thoughts".—9th commandment : "Thou shalt not steal from nor rob any one".—10th commandment : "Thou shalt not fraudulently overreach others even to the value of a copper coin".—11th commandment : "Thou shalt not make attempts against any kind of property belonging to others".—12th commandment : "Thou shalt not unrighteously covet the possessions of others."

14th commandment : "Thou shalt not be ungrateful for the kindness and affection of thy teachers".—15th commandment : "Thou shalt not envy the noble nor be jealous of the good".—18th commandment : "Thou shalt not deceive and hoodwink old people and children".

115th commandment : "Thou shalt not repulse beggars nor treat them with contumely".—145th commandment : "Thou shalt not boast of thy ability to cure others".—218th commandment : "Thou shalt be careful first to save others, afterwards thyself".

The well-known commandments of compassion for animals from the Kan-Ying-P'ien are also found in these monastic Rules.[4] 34th commandment : "Thou shalt not whip not beat... domestic animals"—35th commandment : "Thou shalt not with intention crush beneath thy feet insects and ants".—36th commandment : "Thou shalt not take delight in fish-hooks or arrows in order to get amusement".—37th commandment : "Thou shalt not climb trees to take nests and destroy the eggs".—63rd commandment : "Thou shalt not catch birds or animals in snares and nets".—64th commandment : "Thou shalt not alarm and scare away birds sitting on their nests".—65th commandment : "Thou shalt not pick flowers nor pluck up grass without reason".—66th commandment : "Thou shalt not cut down trees without season".—67th commandment : "Thou shalt not burn commons nor hill-side woods".—68th commandment : "Thou shalt not dig out animals hibernating in the earth in the winter months".—112th commandment : "Thou shalt not pour hot water on the ground for the purpose of destroying insects and ants".

According to a belief already found in China in the 2nd century A.D., Lao-Tse—who, says an old tradition, wandered westward after writing down the Tao-Te-King and ended his days in a foreign land—went to India and appeared there as the Buddha. It is a fact that Lao-Tse, the Buddha and Confucius were contemporaries.

Buddhism, at all events to begin with, found most of its patrons and followers in the circles of Taoist philosophy and Taoist popular religion.

In Chinese as in Indian Buddhism whole series of schools and communities (Tsungs) were formed. The question of the reality and non-reality of material and spiritual Being was discussed in them in all its bearings.

But the chief difference between them is that in some of them Buddhism was principally the religion of faith in Buddha Amitābha and bliss in a "pure land", that is to say, in the Sukhāvatī Paradise, whilst in the others was fostered rather the true Buddhist meditation. The founder of the great school of meditation, also called the School of Inwardness (Hsin-Tsang), was the great Indian teacher Bodhidharma, who came—by the sea route—to China somewhat about A.D. 525 and worked there upto his death (A.D. 535). Bodhidharma exhorted his pupils to practise self-submergence. Through this alone, not through letters and learning, was the knowledge of the unspeakable truth of Being and redemption from the illusion of Being to be won. Later on—towards the end of the 6th century A.D.—the Chinese Buddhism of meditation also constructed for itself of cult.

A lower form of Buddhism, which like the most primitive Taoism sought to satisfy the superstition and belief in magic of the people, also developed, especially after the 8th century A.D. It called itself "The School of Secrets" (Mi-Tsung).

About A.D. 1050 a Buddhist monk issued a work with the title *Support of Religion,* in which he developed the view of Chinese Buddhism that the Buddha, Lao-Tse and Confucius preached one and the same doctrine. In the period which followed, statues of Lao-Tse and Confucius were erected in Buddhist monastries and chapels by the side of those of the

Buddha. Lao-Tse was given the place on his left, which is regarded in China as the place of honour, and Confucius that on his right.

About the year A.D. 1000 the spiritual and mental development of Chinese Buddhism came to a stand-still. It really possessed no creative force of its own, but lived by the stimulation it received from India. This is the only comprehensible way in which we can account for the absence of controversy between the ethical world and life affirmation of the Chinese mind and the ethical world and life negation of Buddhism.

Chinese Buddhism could not constantly enjoy peace. At times it had to undergo severe persecutions. It was Confucianism that waged war against the foreign faith.

Under the T'sang Dynasty the Confucian dignitaries Fu-Yi (A.D. 624), Yao-Ch'ung (A.D. 714) and Han-Yü (A.D. 819) brought bills of indictment against Buddhism before the Emperors. In the year A.D. 844, under the Emperor Wu-Tsang, the first harsh persecution aimed at all foreign religions broke out, and it meant the end of Manichaeism and the religion of Zarathustra in China and dealt to Buddhism blows from which it never fully recovered. Fortunately Wu-Tsung's successor, Hsüan-Tsung, brought the persecution to an end.

In the following centuries the rulers sought to put a stop to the undue multiplication of Buddhist monasteries. The founding of monasteries and entrance to the monastic life were made dependent on the permission of the authorities. Monasteries were often broken up, their estates confiscated, their bronze statues melted down to mint coinage, and their monks and nuns forced to go back and earn their living in ordinary life. In the year 1019 the pious Emperor Chen-Tsung (998-1022) of the Sung Dynasty (960-1127) for a time granted full liberty to Buddhism and Taoism alike, and in that same year upwards of 230,000 men and 15,000 women entered Buddhist cloisters! Chen-Tsung's successors found themselves compelled to return to the former measures in order to prevent the life of the people being endangered by Buddhism.

The Emperor Hui-Tsung (1101-1125) of the Sung Dynasty forbade the erection of statues of Lao-Tse and Confucius beside those of the Buddha, but without great success.

These measures taken by the authorities against Buddhism stopped it from spreading among the upper classes, but could do little to weaken its prestige among the masses.

And from time to time also there were reigning princes who more or less favoured it. Among these were Genghiz-Khan (1162-1227), the Mongol conqueror of Peking, and his grandson Kublai-Khan (*d.* 1294), the first Mongol Emperor of China.

Under the Ming Dynasty (1368-1644) and the Ch'ing (Manchu) Dynasty (1644-1912) Confucianism gained the upper hand, whilst Buddhism lost its influence more and more.

The outward decline was accompanied by spiritual decay. It became more and more religion of the people, addressing itself to the quite uneducated and hardly continuing to possess any spiritual or ethical interests.

In the last few decades attempts, originating in Japan, have been made to uplift and reform Chinese Buddhism. We cannot yet tell whether they will have any success.

Buddhism reached Tibet in the 7th century A.D. under King Srong-btsan-sgam-po, who had for wives a Chinese and a Nepalese princess. It was at their wish that he introduced it.

The priests of the new religion gradually succeeded in taking possession of the power. In the 11th century they made an end of the monarchy. Tibetan Buddhism developed into a strongly organised church exercising temporal sovereignty.

The man who deserves the credit for the exalted position of Tibetan Buddhism is the monk Tsung-kha-pa ("the man from the vale of onions"), who at the beginning of the 15th century A.D. appeared in its fold as a reformer. He succeeded in introducing monastic celibacy and strove against superstition and magic.

At the head of Tsung-kha-pa's reformed Tibetan Buddhist church are two Grand Lamas (Lama means the chief), who are regarded as incarnations of the Buddha. One—who since 1575 bears the title Dalai Lama (the Lama like the ocean)—resides in Lhassa, the other, the Pantchen-Erdeni-Lama (that is to say, the Lama who is the jewel among scholars), in the Ta-shi-lhum-po Monastery. The first is reputed to be the incarnation of the divine Bodhisattva Avalokiteśvara, the other that of Buddha Amitābha. The Grand Lama at Lhassa rules on earth, the other is more occupied with spiritual things. The successors of the Grand Lamas are sought among the boys born at the hour of their death. The origin of this custom is the belief that the Buddha who dwelt in the deceased Grand Lama is born again in a human form immediately after his death.

The commandment not to kill living creatures is only followed by the Buddhists of Tibet in a quite superficial fashion. They think it sufficiently observed, if they abstain from forms of slaughter which involve the shedding of blood. So when they lust after the flesh of a domesticated animal, they hold its mouth and nose and subject it to a cruel death by suffocation.

From Tibet the Buddhism of the Lamas spread in the

13th century to Mongolia, at the time when the great Mongol rulers conquered Tibet. Under Kublai-Khan the conversion of the Mongols made great progress.

Lamaistic Buddhism maintains its independence in face of Chinese Buddhism. Since China at the end of the 17th century A.D. made Tibet its vassal, a representative of the Dalai Lama at Lhassa resides in Peking. He too is regarded as an incarnation of the Buddha. And it is the same with the highest dignitary of Mongol Lamaism, who is resident at Urga.

The magnificent temples at Jehol, the summer residence of the Chinese Emperors of the Manchu Dynasty, lying north of Peking the other side of the Great Wall, which were robbed of their treasures when the Chinese Empire came to an end, were built in the 18th century for Lama worship.

It was permissible for the Emperors of China to show disfavour to Chinese Buddhism. But in order not to endanger their dominion over Tibet and Mongolia they were obliged to maintain an attitude of good-will towards the religion of the Lamas in North China as well, where it had spread. Since 1911, the Dalai Lama at Lhassa has been dependent on England. The Pantchen Lama, who is faithful to China, left Tibet years ago to reside in that country. But he will not be able to live permanently outside Tibet.

REFERENCES

1. On Chinese ethics, see also pp. 84-87.
2. H. Hackmann, *The 300 Monastic Commandments of Chinese Taoism,* 1931.
3. This means certain plants of the Allium family (garlic).
4. For the Kan-Ying-P'ien, see pp. 84-87.

CHAPTER-VIII

BUDDHISM IN JAPAN

—Albert Schweitzer

Chinese Mahāyāna-Buddhism reached Japan in the 6th century A.D. from Korea. It at once spread at the court and among the nobility.

At the beginning of the 9th century A.D. Buddhism and the national Shintō religion joined forces. The gods of the Shintō religion were recognised as appearances of the celestial Buddhas and Bodhisattvas. This fusion was the work of the Buddhist monk Kōbō (774-835).

The original Shintō religion was a form of polytheism in which ethics played hardly any part. The gods were personified forces of Nature, appealed to for their protection. The sun, conceived as feminine, was regarded as the chief divinity. It is probably incorrect to say that Shintōism was essentially the religion of ancestor-worship, as the modern Japanese would like to believe.

Shintō-Buddhism therefore, called Ryōbu-Shintō (two-sided Shintō), received from Buddhism religious and ethical ideas. In ethics, furthermore, it was strongly influenced by Confucianism.

Japanese Buddhism was at first only connected with the Buddhism of China through the Korean form, but very soon it entered into direct relations with, and was strongly influenced by, Chinese Buddhism. Japanese monks journeyed, as Kōbō had already done, to China for the purpose of study.

From the beginning of the 10th century onward intercourse with China was interrupted for some 250 years, as Japan, for political reasons, closed its doors against it. But even during this period Japanese monks occasionally went to China. Along with Buddhism, Confucianism also spread in Japan.

From the end of the 12th century, from the time when Japan resumed intercourse with China, a vigorous religious life made itself felt in Shintō-Buddhism. Movements were developed within it which corresponded to the great Chinese schools.

The Buddhism of Meditation of the "School of Inwardness", founded by Bodhidharma in the 6th century, was spread in Japan by Myōan Eisai (1141-1215), the founder of the Zen sect.[1] This sect counted its followers principally among the members ... of the warrior caste.

There is a tradition that in order to be able to keep awake during the nocturnal exercises in meditation by drinking tea as did the Chinese disciples of Bodhidharma, the Zen Buddhists brought seeds of the tea-plant from China to Japan and introduced its cultivation. Tea-planting had already been tried in Japan at an earlier period, but had been given up.

The Jōdo sect (Sect of the Pure Country that is to say, of Paradise), which also sprang into being at the end of the 12th century A.D., stands for the Chinese Buddhist doctrine of redemption through the grace of Buddha Amitābha, who in Japan is called Amida-Butsu (Butsu is the Japanese name for the Buddha). Its founder was the monk Genkū (1133-1212), the spiritual adviser of three Japanese Emperors.

At the age of seventy-four, however, he was banished for three years to the island of Shikoku by the third of these Emperors, Go-Toba, because he had persuaded one of his favourite wives to become a nun.

The thoughts of Genkū were further developed by his pupil Shinran (1173-1262), the founder of the Jōdo-Shinshū sect, that is to say "the True Sect of the Pure Country". Whilst Genkū taught that entry into Paradise follows on faith in the grace of the Amida-Buddha and good works, Shinran, asserted that faith in the grace of the Amida-Buddha alone comes into cosideration. Man is not in a position in any way to earn bliss by his own merits. In spite of this, Shinran required ethical conduct, and, be it noted, required it like Luther, as the expression and fruit of faith in redemption.

Like Luther, Shinran rejected pilgrimages, exercises in penance, fasting, superstition and all magical practices. He abolished the celibacy of the priesthood, of the monks and of the nuns. True piety was to be preserved in the family and in the worldly calling. He recommended to the laity the diligent study of the holy scriptures. And he demanded that the people should be delivered from their ignorance by good schools.

He did not admit that women are less capable than men of attaining to the state of bliss.

Like Luther he composed hymns intended for use at divine service in praise of the redemption which follows upon grace. In the conduct of worship he assigned an important place to the sermon.

The Jesuit missionaries who came to Japan in the middle of the 16th century at once became aware of the relationship between Jōdo-Shinshū-Buddhism and the "Lutheran Harsey". Father Francesco Cabral reported on it in a letter dated 1571.

In Japan, then, there arose a Buddhism in which world and life affirmation took the place of world and life negation. There was no argument between the two; the former with magnificent ingenuousness simply reinterpreted Buddhism in its own sense. So what the Chinese mind could not do, the Japanese mind accomplished. But the ethical world and life affirmation of Confucius, with which it had been familiar for centuries, came to its aid in this.

It was because of its ethics that Buddhism was able to enter into alliance with world and life affirmation.

Although Buddhism and Christinity have their roots in world and life negation, they nevertheless have affirmity with world and life affirmation because their ethics of perfection of heart contain the principle of love and within that principle lies the impulse to activity. They can be lifted out of world and life negation and transplanted into world and life affirmation.[2]

Thus Japanese world and life affirmation transforms Buddhism and makes it harmonise with its own spirit. In similar fashion modern European world and life affirmation gives a fresh interpretation, in its own sense, of the teaching of Jesus. In both cases violence is done to history, but violence which is justified, in so far as the Buddhist and Christian ethics of love, by their instinct to activity, strive to escape from world and life negation, and can only attain to full development in world and life affirmation.

How greatly a world and life affirming form of religion appeals to the Japanese nature is seen in the great response evoked by Jōdo-Shinshū-Buddhism. At the present day at least two-fifths of the population are followers of this faith.

Of course the doctrine of Shinran is an outrage on Buddhism. The monk Nichiren (1222-1282) rebelled passionately against the betrayal of the original spirit of Buddhism. His self-adopted name means Sun-lotus. He condemned together the Zen sect, the Jōdo sect and the Jōdo-Shinshū sect. Faith in the saving grace of the Amida-Buddha he characterised as a damnable heresy. Redemption can only be won by the "path of holiness", that is to say, by renunciation of the world.

Nichiren believed he was sent by the Buddha to renew his true doctrine. And this indeed he did when he emphasised the value of world-renunciation and the monastic life. But his doctrine of Being is not that of the Buddha, for he thinks on pantheistic lines. All that is, according to him, participates in the essential nature of the Proto-Buddha. On this he based his hope of world-redemption, and from this standpoint he concluded that animals, plants, stones and all lifeless objects are called to the attainment of the glory of Buddha.

It was because Nichiren appeared not only as the accuser of rationalistic world and life affirming Buddhism, but also of the government which tolerated it, that he suffered persecution and for many years banishment. He was even condemned to death, but was reprieved at the last moment when he had already knelt down to suffer decapitation.

His doctrine, which was of a nature to gain the sympathy of primitive religious feeling, spread especially among the common people.

The Catholic Christianity which the famous Jesuit missionary Francis Xavier began to preach in Japan in the year 1549 had remarkable success there at first. A great outlook opened before it when after thirty years the Vice-Regent of the Empire, Nobunaga, who would have liked to break the political power of the Buddhist priesthood, showed it favour. But after his murder in the year 1582 it was completely exterminated in cruel persecutions.

From the 17th century onward we see the gradual rise of a national movement aiming at the restoration of the imperial power, which had been encroached upon by the nobility, and at the same time at that of the pure Shintō religion. By a series of imperial edicts issued between 1868 and 1873, the connection between Shintōism and Buddhism which had endured for centuries was ended and Shintōism was proclaimed the State religion. Buddhism lost its share in the temples and their estates. But in the year 1884 Shintōism again ceased to be the national religion; in 1889 full religious freedom was granted. So Japanese Buddhism, which had adapted itself to the Japanese nature by its world and life affirming ethics and had achieved so much of importance in its social activities, was able again to develop side by side with Shintōism without let or hinderance.

There is scarcely any conflict between the two. Modern official Shintōism really has not the significance of a religion. It makes it the duty of all who belong to this people to venerate their ancestors, the Emperor and the Nation. But this can be reconciled with their adherence to another religion which is capable of satisfying their personal needs.

The original Shintō religion must be distinguished from modern official Shintōism. Countless Japanese, especially country people, live in the faith to-day just as they did centuries ago. Many of them at the same time profess Buddhism.

In the last few years Japan has begun to work very energetically for the propagation of Buddhism in the world. The recently founded International Buddhist Society has its headquaters in Tokyo. This Society is aiming at founding a Universal Buddhism based on the Ancient Buddhism of India.

But it is impossible to conceive how it will manage to reconcile Ancient Buddhism and Later Buddhism, and in particular the world and life negation of Indian Buddhism, with the world and life affirmation of Japanese Buddhism.

REFERENCES

1. For Buddhism of Meditation of Bodhidharma, see p. 144.
2. On this, see also pp. 113, 114.

CHAPTER-IX

THE LAW OF THE BUDDHA

—H. Kern

1. Fundamental Principles

When the Buddha had taken possession of the seat of full enlightenment, he evolved from within two formulas, ever since revealed by him to all beings, and represented as the fundamental truths of his teaching. These formulas are the four Āryasatyāni[1] and the twelvefold Pratītyasamutpāda.

The four Satyāni, i.e. Axioms or Certainties, summarily denoted by the four terms *duḥkha,* suffering, *samudaya,* cause, *nirodha,* suppression, and *pratipad* or *mārga,* path, way, state it as undeniable that there *is* suffering; that suffering necessarily has a cause, that in order to suppress the evil one must know the right way.[2]

It is not difficult to see that these four Satyas are nothing else but the four cardinal articles of Indian medical science, applied to the spiritual healing of mankind, exactly as in the Yoga doctrine.[3] This connection of the Āryasatyas with medical science was apparently not unknown to the Buddhists themselves, for in Lal. V. p. 448 we find immediately after the announcement of the discovery of the two formulas the significant words : *"utpanno vaidyarājaḥ pramocakaḥ sarvaduḥkhebhyaḥ, pratiṣṭhāpako nirvāṇasukhe, niṣaṇṇas Tathāgatagarbhe Tathāgatamahādharmarājāṣane"*. And again p. 458;

virāture jīvaloke kleśavyādhiprapīḍite /
vaidyarāṭ tvaṃ samutpannaḥ sarvavyādhipiamocakaḥ //

The second formula, the Concatenatiom of causes and effects, the twelvefold Pratītyasamutpāda or causal production, otherwise termed "the 12 Nidānas (causes)" is intended to lay bare the root of evil, and stands to the 4 Satyas in the same relation as Pathology, (Nidāna or Nidāna-śāstra), to the whole system of medical science. The terms of the series are : *avidyā,* ignorance; *saṃskāras,* impressions; *vijñāna,* clear consciousness; *nāmarūpa,* name-and-form;[4] *ṣaḍāyatana,* the six organs of sense; *sparśa,* contact (of the senses with exterior objects); *vedanā,* feeling; *tṛṣṇā* desire; *upādāna,* clinging effort:[5] *bhava,* becoming, beginning of existence; *jāti,* birth, existence; *jarāmaraṇam, śakaparidevanaḍuḥkhadaurmanasyo-Payāsāḥ,* old age and death, sorrow, lamentation, pain, grief, despondency.[6]

It seems probable that the whole series, in which the difference between the *post hoc* and the *propter hoc* is utterly ignored, is like the corresponding Yoga tenet, stating *avidyā* to be the ultimate cause of *duḥkha.*[7] An imitation of adaptation of some ancient cosmogonical myth; poetically describing the creation, and the destruction of the world, i.e. the successive stages in the daily phenomena, beginning when light emerges out of darkness, the world of chaos, up to the end of day after its trobles. A similar adaptation is the Pratyaya-sarga of the Sāṅkhya. The very name of which suggest some connection with the Pratītya-samutpāda. The connection, however, is not such as to warrant the assumption of a mutual dependence between the Buddhist and the Sāṅkhya series; we only surmise that both systems derive from a common remote source.[8]

When we try to connect the twelvefold formula with cosmogonical notions, we arrive at the following conclusions. *Avidyā,* ignorance, is the state of the not-knowing of sleep. An allusion to this state of man is found in Lal. V., p. 458 :

ciraprasuptam imaṇ lokam tamaḥskandhāvaguṇṭhitam/
bhavā prajñpradīpena samartaḥ pratibodhitum//

Man at the first awaking enters into a state of half-consciousness; his mind is affected by vague impressions *(saṃskāras)* before he has reached the state of clear consciousness. Then the phenomena appear to him, and the activity of his organs of sense commences. By the contact of the organs with some exterior object (either real or ideal) a certain feeling or sensation is produced. Feelings leads to the wish *(tṛṣṇā)* of getting what seems desirable, and that wish, steadily increasing[9] produces a strong clinging and effort to bring about a state of things differing from the present state. So a new state begins, and immediately after the process of becoming, of transition, the new existence springs to light. That existence, having a beginning' must also have an end, which is ushered in, so to say, by all kinds of misery.[10]

The Northern Buddhist know more than one explanation of the process. The next approach to the interpretation just proposed is that prevailing in the 'Kārmika school'.[11] It can be formulated as follows; from them, contact; from it, definite sensation; from it desire; from it, embryonic 'existence'; from it, actual physical existence; from it, all the distinctions of genus and species among animate things; from them, decay and death. According to another theory[12] the series represents the history of human life, in twelve acts; a history beginning *above* or even earlier, and ending with decay and death. The root of all is Avidyā, i.e. the error of deeming transient things to be permanent; from error spring Saṃskāras, affections, temporary dispositions, as love, hate and infatuation; from them springs Vijñāna, incipient consciousness of the embryo; from this proceeds Nāmarūpam, i.e. the rudimentary body consisting of *nāman,* earth and the other three elements, and *rūpa,* from.[13] Thence proceed the Ṣaḍāyatanas, organs of the senses; when the organs come in conjunction with Name-and-Form, there is Sparśa, contact. Thence follows Vedanā feeling, sensation; then arises Tṛṣṇā, longing (for renewal of pleasant feeling and desire to shun what is painful). Hence Upādāna, effort, beginning of action; then Bhava, state (of merit or demerit). Then comes Jāti, birth, i.e. the aggregation of the 5 Skandhas. On birth will follow decay, death, etc.

A recent discovery[14] among, the flescoes of the caves of Ajanta has brought to light a picture which portrays the Nidānas in concrete form. This picture, supplemented by its Tibetan versions and its explanation by the Lamas, shows unmistakably a diagram of Human Life. This agrees with the theory known to Govindānanda, notwithstanding discrepancies in the rendering of some terms in the Wheel of Life. Whatever we may see in it "a complete authentic account of human life from the absolute standpoint of the earliest Buddhist philosophy"[15] does not seem to be beyond all doubt. This much, however, is plain that the purport of the Prantītya-samutpāda is to show how all evil, death etc. ultimately springs from Avidyā. Formally this does not differ from the Yoga axiom : "Avidyā, is the germ from which the whole mass of evil proceeds", but the sentiment underlying the phrase is another. For the Yoga philosopher has a craving for permanency, he is a *śāsvatāvādin*. Hence all that is impermanent and changeable is to him an evil,[16] and therefore he seeks after true knowledge, the right insight that the *puruṣa* is in reality not affected by its union with *prakṛti,* and that it is only *avidyā,* the wrong notion about that union which is the cause of evil and grief.

The two fundamental formulas, to which may be added the stanza "*Ye dhammā hetuppabhavā,*[17] do not presuppose the belief in retribution and rebirth, the Karman theory nor do they contain anything decidedly opposed to it. The same can not be said of the Buddhist doctrine regarding the Ātman, self, soul, individuality.

A concise and clear exposition of the three principal contending theories regarding Ātman is found in Pugg. P., p. 38.[18] These theories are the *Sassatavāda,* the *Ucchedavāda,* and the doctrine of Buddha. The first holds that the soul is truly existing, both in this life and in the life to come; the second, that the soul is truly existing, but only in this life the Buddha teaches that soul is not truly existing neither in this life, nor in the life to come.[19]

The categorical and absolute denial of an *ātman* is evidently in conflict with the common Hindu view of *karman,* which is based upon the assumption of the existence of a soul. Therefore the Buddhists could not adopt the theory in their own system without modifications. The shape which the dogma has received under their hands is admirably described by CHILDERS.[20] "When a man dies the khandhas of which he is constituted perish; but by the force of his Kamma a new set of khandhas instantly starts into existence, and a new being appears in another world, who though possessing different khandhas and a different form is in reality identical with the man just passed away, because his Kamma is the same. Kamma then is the link that preserves the identity of a being through all the countless changes which it undergoes in its progress through Saṃsāra."[21]

Such a theory, it will be admitted, is beyond the reach of human reason, but that is no argument against its appropriateness in the original system of the creed. For Buddhism is professedly no rationalistic system, it being a superhuman *(uttarimanussa)* Law founded upon the decrees of an omniscient and infalling Master, and in such a creed mysteries are admissible. A somewhat greater difficulty arises if we wish to reconcile the maxim *sarvam-anityam,* "all is impermanent, with this theory; for if all is impermanent, the Karman can not be productive *ad infinitum.* Yet, even this difficulty can be got rid of, on the assumption that the phrase is only a certain way of speaking to denote that all is changeable except the ideal link connecting the successive stages of being. It is less easy to account for such examples of punishment as are related of Ciñcā and others, who are represented as being swallowed by the earth and going down to hell before the eyes of all present. Does this belong to the mythology of the creed? If so, why should not the Karman theory pertain to the same category?

The more we try to remove the difficulties, the more we are droven to the suspicion that original Buddhism was not exactly that of the canonical books. If we suppose that the teaching of the founder of the Order was free from mythology and the Karman theory, we get a system intelligible, self consistent and perfectly apt to lead persons possessing a contemplative bent of mind, by means of a dignified and harmless solitary and canobitic mode of life, to the blissful state of calm beautitude, called Nirvāṇa,[22] a state only surpassed by the final Nirvāṇa or Parinitvāṇa, when all suffering is absolutely and for ever at an end.[23]

Whatever may be our doubts about the original form of Buddhism, it is certain that the dogma in question made part and parcel of the whole system of Dharma before the great bulk of the canonical books were composed. The hypothesis that in course of time some elements were incorporated into the creed to which originally they were foreign, does not involve the belief in a radical change. In our view Buddhism was from the very beginning ***essentially*** such as we find it in the Tripiṭaka; a creed aptly characterized[24] in the following words : "As a philosophy, Buddhism thus seems to be an Idealistic Nihilism; an Idealism which, like that of Berkeley, holds that "the fruitful source of all error was the unfounded belief in the reality and existence of the external world"; and the man can perceive nothing but his feelings, and is the cause to himself of these. That all known or knowable objects are relative to a conscious subject, and merely a product of the *ego,* existing through the *ego,* for the *ego,* and in the *ego.*[25] But, unlike Berkeley's Idealism, this recognition of the relativity and limitations of knowledge, and the consequent disappearance of the world as a reality, led directly to Nihilism, by seeming to exclude the knowledge, and by implication the existence, not only of a Creator, but of an absolute Being".[26]

2. *The Elements of existence Karman—the Road to Deliberance*

Every organized being consists of Name and Form. The former denotes all mental or internal phenomena; the latter, all physical or external phenomena.[27] *Nāman* generally includes four of the five Skandha, viz. *vedanā,* feeling; *sāñjñā* notion; *saṁskāras,* mental dispositions, and *vijñāna* clear consciousness, discrimination. *Rūpa* compreheneds the four elements *(mahābhūtāni) :* earth water, fire, air, and every form springing from, them.[28]

It appears from this enumeration that Nāmarūpa and the 5 Skandhas are co-extensive terms, definition of the mental Skandhas is attended with considerable difficulties, owing to the ambiguousness of most terms, and the loose way in which they are used. Not to go farther than the Pāli texts, we see how *saññā,* notion or first perception, and *vedanā,* feeling, sensation, form each a separate Khandha and at the same time occur as two subdivisions of the Saṃkhāra-kkhandha. This, however unlogical, is not inexplicable, provided we do not assign to Saṃkhāra the meaning of "discrimination", as HARDY has done. The first of the 52 Saṃkhāras is *phassa,* touch, contact whereas the sentiments as fear, joy, shame etc. are likewise Samkhāras; which would be impossible if the term had the meaning assigned to it by HARDY.[29] Saṃkhāras are, in our opinion, passing impressions, mental dispositions, comprising both intellectual affections and sentiments. Hence the first step in the line of Saṃkhāras is *phassa,* contact;[30] the second *vedanā,* feeling the third *saññā,* notion (e.g. of different colours); *cetanā,* thought, intention; *manasikāra,* attention; *Jīvitindriya,* vitality;[31] *cittekāggatā,* concentration of the mind; *vitakka* consideration; *vicāra,* deliberation and soon.[32]

Viññāna, clear consciousness, has 89 subdivisions, and comprises clear consciousness of what is transmitted by the organs of seeing, hearing, smelling, tasting, touch, and the sixth sense, *manas;* father the clear consciousness or discrimination of what is good, bad or indifferent. In the latter case the term denotes spontaneous or instinctive moral discrimination.[33]

The N. definition of the four mental Skandhas[34] is, shortly formulated, as follows : *Viñānā* is clear consciousness of what is going on in our interior. Form it in combination with the Rūpaskandhas springs *vedanā* feeling of what is pleasant, painful, etc. *Sañjñā* is the distinct notion of an object, by which we are enabled to recognize the object. *Saṁskāras* are affections, temporary mental or moral dispositions, having their motive in *vedanā;* to them belong the *kleśas* (defiling passions)[35] as love, hatred, etc.; the *upakleśas* (secondary *kleśas),* as pride conceit etc., piety and impiety.[36]

The aggregation of the five Skandhas constitute the *pudgala, puggala* what we would call the individual, but what in the idealistic system of Buddhism is a being without real individuality. Although the Skandhas constitute the Pudgala, it is explicitly asserted that neither separately nor conjointly they *are* the Pudgala.[37]

The cause of the aggregation of the Skandhas, i.e. of birth and rebirth, is Karman. Hence it is said : "It is Name-and-form which is reborn".[38] We have seen that Nāma-rūpa is coextensive with the 5 Skandhas. The passage through a succession of existences, transmigration, bears the usual name of Samsāra.

The Karman is supposed to have no beginning, but it *can* have an end. The means of attaining that end, of destroying the working of Karman is the Eightfold Path, as the Master set forth in his first discourse.[39]

According to the stage one has reached in one's course towards deliverance, Nirvāṇa, there is a fourfold division. Those who are walking in this path of Sanctification in four stages are called, respectively; Śrotāpanno, Sakṛdāgāmin, Anāgāmin, Arhat (Pāli; Sotāpanna, Sakadāgāmin, Anāgāmin, Arahā), and with a common designation Śrāvaka, Sāvaka, disciple. Each of the stages or path-divisions is subdivided into a higher and lower degree, the *mārga, magga,* and its *phala* result, fruition.[40]

The Srotāpanna is he who has entered the first stage *(srotāpatti, sotāpatti)*, the nophyte. He has got rid of the first three bonds of human passion, *saṁyojana;*[41] the doors of the states of punishments, *upāya,* are shut for him.

The Sakṛdāgāmin is so termed because he will once be reborn in the world of men. He is not only free from the first three bonds, but has in addition reduced to a minimum *rāga,* affection, *dveṣa;* P. *doṣa,* hatred, and *moha,* infatuation.[42]

The Anāgāmin is he who has freed himself from the first five or lower *(avarobhāgīya, orambhāgiya)* bonds[43] and will not be reborn on earth or in a Kāmalaka, but in a Brahmaloka.

The Arhat is he in whom the causes of mortal infection[44] are exhausted, the impurities washed away, the Kleśas[45] rejected; who has fulfilled his task, laid down his burden, removed all bonds,[46] obtained the four kinds' of transcendent faculties.[47] He is no more subject to rebirth.[48]

One who, without having entered the first stage, is in possession of those conditions upon which the commencement of sanctification immediately ensues, is called a Gotrabhū.[49] Such a previous stage, which is, so to say, the court-yard of Holiness, is known to the N. Buddhists by the name of Gotrabhūmi.[50]

Those who are walking in the four paths in their progress towards final beautitude rank as true Āryas in contradistinction to the *profanum vulgus'* the Pṛthagjanas. Their power far surpasses that of common mortals, which is nothing strange, as the notion that transcendent power is attainable by man is prevalent among Hindu sects; the Yogin more especially is, to vulgar apprehension, a worker of miracles. Further on we shall have occasion to revert to this subject.

The object of the Ārya is to reach Nirvāṇa.[51] It is impossible within a short compass to refer to all the opinions emitted on the subject; it would fill a volume. We will, therefore, limit ourselves to the main points.

In the first place we must distinguish between the secondary Nirvāṇa and the final or absolute one. The former Nirvāṇa, attained by Arhats in this life, is virtually the same as the Jīvanmukti of the Vedāntins. It is specified by the addition of *upādisesa* or *sa-upādisesa* in Pāli, *upādhiśeṣa* with the N. Buddhists,[52] i.e. having the residuum of a substratum.

The second or final, absolute Nirvāṇa *(nirupādhiśeṣa, P. anupādhiśeṣa)* in case of the Buddha usually styled Parinirvāṇa—can only be reached after death. By it all suffering ceases, completely and for ever, and in so far it may be extolled as a blissful state, and as eternal, *amṛta (aṁata)*. Does it imply a complete cessation of consciousness? It does, of course, if we draw the logical conclusions from the fundamental principles underlying the creed.[53] But not every one draws logical conclusions, and it would seem that even in the bosom of the Congregation there reigned some uncertainty event the point in question. This would not be very wonderful; when the brethren repeatedly heard how the Buddha was conscious of all occurences in his former births some of them may involuntarily have been led to believe that memory, consciousness survives after death. We may understand how in order to prevent fruitless discussions among the brethren the Euddha is represented to have laid down the rule that the question : "Does the Tathāgata exist after death, or does he not?" Is one of those questions that must be set aside as useless and remain unanswered.[54]

Practically, Nirvāṇa means a happy death without fear of rebirth. If so, how then can the Buddha be said to have conquered Māra? Because he conquered, not, indeed, physical death, but the abject fear of death. The means of bringing about that result, consists in representing death as something extremely blissful.

3. Spiritual Exercises

The striving for Nirvāṇa requires a 'good deal of constant spiritual exercise, meditation and comtemplation, such as with insignificant variations are practised by all Indian ecstatics.

As a preparatory to soaring into the higher regions of thought, must be considered the *bhāvanā,* cultivation, cherishing of the sentiments of *maitrī,* benevolence, *karuṇā,* compassion, *muditā,* cheerfulness, and *upekṣā* indifference, equanimity. These four Bhāvanās, identical in name and character with those of all Yogins,[55] are otherwise termed *brahmavihāra,* living in the spiritual world, and P. *appamaññā* Skr. *ayramāṇa.*[56]

Sometimes a fifth Bhāvanā is added to the four Brahmavihāras, to wit the Aśubhabhāvanā, realisation of the loathsomeness of the body, but in this case *bhāvanā* means conception, realisation; synonymous terms are *asubhasaññā* and *aśbhapratyavekṣā.*[57] There are 10 Aśubhas, notions arising from the contemplation of a dead body; the names in P. are; *uddicumātaka,* bloated; *vinūlaka,* blakish; *vipubbaka,* festering; *vicchiddaka,* fissured from decay : *vikkhāyitaka,* gnawed by animals; *vikkhittaka,* scattered; *hatavikkhittaka* injured and scattered; *lohitaka,* bloody; *pulavaka,* full of worms; *aṭṭhika,* bones.[58]

The ten Aśubhas, as well as the four Brahmavihāras, belong to the 40 philosophical Operations or Kammaṭṭhānas[59] these Operations include the tenfold Kasiṇa, a kind of mystic Bhāvanā. The ten objects on which the attention at this operation must be fixed are : earth, water, fire, air, blue, yellow, red, white, light, and ether or space.[60] The same rite is practised by the N, Buddhists, who term it *kṛtsnāyatana,* object or base of Kṛtsna. The ten modes of operation are given in the following order; *nīla, pītalohita, avadāta, pṛthivī-, op-, tejas-, vāyu-, ākāśa-* and *vijñāna-kṛtsnāyātana.*[61]

The 40 Operations further comprise the 10 kinds of *anusmṛti,* P. *anussati,* recollection, constant thinking : on the Buddha, the Dharma, the Saṅgha; morality; liberality *(cāga, tyāga);* the gods; death; the body; the regulation of inspiration and expiration *(ānāpānasmṛti)* and quiettude.[62]

The exercise, of Ānāpānasmṛti consists in fixing the mind intently on one's own breathing, in connection with certain set subjects of reflection; it is a highly valued kind of Samādhi.[63]

Four species of Kammaṭṭhāna are termed Āruppa, belonging to the 4 incorporeal Brahmalokas : *Ākāsānañcāya-tana,* place of infinity of space; *Viññānañcāy* P. of infinity of clear consciousness; *Ākiñcaññāy;* P. of nothingness; *Nevasaññā-nāsaṇñāy;* P. of neither-consciousness-nor-unconsciousness; in Skr. Ākāśānantyāyatana, Vijñānānantyāy, Ākiñcanyāy; Naiva-sañjnā-nāsañ-jñayatana.[64] Those who by dint of ecstatic meditation soar into those regions have reached a very high standpoint there remaining but one superior : the *Saññāvedayitanirodha,* Skr. *Sañjñā-veditanirodha* cessation of consciousness; the same have arrived at the corresponding exalted states of *vimokṣa,* P. *vimokha* emancipation, deliverance.[65] There is, of course, not much that is particularly Buddhist in this system. For we know that Ārāḷa Kālāma was proficient in the state of Nothingness, and Udraka Rāmaputra in that of Neither consciousness nor unconsciousness, but they were surpassed by the Buddha, who attained to cessation of consciousness.[66]

It results from the foregoing that the four degrees of Dhyāna, P. jhāna, abstract meditation, though nominally, excluded from the system of Kammaṭṭhānas, are nothing else but the four lower stages of ecstasy. Since the exercise of Dhyāna is confessedly anterior to Buddhism.[67] We content ourselves with producing the following passage from the racy description by CHILDERS.[68] "The priest—concentrates his mind upon a single thought. Gradually his soul becomes filled with a supernatural ecstasy and serenity, while his mind still reasons upon and investigates the subject, chosen for contemplation; this is the first Jhāna. Still fixing his thoughts upon the same subject, he then frees his mind from reasoning and investigation, while the ecstasy and serenity remain, and this is the second Jhāna. Next his thoughts still fixed as before, he diverts himself of ecstasy, and attains the third Jhāna, which is a state of tranquil serenity. Lastly, he passes to the fourth Jhāna, in which the mind, exhalted and purified, is indifferent to all emotions, alike of pleasure and pain." Each of the first three Dhyāna is subdivided into three degrees, the inferior, the medial and the superior meditation; the attainment of the first Dhyāna gives the power of working miracles, *ṛddhi* P. *iddhi'*. In general the Dhyānas secure access to the sixteen corporeal *(rūpa)* Brahmnakas the peculiar *loka* being determined by the degree of Dhyāna attained.[69] It is, consequently, plain that the 4 Dhyānas represent a lower stage of ecstatic contemplation than the 4 Āruppas.

Sometimes there is question of 5 Dhyānas *(pañcangikaṃ jhānaṃ)*. They differ in no essential point from the 4 Dhyānas, the second stage being separated into two.[70]

In connection with Dhyāna we have to speak of Samādhi, properly a state of most intense concentration and absorption.[71] But in Buddhist writings a wider term. There are different sets of Samādhi. The 3 Samādhis are Savitakka-savicāra. Avitakka-vicāramatta, and Avitakka-avicāra. Three others are Suññata, void, Animitta, groundless, reasonless, and Appaṇihita without fixed purpose, to which[72] correspond 3 states of emancipation.[73] A set of 4 Samādhis is designated by the qualifications of *hānabhāgiya,* leading to rejection; *thitibhāgiya,* 1. to firmness; *visesabhāgiya* 1. to distinction, and *nibbedhabhāgiya,* 1. to excellence.[74]

In Samādhi one distinguishes two degrees, the inferior called Upacāra samādhi, and the superior, Appanā-S., i.e. initiatory, and penetrating, thoroughly grasping.[75]

The original meaning of Samādhi is such that any profound pious meditation can be brought under that head. Hence it is not to be wondered at that the Mahāyānists with their ritualistic propensities invented a series of Samādhis adorned with more or less sensationate names, but with no definite meaning. The number in the Prajñā-Pāramitā is no less than 108.[76]

Theoretically there should be as many Samāpattis as Samādhis. For the latter does not differ more from the former than a process going on does from its accomplishment. It is, in fact, expressly stated that there are eight Samāpattis, coinciding with four inferior kinds of Samādhi. i.e. the four Dhyānas, and with the four Āruppa Kammaṭṭhānas. The ninth, Nirodha-samāpatti, answers to the Saññāvedayita-nirodha.[77]

Reverting to the Kammaṭṭhānas, we further come across the *Āhāra, paṭikkūlasaññā,* consciousness of the impurity of material food.[78] The last of the list is *Catudhātu-vavatthāna,* determination of the four elements.

Besides the forty Operations occasionally occur some exercises not included in the list, and yet termed Kammaṭṭhānas; e.g. the Suññatā-kammaṭṭhāna, but this is obviously merely another name for Suññato (sic) samādhi.[79]

The base of substratum of and idea, and as such the subject for meditation is called *ārammaṇa,* Skr. *ārambaṇa* or more usually, *ālambana.*[80]

In the foregoing we have had occasion to name several ideal worlds, the corporeal and the incorporeal Brahmalokas. These and similar world are spoken of in a way as if they constituted parts of the universe. The Buddhists, being idealists, make no marked difference between cosmical facts based on observation[81] and the products of fancy. The one and the other belong to their cosmical system, where of we will try to give a succinct view.

4. Cosmical System, Classification of Living Beings

The universe consists of innumerable spheres, Cakravālas, each of which has its own earth, sun, moon, heavens and hells.[82] Between those spheres are situated certain hells, termed Lokāntrika. The centre of our earth is occupied by Mount Meru of Sumeru (P. also Siṇeru), around which are the principal mountains, Kulācalas[83] and beyond these the four continents of Mahā-dvīpas, viz. Uttara-Kuru, the country of the Hyperboreans; Jambudvīpa, India, to the South of the Meru; Apara-Godāna or Godānīya (P. Apara-Goyāna) to the West; Pūrva-Videha (Pubba-V.) to the East.[84]

Each of the spheres consists of three Avacaras, regions, also styled Lokas, worlds, or Dhātus, layers, floors, the lowest being the region of Kāma, sensual pleasures; higher is the region of Rūpa, form, divided into four stages of Dhyāna; the highest is the region of Arūpa, formlessness.[85]

The lowest region is the abode of six classes of gods: 1. the four Rulers of the cardinal points; 2. the Thirty-three gods; 3. the Yāmas; 4. the Tuṣitas; 5. the Nirmāṅaratis; 6. the Parñanimita-vaśavartins.[86] These six Devalokas constitute with the world of men, of Āsuras, of Pretas, the animal kingdom and the hells, the eleven Kāmalokas.[87]

The second region that of Rūpa, or more accurately the Rūpa-brahmaloka—for Rūpaloka in a wider sense Include the Kāmaloka—is divided into sixteen sections, the abodes of as many classes of gods who are free from *kāma*. Beginning from below we have: 1. Brahmapārisajjas; 2. Brahmapurohitas; 3. Mahābrahmas; 4. Parittābhas; 5. Appamāṇābhas; 6. Ābhassaras; 7. Parittasubhas; 8. Appamānasubhas; 9. Subhakiṇṇas; 10. Vehapphalas; 11.

Asaññasattas; 12. Avinas; 13. Atappas; 14. Sudassas; 15. Sudassins; 16. Akanīṭṭhas.[88] The absses of 1-3 are attained by those who exercise the three degrees of the four Dhyāna severally. The next three by profficients in the second Dhyānas the next three by the adepts in the third Dhyāna; 10 and 11 are assigned to the fourth Dhyāna, and the remaining five to the Anāgāmins.[89]

The Northern texts contain nearly the same names. The first group is made up of Brahmakāyikas, Brahmapāriṣadyas, Brahmapurohitas Mahābrahmas;[90] the second, of Parittābhas, Apramāñābhas, and Ābhāsvaras; the third of Parīttaśubhas, Apramāṇaśubhas, and Ābhāsvaras; third, of Parīttaśubhas, Apramāṇaśubhas, and Subhakṛtsnas, the fourth, of Anabhrakas, Puṇyaprasavas, and Vṛhatphalas.[91] The latter five are Avṛhas, Atapas, Sudṛśas, Sudarṣanas and Akaniṣṭhas.[92]

Higher than the Rūpabrahmaloka is the Arūpabr, divided into four degrees which bear the same names as the Āruppakammaṭṭhānas.[93]

The very lowest of the thirtyone abodes of living beings are the hells or places of punishment *(naraka, niraya)*. The principal hells are eight in number and known by the names of Sañjīva. Kālasūtra, Saṅghāta. Raurava Mahāraurava, Tapana, Pratāpaba, and the very deepest, Avīci.[94] Apart from these three is the Lokāntarika hell, already mentioned, and many minor hells. In the old system of the N. Buddhists there are besides the eight hot hells just enumerated as many cold hells: Arbuda, Nirarbuda, Aṭaṭa, Hahava, Huhava, Utpala, Padma and Mahāpadma;[95] in the Pāli canon we meet with the same and a few more; Aṭaṭa, Abbuda, Nirabbudha, Ahaha, Ababa, Kumuda, Uypalaka, Sogandhika, Puṇḍarīka and Paduma.[96] In later N. works the number of hells is still greater.[97]

Above the hells is placed the animal kingdom or brute creation. Not unlikely we have to see in this notion the survival of ancient myths, for real animals are living on our planet, the world of men. Higher than the animal kingdom is the abode of Pretas, ghosts, spectres, though these beings are also placed in the Lokāntarika hell.[98] Still higher is the domain of Asuras, demons among whom ranks foremost Rāhu, the personified eclipse.[99] The hells, together with the next three worlds, constitute the four Apāyalokas,[100] places of suffering. Adding to them the state of men, we get the 5 Gaits or states of existence.[101]

It is difficult for us to realise in how far such theories were matter of serious belief. This much is certain that in the canonical books, both of the South and the North, we repeatedly hear the Master gravely and in a tone of perfect earnest discoursing on his visits to various heavens etc. A visit to the Brahmaloka is vividly described by him in the Brahmanimantaṇika Sutta.[102] In another passage he asserts that he had received a visit from Brahman Sahampati.[103] Such like declarations are numberless, not to speak of the passages where in the history of the Buddha the gods especially Brahmā and Indra enter as actors, represented with as much reality as the Tathāgata himself. The Master knows all about the destiny of persons in the life to come, and freely predicts where so and so will be reborn, at the same time expressly—and suspiciously—stating that he does not use his transcendent faculty, as other teachers do, out of greed or in order to deceive the world.[104]

What have we to infer from all this? Whatever may have been the conviction and purpose of those who composed the canonical texts, it can hardly be doubted that the majority of the believers, both among the laity and the monks, have, up to this day, put implicit faith in the contents of their sacred books.[105]

Besides this system of 31 worlds and their inhabitants, there is another in which living beings are distinguished according to their higher and lower degree of spiritual excellence: a distinction, it must be obserbed, of a temporary character. For the lowest beings of the scale may by dint of Karman rise to the highest rank, and the most elevated can descend, with the exception of Buddhas, Pratyekabuddhas and Arhats, who are certain of reaching final Nirvāṇa.

According to this classification the highest beings are: 1. the Supreme Buddhas; then follow: 2. Pratyekabuddhas: 3. Arhats; 4. Devas; 5. Brahmas; 6. Gandharvas, celestial musicians; 7. Garuḍas, winged beings flying through the sky like lightening; 8. Nāgas, snake-like beings, resembling clouds; 9. Yakṣas;[106] 10. Kumbhāṇḍas, goblins; 11. Asuras, demons, 12. Rākṣasas, giants, monsters; 13. Pretas, ghosts, spectres; 14. the inhabitants of hell.[107]

Of all these only the first three will occupy us; the others need no particular notice, the less so, because they belong to Indian mythology in general.

5. *Arhats, Pratyekabuddhas and their Characteristics*

Arhats are, dogmatically, all those who are walking in the fourth and highest stage of the path leading to Nirvāṇa. They are distinguished by faculties far surpassing those of common mortals. First of all then they possess the four sorts of *paṭisambhidā*—in N. texts. *pratisaṃvid*—regarding 1. Artha; 2. Dharma; 3. Nirukti; 4. Pratibhāna. The purport of these terms seems to be; a transcendent faculty in grasping the meaning of a text or subject; in grasping the Law of all things as taught by the Buddha; in exegesis; readiness in expounding and discussing.[108]

Besides the four distinctive faculties just named, the Arhat possesses five kinds of transcendent knowledge,

Abhijñā (Abhiññā); to wit, Ṛddhi (Iddhi), the power of working miracles.[109] Further the Divine ear by which he is enabled to hear and understand all sound in the universe;[110] knowledge of the thoughts of others; memory of former existences; and the Divine eye, by which he sees all that is occurring in the world and perceives how beings in different worlds die and are reborn. There is also a sixth Abhijñā, being the transcendent knowledge which causes the destruction of defiling passions.[111]

The Arhat is also endowed with eight Vidyās, branches of knowledge, which, however, are nothing else but the six Abhijñas with the addition of *vipassanañāna* and *manomayiddhi*. The latter is properly only one of the 10th Ṛddhis.[112]

Vipassanā Skr. Nipaśyanā and more correctly Vidarṣanā, is contemplation and the true insight connected with it. It is often mentioned together with Samatha, Skr. Samatha quietude, as an attribute of Arhats. Accordingly it is said that there are two orders of Arhats, the Sukkhavipassaka, the barely contemplative philosopher, and the Samathayānika, he who is devote to quietude.[113]

The power of working miracles requires the aid of the fourfold Pradhāna of Sammā. P. right exertion or application,[114] consisting : 1. in the estraint of the senses, Saṃvara-P.; 2. in the abandonment of sinful thoughts; 3. in the Bhāvanās; 4. in steady perseverance.[115]—Certain spiritual qualities which the Arhats share with the Boddhisattvas will be noticed in the sequel.

The prominent characteristic of the Arhat is Wisdom, Prajñā. It is by Wisdom that he crosses the ocean of existence; hence he is said to by Prajñāvimukta. His inferior, the Anāgāmin, cannot yet reach that ultimate goal, but becomes a denizen of the Brahmaloka, by means of Samādhi, whilst the Sakṛdāgāmin and Srotāpanna by virtue of Morality, Sila, occupy places intermediate between the Brahmaloka and the Apāyas.[116]

The Arhat is the Ārya *par excellence,* though all others who are progressing towards Deliverance are entitled to that denomination. In many cases Ārya, Arhat and Srāvaka are controversible terms. Primarily Srāvaka is a hearer, a disciple of Buddha, but it is not seldom used synonymously with Arhat or Ārya,[117] and the compound Ariyasāvaka in general denotes a pious believer.[118]

In a later period we see the Mahāyānists apply Śrāvaka to denote the primeval Buddhists, but it is with them also a comprehensive term for their opponents, the Hinayānists, whom we may call Old Buddhists.

The Mahāyānists divide all sons of Buddha into three classes, according to the *yāna,* the vehicle they use, the curriculum they go through: 1. the Yāna of the Śrāvakas, the lowest; 2. that of the Pratyekabuddhas; 3. that of the Bodhisattvas.[119] In connection with the whole renor of the passage in Saddh. P. where the three Yānas are spoken of, it would seem that by the followers of the Śrāvaka-yāna are meant the Sthaviras of Buddhists of the old orthodoxy; with the second class the solitary contemplative philosophers.[120] with the third accomplished teachers and preachers.

Although such a distinction is made, one should know that essentially there is only one Yāna, the Buddhayāna, because ultimately all beings, at one time or another, shall reach the same goal. Therefore the Tathāgata declares that he will lead all beings to final Nirvāṇa, adding: "all beings are my children."[121]

Both with the Mahāyānists and the adherents of the creed the Arhats are inferior to the Pratyekabuddhas or private

Buddhas. Dogmatically the Pratyekabuddha. P. Pacceka-b. is a being who has attained like a Buddha, by his unaided powers the knowledge necessary to Nirvāṇa, but does not preach it. He is not omniscient, and is in all respects inferior to a supreme Buddha. It is a law of nature that he can not live at the same time with a Buddha.[122]

6. Buddhas and their Characteristics

The Buddhas are the highest spiritual beings. So the supreme Buddhas has said himself, and repeatedly. Now what kind of being is a Buddha? Before attempting to answer this question, we have to take a survey of his characteristics, external and internal.

Among the external characteristics of a Buddha the most remarkable are the 32 Mahāpuruṣa-lakṣaṇas, which he shares which Cakravartins, Arhats and other eminent persons.[123] The number of secondary characteristics, Anuvyañjana, is 80. The enumeration and description of those primary and secondary marks, which with insignificant variations are equally found in S. and in N. texts, is too long to be here inserted. It will suffice to indicate the chief sources of information.[124] Besides these marks, 216 Māṅgalya-lakṣaṇas or auspicious marks, 108 on each foot, are attributed to the Buddha.[125]

It is a remarkable custom of all Buddhas that with their Divine eye they survey the world six times every day.[126] As something peculiar to Gautama Buddha, it is recorded that he measured 12 cubits, or as others have it, 18 cubits in height. This tradition is somehow countenanced by the dimensions of his sacred footstep, Śripāda, on the Adam Peak in Ceylon, measuring more than 5 feet in length and 2½ feet in breadth.[127]

The mental characteristics of a Buddha are divided into three categories, each of them comprising a certain sum of qualities : I. the 10 Balas or forces, powers; II. the 18 Āveṇika Dharmās or peculiar properties; III. the 4 Vaiśāradyas; or points of self-confidence, of assurance.

The 10 Balas are : 1. the knowledge of what is fit or unfit; 2. of the necessary consequences of Karman; 3. of the right road leading to any end; 4. of the elements; 5. of the different inclination of beings; 6. of the relative powers of the organs; 7. of all degrees of meditations and ecstasy, as well as of their power to purify and fortify the mind; 8. of remembering former births; 10. of removing moral corruption.[128] On account of these powers a Buddha bears the epithet of Daśabala.

Sometimes we read of a set of four, of five, and of seven Balas.[129] These, however, are not peculiar to Buddhas.

The 18 Āveṇika Dharmas, otherwise termed Buddha-dharmas or qualities of a Buddha, are shortly stated, the following : 1. the seeing of all things past; 2. of all things future; 3. of all things present; 4. propriety of actions of the body; 5. of speech; 6. of thought; 7. firmness of intention; 8. of memory; 9. of Samādhi; 10. of energy; 11. of emancipation; 12. of wisdom; 13. freedom from fickleness or wantonness; 14. from noisiness; 15. from confusedness; 16. from hastiness; 17. from heedlessness; 18. from inconsiderateness.[130]

The 4 Vaiśāradys (Vesārajjas are : 1. the assurance of the Tathāgata that he has attained omniscience; 2. that he freed himself from sin; 3. that he knows the impediments *(antarāyika-dharma)* to Nirvāṇa; 4. that he has shown the right way to salvation.[131]

It is quite in keeping with Indian habits that the qualities and functions of such a sublime being as the Tathāgata are indicated by a host of epithets which more or less assume the character of proper nouns. The most common appellations are Buddha, Jina Sugata, Tathāgata; decidedly titles are Arhat, Śāstṛ, Bhagavat; many other descriptive epithets, as Daśabala, Lokavid, Puruṣadamyasārathi, Sarvajña, Ṣaḍabhijña, Anuttara, Narottama, Devātideva, Trikālajña, Triprātihāryasampanna, Nirbhaya, Niravadya, and the like.[132]

Apart from the epithets applying to Buddhas in general, there are special names for the Buddha of the present period; as Śākyasinha, Śākyamuni, Śākyapuṅgava, Śākya, Sauddhodani, Ādityabaṅdhu (in contradiction to Kṛṣṇabandhu, i.e. Māra) Sūryavaṃśa, Siddhārtha, Sarvārthasiddha, Āṅgirasa, Gautama.[133]

In the oldest system of historical Buddhism, we have cognizance of, the Buddha of the present period had been preceded by 24 others. Their names are, in Pāli : Dipaṃkara, Kondañña, Maṅgala, Sumanas, Revata, Sobhita, Anomadassin, Paduma, Nārada, Padumuttara, Sumedha, Sujāta, Piyadassin, Atthadassin, Dhammadassin, Siddhattha, Tissa, Pussa, Vipassin, Sikhin, Vessabhū, Kakusandha, Koṇāgamana and Kassapa.[134] Each of them has his peculiar Bodhi tree, e.g. Dīpaṃkara the Ficus religiosa, just as Gautama Buddha.

Many of these Tathāgatas are also mentioned in N. writings, but not systematically, and lumped together with others of later invention.[135] The last seven Tathāgatas, to wit, Vipaśyin, Śikhin, Viśvabhū, Krakucchanda, Kanakamuni.[136] Kāśyapa, and Śākyamuni are common to the North and the South, and are designated in N. texts as the Mānuśibuddhas. Sometimes we find that the four last Buddhas, Śākyamuni included, received special worship.[137]

Just as there were Tathāgatas in the past, so there will be in future. The Buddha of the next following period is

Maitreya, P. Metteya, surnamed Ajita, at present still a Boddhisattva living, it would seem, in the Tuṣita heaven.[138]

All Tathāgatas are alike, save in a few points of no importance : they differ e.g. in size, and in duration of life; some are born as Kṣatriyas, others as Brāhmaṇas.[139] The Law proclaimed by all Tathāgatas is likewise one and the same, and when it is stated that Gautama Buddha evolved the Law from within himself without the aid of a master, the meaning is that by his intuition he re-discovered the old truths which had been forgotten in the night of dark times.[140]

A peculiar sort of Buddhas, wholly anomalous—for they are eternal and never were Boddhisattvas,—are the five Dhyāni-Buddhas of the Mahāyānists: Vairocana, Akṣobhya, Ratnasambhava, Amitābha or Amitāyu(s), and Amogha-siddhi. Their female counterparts, Tārās, or Śaktis, are : Vajradhātvīśvari, Locanā Māmakī, Pāṇḍarā and Tārā.[141]

It is a common opinion among European *savans* that the Buddhas preceding Śākyamuni are mythical latter alone being historical. That theory, whether true or false, is entirely opposed to the fixed dogma of *historical* Buddhism. Of course, we may surmise that in original Buddhism the matter stood otherwise. Such a supposition is allowable, provided we do not confound an hypothesis of our own making with the facts of sober history.

Having surveyed the external and internal characteristics of a Buddhas, we revent to the question; "What kind of being is a Buddha?" The answer is given by the Lord himself. Once upon a time the Brahman Doṇa, seeing the Lord sitting at the foot of a tree, asked him; "Are you a Deva?" And the Lord answered; "I am not". —"Are you a Gandharva?"—"I am not".—"Are you a Yakṣa?"—"I am not". —"Are you a man?"—"I am not a man.". On the Brahman asking what then he might be, the answer was, "Know, O Brahman, that

I am a Buddha."[142] Here the Buddha denies flatly and categorically that he is a man. This dogma has not undergone any change by the later development of the creed in Mahāyānism. In such an authoritative book as the Lotus the anthropomorphism of the Tathāgata has been reduced to a minimum, and the traits lent to him are not a whit more real than e.g. those of Avalokiteśvara.[143] Consequently, in all periods of the creed the Buddha is only anthropomorphic, not a man. What he may have been in prehistoric Buddhism, must be left to individual taste and fancy; it is no matter of science.

7. Bodhisattvas and their Qualities

The sublime place occupied by the Buddha cannot be reached before his having gone through numerous, nay innumerable existences, and having lived in lower and higher states. A being destined to develop into a Buddha is called a Bodhisattva; he is, we may say, a Buddha *potentiā,* not yet *ye facto.* Properly "Bodhisattva" simply means "a sentient or reasonable being", possessing *bodhi,* but this faculty has not yet ripened to *samyak-sambodhi,* perfect sensibleness. He is, in a word, the personification of what the Yogins call *buddhisattva,* potential intelligence, just as the Buddha, the Samyaksaṁbuddha, personifies *buddi.* The highest product of nature in most Indian systems of philosophy based on cosmogony.

In the evolution of a Bodhisattva—usually called his course, *caryā*—one distinguishes three periods : 1. that of the aspiration *(abhinīhāra);* 2. of the prediction *(vyākaraṇa)* by the Tathāgata of the period that the aspirant once shall become a Buddha; 3. of the tumultuous acclamation *(halāhala)* at the approach of his last birth.[144] Others distinguish four periods: 1. that of the intention *(manas);* 2. of the vow or firm resolution *(praṇidhāra);* 3. of pronouncing that vow *(vākpranidhāna);* of the revelation *(vivaraṇa).*[145] Similarly in N. writings albeit with some variations; 1. Prakṛticaryā, original course; 2. Praṇidhāna-c., course of the vow or firm resolution; 3. Anuloma-c., course in accordance with the vow taken; 4. Anivartana-c., the course in which no sliding back is possible.[146]

The Bodhisattvas, like the Buddhas, are honoured with various epithets, the most common being Mahāsattva.[147] A great number of them are honoured by the Mahāyānists. This most celebrated, apart from Maitreya, who is also known in the South, are Avalokiteśvara or Lokeśvara and Mañjuśri.[148] It is hardly to be doubted that these worthies, like so many other Buddhas and Bodhisattvas, have been canonized after the time of Aśoka.

The being who one day should appear as Gautama Buddha, went through numberless births during incaculable ages before he attained Buddhahood, after receiving the prediction to his future destiny from 24 Buddhas.[149] The prehistory of Śākyamuni, the Buddha of the present Bhadra-kalpa, in connection with the predictions of former Tathāgatas, is recorded in S. and in N. Buddhist texts without material discrepancies.[150] Memorable occurrences and great feats *(apadāna-avadāna).* In his prehistory, are related in a number of lates called Jātakas and Avadānas. Such stories occasionally occur inserted in other works, but there exist also separate collections of Jātakas and Avadānas, some of them reckoned to belong to the canonical books, others composed or rather retouched by profane authors. The P. Cariyā-Piṭaka contains 35 stories exemplifying as many proofs of Pāramitā frunished by the future Gautama Buddha; a Skr. composition by Ārya Sūra, the Jātaka-Mālā, desentes 34 Jātakas or Bodhisattvāvadānas.[151] There is certainly some connection between the number of stories in Śūra's composition and the epithet Catustriṃśajjātakajña of Buddha, although in the absence of a fixed date to be assigned to the origin of the epithet, the cause of the coincidence is not traceable. As to the 35 tales of the Cariyā-Piṭaka, we suspect that the number has something to do with the number of years passed by the Bodhisattva Siddhārtha-Gautama before he attained perfect and complete Enlightenment. However that may be, it is not easy to see how both numbers can be commeasurable with the 10, or, if we reckon the subdivisions, 30 Pāramitas.

The Bodhisattvas are endowed with many eminent moral and intellectual qualities. Their most striking characteristic is compassionateness. They represent, in general, active and himindedness, in contradiction to the Arhats, who are inative. One might mark the difference between the two classes of persons by saying that the Bodhisattvas are compassionate, the Arhats unpassionate or passionless.

The 10 Pāramitās or Pāramīs, perfect virtues, are, in Pāli, the Pāramitās of *dāna,* almsgiving; *sīta,* morality; *nakkhamma,* renunciation of the world; *paññā,* wisdom; *viriya,* energy; *khanti,* forbearance; *sacca,* truthfulness; *adhiṭṭhāna,* resolution; *meita,* charity; and *upekkhā,* in difference equanimity; each of them divided into three degrees.[152]

Along with their eminent moral virtues the Bodhisattvas possess such intellectual qualities as are conducive to enlightenment, and which are therefore termed Bodhipākṣika dharmas, Bodhipakṣadharmas, P. Bodhipakkhila, pakkhiya, or Bodhapakkhiya, thirty-seven in number.[153] These qualities are not as is the case with the Pāramitās, peculiar to the Bodhisattvas, for they belong likewise to the Arhats. They comprize seven categories.

I. The four kinds of Smṛtyupasthāna,[154] presentness of memory, thoughtfulness; 1. in regard to the body; 2. to sensation; 3. to rising thoughts; 4. to Dharma.

II. The four kinds of application, right exertion, Sammappaddhāna N. Samyak-prahāṇa, already enumerated.

III. The four parts of miraculous power. Ṛddhipāda, Iddhipāda; as above.

IV. The five Indriyas, mental energies, faculties: faith, energy, memory or thoughtfulness, concentration of mind, and wisdom.[155]

V. The five Balas, mental powers, not differing from the Indriyas, unless in intensity.[156]

VI. The seven constituents of Bodhi, Bodhyaṅga, Sambodhyaṅga, to wit : memory, investigation *(dharmavicaya),* energy, contentment *(prīti),* calm, concentration of the mind, contemplation *(samādhi),* and indifference or equanimity.[157]

VII. The Eightfold Path, Aṣṭāṅgika-mārga of the Āryas; already treated of.

Occasionally we come across other qualifications or faculties of Bodhisattvas, but they do not belong to the system of 37 Bodhipākṣika dharmas, and are partly common to Bodhisattvas and Arhats.[158] To the latter amiable qualities, which should by no means be confined to those saintly persons, may be reckoned the four Saṅgrahavastus (Saṅgahavatthus), elements of friendly treatment; to wit: liberality in almsgiving; affability officiousness, and cooperation.[159]

In N. texts the whole career of a Bodhisattva is divided into ten degrees or stages, Bhūmis, the system of which is amply described in Mahāvastu.[160] The most usual names are Pramuditā, Vimalā, Prabhākarī, Arciṣmatī, Sudurjayā, Abhimukhī, Dūraṅgamā, Acalā. Sādhumatī (or Madhumatī), and Dharmameghā.[161]

The prerogatives or immunies of being a Bodhisattva are numerous,[162] and proportionate to their duties.

Before leaving this chapter we ought to note that the Bodhisattva births of Śākyamuni are frequently called his Avatāras, at least with the N. Buddhists. In the creed of the N. Church, or of some sects, it is admitted that those Avatāras had occurred not only in former times, but that the Buddha retained his power of Avatāra, of appearing on earth as a Bodhisattva, even after his complete Nirvāṇa. Such an Avatāra of Śākyamuni was the prince Kuṇāla, the virtuous son of Aśoka.[163] If we remember that in the Lotus Śākyamuni declares his Nirvāṇa to be only a feint for the benefit of mankind, we cannot refrain from supposing that the masters of the Mahāyāna had no belief in an historical Nirvāṇa.[164] In fact, we have seen that with then the very idea of Nirvāṇa is a delusion.

8. Morals

The moral code of the Brahmanist Indians has professedly its roots in the Veda, tradition, the custom observed by good men, and one's own conscience.[165] Buddhist morality is dogmatically founded on, and referrible to the Buddha, for we read; "*Bhagavammūlakā no dhammā Bhagavamnettikā Bhagavampatisaraṇā*".[166] Yet it does no necessarily follow from this dogma that the Buddha was supposed to have invented the whole of morality. On the contrary, the Master himself repeatedly extols the morals and virtues of the ancient Ṛṣis. "The Dharma", says he, "is the ensign of the Ṛṣis".[167] The exemplary life and the great feats of generosity, self-sacrifice etc. of the Bodhisattvas might be adduced as an implicit evidence of what the Buddhists themselves believed about the moral faculties of mankind in prebuddhist times. But more significant is the explicit statement by the Master that the Brahmans of yore were distinguished by the highest moral qualities.[168] Even the fact that the true, the genuine Brahman is not seldom represented as the noblest of creatures, in contradiction to those who are merely Brahmans by birth, Bhovādins, or as the unbelievers call them, Brahmabandhus, would have been impossible if the type had wholly failed in common life.

In spite of the fore-mentioned dogma, Buddhism has wisely adopted many articles of morality and pious customs flowing from the sources of the Brahmanist code. When the Master commands that the pious Buddhist householder, *gahapati ariyasāvaka,* ought to perform the five Balis: to the family, the guests, the Pitaras, the king, and the gods.[169] It is manifest that he draws from the Smṛti; and when he appeals to conscience, *ātman,* notoriously a non-entity in Buddhism,[170] he authorized a view thoroughly at variance with the fundamental maxims of the creed.

The other sources, the *smṛtiśīle tadvidām* and the *ācāraḥ sādhūnām* of Manu, have not been lost sight of by the Buddhists. To these categories belong the duties qualified as *Paṇḍitapaññatta* and *sappurisapaññatta,* and consisting in almsgiving, in *ahiṃsā,* and in supporting father and mother.[171]

It is hardly accidental that almost all passages where moral duties are enjoined are either wholly or-partly in metrical form, and this circumstance in combination with the fact of those passages containing so much that is contrary to the fundamental articles of the creed, leads us to the inference that the sect originally had no moral code at all, except the prohibitious and duties prescribed to the members of the Order, which only partly coincide with the laws of society in general.

If we wish to form a just estimate of the character of Buddhist morals, such as laid down in the final redaction of the canonical books, we must bear in mind : 1. that the prescriptions were indended to supply the wants both of the ecclesiastics and of the laity; 2. that the Arhats are, to a certain extent, above common morality. The Sage, *muni*, has no attachment, does nothing what is pleasant nor what is unpleasant.[172] Those who are wise abandon their children.[173] A man who leaves his poor wife, the mother of his child, in order to become a monk, and obstinately refuses to take care of her and the child, is held up to the admiration of the world as having done something very grand. Still at other times we read that one's wife is the best friend, and that a wife is the most excellent of goods, though repeatedly women are described as horribly wicked creatures with hardly any exception.[174] Such inconsistencies are endless.

There is no formal discrepancy between the two great branches of the Church as regards their moral code; but as a rule it may be said that with the N. Buddhists moral activity comes much more into the fore-ground than with their brethren in the South. Not the Arhat, who was shaken off all human feeling, but the generous, self-sacrificing, active Bodhisattva[175] is the ideal of the Mahāyānists, and this attractive side of the creed has, more perhaps than anything else, contributed to their wide conquests, whereas S. Buddhism has not been able to make converts except where the soil had been prepared by Hinduism and Mahāyānism.[176]

All moral laws, either in India or elsewhere, may roughly be brought under two heads : 1. prescriptions the infringement of which is followed by penalty; 2. injunctions the fulfilment of which is meritorious and somehow meeting with its reward. The former commandments are everywhere the strongest, because they are absolutely necessary for the maintenance of society. Therefore they are expressed in the form of prohibitions, as only forbidden acts are liable to punishment. The usual Indian term for this category of obligations in *yama,* the second being known by the name of *niyamas,* i.e. obligations only binding for certain classes of persons, or under certain circumstances, though meritorious for all. The principle underlying the division of the commandments into two categories is visible also in the Buddhist Decalogue, the Daśaśīla, otherwise termed the ten Sikṣāpadas (Sikkhāpadas), percepts of training. The ten Śīlas are all of them binding on the members of the Order: the first five on lay devotees.[177] These forbid: 1. the destruction of life; 2. theft; 3. unchasity; 4. lying; 5. the use of intoxicating liquors; the other five prohibit: 6. eating at forbidden hours; 7. attending worldly amusements; 8. the use of unguents and ornaments; 9. the use of a large or ornamented couch; 10. the receiving of money.

The prohibitions 1-5 are conched in the same terms for all persons, but there is some difference in the application. Thus chastity, *brahmacarya* means in the case of monks and nuns absolute abstinence from sexual intercourse, just as in the case of Brahmacārins; for lay devotees it means refraining from adultery.[178] Theft is, in common life, taking anything that has not been given, but a monk commits a thievish act even if he smells at a flower.[179]

If persons appertaining to the laity keep besides the first five precepts the three next following, at least on Sabbath-days, it is a highly meritorious act for which heaven will be their reward.[180]

The moral obligations of those who have renounced the world extend beyond the Dasaśila. In their morality three degrees are distinguished, the inferior, the middling, and the superior degree. The first two degrees are co-extensive with the Daśaśila in its strictest interpretation; the third consists in refraining from pagan sacrifices, prognostifica-tions, astrology and such-like professions.[181] No one, unless unacquainted with Brahmanic literature, will fail to perceive that this superior morality is nothing else but the rule of life of the Dvija in the fourth Āśrama, when he is a Yati or Mukta. It is difficult to explain why and at what time all such minute prescriptions were deemed necessary for Śramaṇas, as their vow of embracing a spiritual life would seem to be sufficient. The only plausible explanation is that all those superfluous details were bodily or with some modifications[182] taken from Dharmasūtras and Dharma-śāstras, in which they were appropriate, because Brahmans and other Dvijas are not obliged by any vow to observe the rules specified.

Buddhism deserves credit for its having discountenanced the coarser forms of superstitious rites and degrading ascetic observances.[183]

The sons of Śākya have as a rule respected the moral-feeling and social customs of their hetreodox countrymen and contemporaries.[184] Far from being indifferent to public opinion, they anxiously avoided giving offence. Repeatedly we read how people are scandalized by the behaviour of some monks; how the question whether such a behaviour is or is not lawful is brought before the Master, and how his decision is always conform to public opinion.[185] In all such cases the Buddha is simply the echo of the public voice. This difference for the opinion of the world, *lokādhipateya, P. lokādhipateyya;* goes so far that the Congregation, for aught we know, never straightforwardly attacks the family and matrimony. Therefore we cannot wonder if we meet in the canonical books with a detailed exposition of the various duties which children and parents, man and wife, master and servant, friends, ecclesiastics and lay men have to observe toward each other. A treatise in which the Buddha teaches a young layman the duties that were generally acknowledged in the Indian Smṛtis, is the Sigālovāda, known in a S. and a N. redaction.[186] Of maral lessons in poetical form there is no lack. Collections containing beautiful maxims, partly universally Indian in character, partly more specifically Buddhist, are the Dhammapada, the Maṅgala-Sutta, and the Udānavarga.[187]

As a whole the moral teaching of the Church bears witness to a certain breadth of view, not superior, indeed, to what is professed by individuals of other persuasions in India, but certainly to the usual catechism of the other Indian creeds, which are moreover mixed up with offensive superstitions. A striking example that exclusiveness is matters of trifling importance cannot be laid to the charge of Buddhism is the answer given by the Lord to Devadatta, when the latter urged him to command that the monks should during their whole life abstain from fish and meat.[188] We know that the Tathāgata declined the demand.

Highly characteristic, too, is the discourse between the Buddha and the Licchavi Duke Sīha, at Vaiśālī. On that occasion the Master declares that in a certain manner he teaches the value of action *(kiriyavāda),* and in another respect the value of non-action *(akiriyavāda)* : that in a certain sense he teaches annihilation *(ucchedavāda),* etc. Whereupon the terms used are subjected to a process of twisting and distoration to such an extent that all definiteness is lost.[189]

In the same discourse there is a trait of liberal-mindedness which should not be left unnoticed. When the Licchavi Duke, who was an adherent of the Jain sect, had become a convert to Buddhism, the Master administered to him the following charitable counsel : "For a long time, Sīha, your house has been a place of refreshment for the Nirgranthas. Therefore you should deem it proper that alms shall be given to them when they come to you."

It does not follow that the sons of Śākya much liked the Jains, not that they were latitudinarians in matters of doctrine. On the contrary, hereby, *mithyādrṣti,* is considered by them, like by many other religious communities, a most damnable sin, to be punished by the torments of hell.[190] Whether erroneous views outside the community were considered all equally wicked, is questionable. At any rate some heterodox sects were more abhorred than others; the gymnosophists of the Ājīvaka sect e.g. had the reputation of being most impious. On a certain occasion the Buddha is asked by a wandering mendicant of the Vatsa clan whether any Ājivaka after death can become a denizen of heaven, not to speak of Deliverance. The answer is : "It the 91 Kalpas, Vātsya, I have remembrance of, I do not remember of any Ājivaka having become a denizen of heaven, except one, and he was one who acknowledged the effect of Karman *(kammavādin)* and the value of actions *(kiriyavālin)*".[191]

It is difficult to characterize the peculiarity of the Buddhist code of worldly morality, and that for two reasons. Firstly, because its articles do not differ from the standard recognized in India; secondly, because the spirit penetrating the prescriptions is different according to the divisions of the Church. Buddhism properly being a monastic institution, and the laity but accessory, it is natural that social customs and obligations were tolerated, after some pruning, if they were not in flagrant conflict with the dogma of the Church. Current moral tales were collected and received into the canon, after some remodelling and by transforming such tales into Jātakas and Avadānas.[192] By this contrivance the stories have acquired a strongly pious tinge, which is less accentuated or wholly wanting in the corresponding tales in the Mahābhārata, Pañcatantra, Bṛhatkathā.

The second difficulty arises if we try to reproduce the

different shades of moral sentiment we discover, on comparing the S. Buddhists with their bretheren in the North, and further Hīnayānists with the Mahāyānists. Hīnayānism has gradually been ousted by its opponents, and it may be said without exaggeration that the Buddhism of medieval India bears the stamp of the Mahāyāna. Now it cannot be denied that charity and mercifulness are more predominant or at least more highly extolled in Mahāyānist texts than in other books, and so it is not to be wondered at that those virtues or sentiments have been looked upon as distinctive of Buddhism, even by Brahmanical authors, like Bāṇa. The ideal of the Mahāyānists, however lofty, is unhappily marred by the fact that to exemplify their own charity and mercifulness they begin with abjudicating those virtues to all other creeds.[193] Even towards their bretheren of the Hīnayān their feelings were far from charitable.[194]

As a whole the Buddhists have shown themselves to be less exclusive and more liberal-minded than the adherents of other Indian religions inasmuch as in propagating their faith they did not attempr to hinduize their converts. By acting upon so sound a principle they have elevated their creed to the rank of a universal religion.

REFERENCES

1. These are taught by all Buddhas; see e.g. Therag. vs. 492.
2. The theme is worked out in the first sermon addressed to the 5 mendicant friars MV. I, 6; 19; Lal. V. 540; and in other passages, e.g. Majjh. N.I, p. 48.
3. E.g. in Yogasūtra II, 15, Comm., "yathā cikitsāśāstraṃ caturvyūhaṃ: rogo, rogahetur, ārogyaṃ, bhaiṣajyam iti, evam idam api śāstraṇ caturvyūham eva, tadyathā, samsāraḥ, samsārahetur, mokṣo, mokṣopāya iti. Tatraḥ duḥkhabahulaḥ saṃsāro heyaḥ; pradhānapuruṣayoḥ samyogo oeyatuḥ; samyogasyātyantikī nivṛttir hānam; hānopāyaḥ samyagdarśanam". Cp. Sarvad, Saṅgr. p. 180. Hence follows that the activity of *buddhi,* which as being an evolution of *prādhāna* belongs to *prakṛti,* ceases at the *nivṛtti* of the union; in

other words : the activity of the *Buddha* ceases at Nirvāṇa or Nirvṛti (which looks like an intentional subsitution for Nivṛtti).

4. i.e. all physical and mental phenomena, the same as *papañca* S.Nip. p. 95, and consequently—*māyā*. In an idealistic system like Buddhism the phenomena are of course, no realistics. Since every human body consists of an aggregate of physical and mental elements, of the 5 Skandhas, such a being can be designed as *nāmārūpa*.
5. The definition Majjh. N.I, p. 266 is; *yā vedansu nandī tad utādānaṃ;* as to the 4 Upadānas, see there p. 66; cp. p. 51, and Samy. N. II. p. 3.
6. MV. I, 1; Lal. V. 442ff. Lotus, p. 109; and the references in Childers s.v. *paticcasamuppāda,* and Dharma-S. XLII, note.
7. Yogas. II, 15 : "duḥkham eva sarvaṃ vivekunaḥ," on which the Comment : "tad asya mahato duḥkhasamudāyasya *prabhavabījām avidyā;* cp. II, 4 : "avidyā kṣetram uttareṣām".
8. It is not in the Pratyaya-sarga, but in the Sāṅkhya theory of creation that there is a partial parallelism to be discovered between the Buddhist, and the Sāṅkhya system; as follows :

Avidyā	parallel	Pradhāna
Saṁskāras	"	*Buddhi*
Vijñāna	"	Ahaṁkāra
Nāmarūpam	"	Tanmātrāṇi
Śadāyatanam	"	Indriyāṇi.

9. *Upādnu* also means "fuel".
10. For a totally different translation and explanation see Prof. Rhys Davids and Oldenberg in SBE. XI, pp. 75 ff, and the latter's "Buddha" (Engl. transl. p. 226 ff.); Childers in "Life and Essays of Colebroke" II, p. 453; Bigandet 1, 93. Cp. also BEBL, SBE. XIX, 161.
11. Hodgson Ess. p. 79. The Nidānas with exception of the first and last term are called the to Karmans, Acts.
12. Mentioned by Govindānaṅda in the Tīkā on Brāhma-Sūtra, p. 549.
13. Hodgson I.C. : "thence proceeds an organised and definite, but archetypal body, the seat of that consciousness."
14. By L.A. Waddell, to whose paper "Buddha's Secret from a sixth century Pictorial commentary and Tibetan Tradition" in JRAS of 1804, p. 367 and Buddh. of Tib. 105—121, we refer the reader.
15. Waddell op., c. p. 370. Curious is the interpretation *bhava.* It is "Pictured by a married woman; and the Lāmas explain the picture by saying that she is the wife of the individual whose life-history is

being traced". Cp. the phrase *taṇhā jageti purisaṃ* Samy. N.I., p. 37. This explains, to a certain extent, how *sañjananī* and *janikā*, Skr. *janikā* (Lal. V. 541) "natural impulse" are nearly synonymous with *taṇhā*, Dh-Saṅgaṇi 1059, where *bhava*, however is not taken in a realistic or material acceptation, as may be inferred from 1312, where *bhāvataṇhā* is explained as "*yo bhaveṣu bhavacchando*", and *bhavaditthi* 1313 as *bhavissati atā cā loko cāti evarūpa diṭṭhi*".

16. The phrase *yad aniccam dukkhām* is Buddhist also, e.g. Saṃy. N. II. p. 244.
17. Ibid., p. 25.
18. Cp. Dīgh N. I, pp. 12ff, 35ff and Samy. N., III, p. 205.
19. Childers s.v. *ucchedo* has the following remarks : "This doctrine was hold in great adherence by the Buddhists, being directly antagonistic to the whole spirit and scheme of Buddhism," This is not very clear. If the *ucchedavāda*, admitting the existence of the soul, albeit only for this life, strikes at the root of the transmigration theory, then Buddhism, denying the existence of soul altogether, does so with double force.
20. Dict. s.v. *khandho*.
21. For a scholastic exposition of the theory see Mil. 40 ff. Cp. Hardy M. of B. 396ff.
22. I.c. the *upādiśeṣa* or *sa-upādiśeṣa* Nivāṇa, the *Jivanmukti* of the Hindus, whereas the final N. is *anupādiśeṣa;* see Childers s.v. The definition of *anupādiśeṣā nibbānadhātu* in Itiv. p. 38 is wrong, and in glaring conflict with the worlds in the stanza there; *anupādiśeṣā pana sāmparāyikā yamhi nirujjhanti bhavāni savvaso*.
23. Cp. Wassilife B.94
24. By Waddell, op. c. p. 384.
25. This is Vedānta.
26. Nihilism is tersely expressed in S. Nip. p. 203 : "*nathi ajjhattañ ca bahiddhā ca kinciti passato*"; cp. p. 194; "*natthīti nissāya tarassu eghaṃ*".
27. Cp. Śatapatha Brāhmaṇa XIV, II, 4, 3.
28. MV. I, 6.36 Dh. Saing. 1309 adds a fifth, viz., *asañkhatā dhātu*. In Samy. N. II, p. 3 the four Skandhas are *vedanā, saṅjñā, phassa* and *manasikāra*. The usual N. enumeration of the 5 Skandas is : *rūpa, vedanā, sajñāa, saṅskāra, vijñāna;* see Burnouf Intr, 511, but Śaṅkara on Brahma. S. II, 2. 18, Dharma-S. XXII, and Sarvad. Saṅg. p. 20 follows a different order, a circumstance connected with the variance in the definitions of the terms—A scholastic

enumeration of the twenty-eight-fold Rūpakkhandha occurs in Vis. M.; see Childers s.v. *rūpaṃ.*—On the 18 Dhātus, Principles or properties of primary substances, see Dharma-S. XXV and the references there. How these are connected and how unconnected with each of the 5 Skandhas, see Dhātuk, P., p. 2; Cp. p. 51f.

29. In Vyu. S. 104 *sprśa* &c. are simply called *caitasikā dharmās,* mental conditions.
30. Somewhat differently Mil. P., 60ff.
31. CP. Dh. Saṅg. 295.
32. Abhidhamma-Saṅgaha, cited by Childers Dict. p. 455 for the whole series Dh. Saṅg. 338. Minor differences in the terms and in the order may be left unnoticed. The list in Vyu. I.c. contains 94 terms; cp. Hardy, M. of B. 404 ff. Dharma-S. Distinguishes Cittsamprayuktasaṁskāras, 40 in number, from 12 Cittaviprayuktasaṃskāras, XXX, XXXI.
33. The enumeration of the subdivisions in Hardy M. of B. 419 ff. Cp. the extracts from Vis. M. and Abhidh. Saṅg. with Childers, p. 577. She list much shorter Vyu. S. 105.
34. Sarvad. Saṅg. p. 20.
35. Dharma-S. LXVI, note.
36. The number in Dharma-S. LXIX is twentyfour; other sources as Pugg, P. II, 1-9 give only twenty; see Dharma-Ś. I.c. note.
37. Mil. P. 25 ff.; cp. 61, where the expression *ekācco puggalo* may not unaptly be rendered with "somebody"; but in an idealistic, i.e. nihilistic, sence.
38. How the process of rebirth is going on, is minutely expounded Mil. P. 43; 72-77.
39. See above p. 23. The Pāli terms are : *sammā-diṭṭhi, s.-saṅkalpa, s.-vācā, s.-kammanta, s.-ājīva, s.-sati, s.-samādhi;* in Skr. *samyag-dṛṣṭi, s.-saṅkapla, s.-vāe, s.-karmānta, s.-ājīva, s.-vyāyāma, s.-smṛti, s.-samādhi*. Definitions Dh. Saṅg. 297-304. Cp. Burnouf, Intr. 519. The Fivefold Path, *pañcaṅgiko maggo* comprises Nos. 1 2. 6, 7 and 8 of the eight; Dh. Saṅg, p. 21.
40. See Childers s. vv. *maggo* and *phalaṃ;* cp. Bigandet I, 153. For the four saints and their characteristics see Vyu. SS 46, 48; and cp. Beal Cat. p. 191; cp. Minayef Recherches I, 217 ff., where sectarian views also are noticed.
41. Viz. *diṭṭhi* or *sakkāydiṭṭhi,* heresy or the heresy of idividuality *vicikicchā* scepticism, and *sīlabbataparāmāsa,* observance of superstitious rites, Aṅg. N. II. p. 238; Dh. Saṅg. 1002-1005;

Dharma-S. LXVIII. There are sesveral classes of Srotā-pannas; the lowest is he who will be reborn 7 times at most, called *saptakrdbhavaparama,* P. *sattakkhattuparama,* Vyu. S. 46; Childers s.v. *paramo; kulaṃkula,* P. *kolaṃkula,* one who will be reborn 2 or 3 times; Pugg. P. p. 16; Aṅg. N. p. 223; Vyu. i.e. Cp. Dharma-S. CIII, note.

42. Synonymous with Sak. is *Ekabījin,* corrupted in Skr. to *Ekavīcika;* Pugg. P. p. 16; Aṅg. N. I. 233 ff. Vyu. S. 46.
43. To wit the 3 specied above, with *kāmarāga,* attachment, and *patigha,* antipathy; Majjh. N.I. p. 432; Aṅg. N. II, p. 238; somewhat different in Dh. Saṅg. 2460. Cp. Divy. 533; 553; Vyu. S. 109—Five classes of Anāgāmins are enumerated Pugg. P. p. 16f. Vyut. S. 46; cp. Childers s.v. *anāgāmi.*
44. *Āsrava.* P. *āsava.* Their number is three : *kāma, bhaua* and *avijjāsava;* or four : the foregoing with addition of heresy; BURNOUF Intr. 823; Childers, s.v. *āsavo.*
45. I.c. besetting evil propensities of the mind, 10 in number; enumerated Dh. Saṅg. 1548 with some variations in Lal. V. p. 59 (where we have to read *rāgo* for *rogo);* 348 (r, *rāgo,* and add mrakṣa) 349.
46. Not only the lower, but also the higher (*ūrdhvabhāgīya,* P. *uddhambhāgiya);* see Childers s.v. *saṃyojana;* the list in Dh. Saṅg. 1460 shows variations. Cp. Vyu. S. 109.
47. *Paṭisambhidā;* more about this term in the sequel.
48. The character and qualities of the four degrees of Saints are fully described in Mil. P. 102 ff. Cp. Vyu. S. 46—The fourfold division of Yogins is : Prāthamakalpika, Madhubhūmika, Prajñājyatis, and Atikrāntabhāvanīya; Yogas. III, 50, Comm.
49. Pugg. P. p. 13; cp. Childers s.v.
50. Wassillef, B. 239.
51. Synonymous terms are Nirvṛti, Nibbuti; Amṛta, Amata and others. The terms are known also to other Indian sects, with a different shade of meaning. The usual term in the Yoga is Kaivalya; in the Vedānta, Mukti, Mokṣa; in the Nyāya, Apavarga; in the system of the Śaiva-monks, Duḥkhānta. In Caraka IV, 5 occurs as synonymous with "final rest" : *śānti, amṛta brahmau, nirvāṇa.*
52. Vyu. S. 95; Burnouf Intr. 590; Childers s.v. *upādiśeṣo,* where the remark that *nirupadhi* is what the S. Buddhists a distinctive epithet of the Arhat must be coupled with what the same author says s.v. *upādhi;* "the term *nirupādhi* may also be applied to one who has attained anupādiśeṣa-nibbāna, has ceased to exist". Now the N.

Buddhists use *nirūpadhi* exactly in the latter sense, and yet they are blamed by the author! On the confusion in Itiv p. 30 see above p. 50.

53. We refer to the exhaustive and masterly article *nibbāna* in Childers Dict. Cp. D'alwis Buddhist Nirvāṇa; Frankfurter, Buddhists Nirvāṇa and the Noble Eightfold Path, JRAS of 1880; Rhys Davids B. 14—For the Mahāyānist the idea of Nirvāṇa is a mere delusion, as we shall see in the sequel.

54. Majjh. N. I, 426 ff.; 484; Saṃy. N. II. p. 222; Mil. P. 145. It is not easy to reconcile, unless by sophisms, this agnosticism with the words spoken by the Tathāgata in Saṃy. N. II, P. 232 : "Puggalam passāmi param maraṇā Nirayam upapannam". And how to explain another passage, Saṃy. N. III, p. 109, where the theory that the "khīṇāsavo ucchijjati, na hoti param maraṇā" is rejected as heterodox?

55. Definition in Yogas, I, 33.

56. Aṅg. N. II, p. 130; Nip. p. 89; Vyu. S. 72; Lal. V. 35; 371; Jāt. Mālā XXXII. Childers' is right in deriving the P. term from *appamāṇa,* as appears from *mettaṃ cittaṃ bhāvanaṃ appamāṇaṃ* S. Nip. i.e.; *appamāṇasamādhi=appamaññā* Aṅg. N.I., p. 236; *appamāṇaṃ cetosamādhiṃ* II, 54; cp. Majjh. N, I, p. 283. We have also *apa rimāṇa* S. Nip. p. 26.

57. Majjh, N. I, p. 424; Vyu. S. 52. Title; Lal. V. 36; Childers, s.v. *asubho*.

58. Dh. Saṅg. 264. The corresponding terms Vyu. S. 52 are *vinilaka, vipūyaka, vipaḍumaka, vyādhmātaka vilohitaka, vikhāditaka, vikṣitptaka, vidagdhaka,* and *asthi-saṅjñā.* This list counts one term less than the P. Asubhas, for a detailed account of which see E. M. 268.

59. Enumerated from Vis. M. by Childers s.v. They are included in the more extensive series of 108 Dharmālokamukhas in Lal. V. 34ff.

60. See Childers s.v. *kasino.* In Majjh. N. I, 423 we find the 5 elements, earth, water, fire, air and ether or space as object of *pathavī-samābhāvanā* &c. The 5 elements with Vijñāna constitute the 6 Dhātus; see Dharma-S. LVIII, note. The following bhāvanās I.c. are *metta-, karuṇā-, upekkhābhāvanā;* then *asubha;* further *aniccasaññā;* finally *ānāpāna-sati*.

61. Vyu. S. 72. The *vijñāna-k* instead of *āloka-k* recurs in a Pāli source, Saṅgrti-S.; see Childers I.c. and Hardy E.M. 252 ff. for a more detailed description.

6. Aṅg. N. I, 42.Out of these 10 the first six are given by Childers s.v. *anussati;* likewise in Lal. V. 34; Vyu. S. 51; Dharma-S. LIV, note.
63. For the details of this mystic operation we refer to Majjh. N.I, p. 425; S. Vibh. I, p. 70; Vyu. S. 53 (where the term is *ānāpāna-bhāvanāvidhi);* Hardy E.M. 267 ff. CP. Wassilife B. 139.
64. Vyu. SS. 68; 119; Burnouf Lotus p. 811; Hardy E. M. 261. Cp. Majjh. N.I, p. 455.
65. Majjh. N.I, p. 456; cp. p. 296; Vyu. S. 70; Dharma-S. LIX; the form Saṅjñāvedayita in Mhv. I, 126— In some passage we meet with a fourfold *cchomutti,* meutal emancipation; viz. *appamāṇā, ākiñcañhā, suññatā,* and *animittā c.;* Majjh. N. I, p. 297; Aṅg. N.I, p. 4; in others, five; see Childers s.v. *vimutti*. The *cittavimukti* in the Yoga is threefold; Yogas. II, 27, Comm.
66. Majjh. N.I, p. 165; Lal. V. 295; 306; Buddhac. XII, vss. 63; 83.
67. See e.g. Jāt. I. p. 58; Mhv. I, 228; Lal. V. 147; Buddhac. XII, vs. 49. Cp. Yogas. III, 2.
68. Dict. p. 160. Original text e.g. in Majjh. N.I. pp. 21 : 117:455; Lal. V. 247; 439; Mhv. I, 228; Vyu. S. 67. Cp. Buddhac. XII, vss. 49ff.
69. The name of these Lokas in the sequel.
70. In Dh. Saṅg. 83 the degrees are *vitakka, vicāra pīti sukha* and *cittassekāggutā*.
71. Mill. P. 38; Yogas. III, 3; Sarvad, S. 164.
72. Aṅg. N.I. p. 299; Mil. P. 337; where the 6 Samādhis are qualified as one of the 7 Ratnas of the Buddha—Cp. Yogas. I, 17f.
73. Dhp. vs. 92. and Comm.; Childers Dict. p. 270. The three Vimokṣas or Vimuktis in Vyu. S. 73 are : Śūnyatā, Animittaṃ, Apraṇihitaṃ. Cp. Dhārma-S. LXXII, note.
74. Vyu. S. 55 *Nirvedhāgiya,* synonymous with *usmagata. mūrdhāna, kṣānti,* and *laukikāgradharma*. Cp. *uṣmagata* &c. Wassilife B. 130:246 Pāli *usāmgata=samaṇateja* Jāt. V, p. 208; *usmīkata* highly proticient, brilliant, Majjh. N. I, p. 132.
75. Hardy, E.M. 257. The same division applies to the Kammaṣṭṭhānas.
76. Enumerated in Vyu. S. 21.
77. Pugg. P. p. 20; Śamy. N. II, p. 216 (nine Vihārasamāpattis); Vyu. S. 68; Burnouf Lot. 348; 789; Wassilife B. 140; 240. Cp. Yogas. I, 42-48.
78. Hardy, E.M. 96, from Vis. M.
79. Aṅg. N. I, p. 299.
80. *Ārambaṇa* in Aṣṭas, Pāram. *passim,* e.g. p. 138; 269; Vyu. S. 21;

cp. *anārambaṇa* Chāndogyopaniṣad 2, 9. But *alambana* Yogas. I, 10; 38; 42, Comm.

81. In an idealistic system where there is no room for absolute reality, as the whole world is a product of imagination; in other words : the world is created by Dhyāna. Cp. Hodgson Ess. 28; Beal, Cat. 124.
82. For details see Childers s. v. *sottalaka*. Hardy M. of B. 1ff.; Legends 80ff. Burnouf Intr., 599 ff.; Waddell Buddh. of Tib. 77-104.
83. Cp. Dharma-S. CXXV, note.
84. Cp. Vyu. S. 154; Lal. V. 170; Divy. 213 ff.
85. Vyu. S. 155; gāma-, rūpa-, arūpya-dhātu.
86. Lal V. 170; Divy. 200; Burnouf Intr. 212. The gods are longived *dīghāyuka,* but not immortal; Aṅg. N. II. 33. The same view is common enough among Hindus; e.g. Yājñavalkya Dharmaś. III, 10; Yogas. II, 5, Comm.
87. Vyu. S. 156 only eight; to wit the worlds of 6 kinds of gods, of terrestrial beings, and of inhabitants of the atmosphere *(antarikṣavāsjñ)*.
88. In Majjh. N.I, p. 329 occur the groups 6-10, followed by Abhibhu; cp. there p. 327.
89. Childers s.v. *jhānaṃ*.
90. Thus Vyu. S. 157; the second name is wanting in Burnouf Intr. 212. As there ought to be only three names, it is probable that Brahmakāyikas properly is a comprehensive term for the whole group, as in Pāli; see Childers Dict. p. 486. Cp. Dharma-S. CXXVIII.
91. Lal. V. 171 adds. : Asañjñisattvas, agreeing with P. Asañjñasattas; so, too, Dharma-S. I.c.
92. The Atapas wanting in Lal. i.c. Vyu. S. 161 adds Aghaniṣṭhas (!) and Mahāmaheśvarāyatana.
93. An account of the exact duration of life of the gods residing in the Ākāsānañcāyatana etc. is found Aṅg. N.I, p. 267.
94. A detailed description of these hells occurs e.g. Aṅg. N. I, pp. 141 ff. Mhv. I, 7ff. Cp. Vyu. S. 214.
95. Burnouf Intr. 201; Vyu. S. 215; Divy. 67. Somewhat different dharma-S CXXII, where Apapa=P. Ababa.
96. S. Nip. p. 123. These terms also denote certain high numerals.
97. E.g. in Kāraṇḍa-Vyūha. Cp. L. Feer, L'enfer indien, JA 1892 and 1893.
98. Cp. the tales in the Books of Ghost stories, Petavatthu, and Childers s.v. *peto*.

99. Childers s.v. *asuro* and Vyu., S. 171.
100. Lal. V. 236 mentions three Apāyas, without specifying them.
101. Or six, if the Asuranikāy be added; Burnouf Lot. 309; cp. Dharma S. LVII, note.
102. Majjh. N. I, p. 326.
103. Aṅg. N. II, p. 20; Majjh. N. I, p. 458.
104. Majjh. N. I, p. 464.
105. On the other hand it cannot be denied that in later Mahāyānist or Tantric works we come across instances of thorough going scepticism. In the Vajramaṇḍā Dhāraṇī the Buddha declares : "The hells, O Mañjuśrī, are of ignorant men who foolishly believe in what does not exist; the hells are a product of their fancy"; Burnouf Intr. p. 544.
106. This word has in B. writing sometimes a wider and older meaning, viz, that of a being to be worshipped or a powerful spirit; Indra e.g. is called a Yakṣa; even the Buddha is glorified by Upāli as an *āhuṅcpvo yakkho uttamapuggalo atulo,* Majjh. N. I, p. 386. The term is used synonymously with *devaputta* Samry. N.I, p. 54. In a more retricted sense the Yakṣas are the attendants of Kubera as in Hindu mythology; cp. Vyu. S. 169.
107. The series in Vyu. 166 is : Devas, Mayas, Yāśas, Gandhrvas. Asuras, Daityas, Garuḍas, Kinnaras, Mahoragas, and Kumbhāṇḍas. Several names of these beings are recorded S. 167-175. Divy. 148. Lal. L. 184 omits Daityas, but adds. Śakra, Brahmā, the Lokapālas, monks, nuns, lay devotees of both sexes.
108. See the dissertation of Childers s.v. *paṭisambhidā*. For *paṭibhāna* cp. Mil. P. 340. Paṭisambhidā, apparently, means speciality, special and distinctive gift. *pratisaṃvid* is wholly inappropriate as has been pointed out by Childers. Cp. Vyu. S. 13.; Dharma-S. LI. note.
109. It has 5 subdivisions, *pādas;* see Childers s.v. *iddhipādo;* the passage there adduced is identical with Vyu. S.40
110. The same faculty belongs to the Yogin; Yogas. III, 40.
111. Hardy E.M. 284; M. of B. 38; Burnouf Intr. 295; Lot. 820. CP. Cv. VI, 6, 2; Lal, V. 184. Slight variations in Vyu. S. 14; the miraculous performances due to Abhijñā are summarized S. 15. Cp. Dharma-S. XX, note.
112. Childers s.vv. *vijjā* and *manomayo*. For the 10 sorts of Ṛddhis see Hardy M. of B. 500. Sometimes there is question of 3 kinds of Iddhi. pāṭihāriya, and we know e.g. from Aṅg. N. I, p. 172, that many monks had the power of performing such miracle. Miracles.,

pāṭihīra, on sacred monuments *(cetyia)* of past Arhats, are not rare; Mil. P. 309. There are 3 species of Prāhihārya : *ṛddhi ādeśanā-* and *anuśāsanī prātihārya;* Dīgh. N. I, pp. 212ff. Vyu. S. 16.

113. Childers s.v. *samatho;* Dhp. p. 425; Wassilief B. 141; Lal. V. 146; 218; Mhv. I, 120; Vyu. S. 90.

114. Aṅg. N, II, p. 15; S. Nip. p. 74; Cp. Dharma-S. XLV; Lal. V. 37; 218; 327. The from Prahāṇa in N. texts is a decidely bludering rendering of a Prākṛt term into Skr. This is proved by the fact that the cerbral expression corresponding to *samyak-prahīṇa* is *samyak pradahāti* Vyu. S. 39; cp. Lal. V. 499.

115. Aṅg. N. II, p. 26; Vyu, S. 39.

116. Vis, M. I, p. 22 and p. 26; cp. Vyu, S. 26.

117. Thus *arryā* Dhp, v.s. 22 is explained p. 180 by *Buedha-paccekabuddha sāvakā* where *sāvaka* takes the place of Arahat, *Sāvaka-bodhi* is the knowledge possessed by an Arhat opposed booth to supreme Buddha-knowledge and to Pratyeka-buddhi; see Childers s.v. *sāvako,* The same results from Vyu, SS 46-48.

118. In Aṅg. N. I, p. 210 the Ariyasāvakas are exhorted to keep the Sabbath in a worthy manner; here the word can only mean a pious believer. So, too, the *gahapati ariyasāvako;* op. c, II, p. 68.

119. Burnaouf Lot. p. 52; 315 *Yānikṛta,* P. *Yānikata* seems to be synonymous with *bahulikata* and *bhāvita* (e.g. Saṇv. N. I, p. 114; II, p. 264, MPS. III, 75; Mil. P. 140); and to mean "gone through, studied, steadily exercised", pretty much the same as Skr. *abhyasta*—For the 3 Yānas see Dharma-S. II, and the references in the note, and Wassilief B. 7. Beal compares the Platonic *öxnua;* Cat. 124.

120. In such passages like Mhv. I, 301, it is not difficult to recognize a hermit under the disguise of the term Pratyekabuddha.

121. Lot. p. 89. Cp. Dharma-S. l.c.

122. Childers s.v. *pacceko* and the references there. From the epithets *khadgavisāṇakalpa,* solitary as the rhinoceros, and *vargacārin*, mixing with society, associating himself. Vyu. S. 45. *(vaggasārin,* S. Nip. p. 151) we may gather that some Pratyekas are rigid hermits of the wilderness; others more sociable, perhaps living as monks, or at least frequenting villages.

123. Mahāpuruṇa-lakkhañaṃ as a branch of science occurs S. Nip. 102; cp. Bṛhat-Saṃhitā Chap. LXIX.—It need not be told that Mahāpuruṣa and Puruṣottama are common epithets of Viṣṇu.

124. See Dharma-S. pp. 53-60; and add Mhv. II, 29 ff. and 213 ff.; Alabaster Wheel of the Law 115 ff.
125. Hardy M. of B. 367.
126. Divy. 95.
127. Hardy M. of B. 264 ff. Burnouf Lot. 622.
128. See Dharma-S. LXXVI, with the references, and add Mhv. I, 159f. where we have to read, instead of Senart's conjecture *manovibhutā: anodhikatā;* i.e. *anavadhikatā,* illimitedness, and *anodhikabalā,* illimited powers, almost as the MSS. have it.
129. Four in Aṅg. N. II, p. 141; seven in Dh. Saṅg. 95-102; three with Childers s.v. *balaṃ,* and cp. Dharma-S. XLVIII, note.
130. The order slightly different in Vyu. S. 9. Cp. Dharma-S. LXXIX, note *Āvenika* or *āveṇiya* means "peculiar, exclusively proper"; e.g. Jāt. IV. p. 358.
131. Aṅg. N. II, 9. See further Dharma-S. LXXVII.
132. A remarkable string of epithets is contained in Upāli's hymn Mjjh. N. I, p. 386, which would afford matter for a complete Buddhology. Rich also is the list Vyu. S. I, and the enumeration Lal. V. 549-564; very poor in Amarakośa I, 8, and Divy. 95.
133. Gautama without the addition of Buddha is a rather irreverential term for a believer. It is only by his opponents and unbelievers (who need not be unfriendly though) that he is called "Sramaṇa Gautama". The most reverential term is Bhagavat, Lord. The rendering of this word with "Blessed One" is hardly right, as is proved by the meaning of the shortened *bhogas* and *bhos.* Bhagavat is essentially the same word as Slavonic *bogatū* rich; Russian *bogacū,* a rich man; a meaning naturally passing into that of "a lord". It bears to the shortened Vedic vocative *bhagos* and the still shorter *bhos* nearly the same relation as French Seigneur to Monsieur, and English Sir. Nothing is more common than that words properly meaning *aominus* are applied to ecclesiastical worthies; e.g. Dom, Domine, Kuningas, Rabbi etc.
134. Their history is recorded in Buddhav. and Jāt. Intr. I, p. 3ff. Properly there are three more Tathāgatas, to wit Taṇhaṃkara, Medhaṃkara, and Saraṇaṃkara, but they are not taken into account, because it was Dīpaṃkara who first predicted the future Buddhaship of Gautama Buddha: Dhp. p. 117, and cp. Mhv. I, 237 ff.
135. See in Hodgson Ess. p. 33 the lists drawn from Lal. V. and other works. Thirty-two Tathāgatas are enumerated Lot. p. 113.
136. Krakutsanda and Konākamuni in Mhv. I, 2; II, 265 : Koṇagamana on a *basrelief* of Bharhut, Pl. XXIX; *Koṇakamana* in the edict of

the Niglīvā (Bühler, Academy of 27 April 1895).—Cp. Dharma-S. VI and note and the translation of the Saptabuddha-Stotra in Wilson Works II, 5

137. Already in the sculptures of Bharhut and Sāñchi; in the time of Fa Hian at Śāṅkāśya, Rec. p. 51.
138. This may be inferred from the story related by Fa Hian, Rec. p. 25; in the Lotus we meet him on the Vulture Peak. His future appearance is predicted by the Lord in Mil. P. 159.
139. The Buddha of the present period is by birth a Kṣatriya, by genius and conduct a Brahman; Mil.p. 225.
140. See the discussion Mil. p. 217; cp. 236.
141. See references at Dharma-S. III and IV, where some variations may be observed. Cp. D. Wright Hist. of Nepāl, Pl. VI; a discussion on the origin and character of the Dhvāni-Buddhas in Versl. Meded. K. Akad, of 1888, p. 38ff. Cp. also Waddell Buddh. of Tib. 346-360; Wilson Works II, 11-25.
142. Aṅg. N. II, p. 38. Cp. such passages as Samy. N. I, p. 67: *Sadevakassa lokassa Buddho aggo pavuccali;* his title *devātideva;* his power to free the Sun and Moon from Rāhu; op.c. pp. 50, 52.
143. The Mādhyamikas, reasoning upon the old Buddhist axiom *sarvam śānyam,* arrive, most logically, at the conclusion that the Buddha himself is as void and nothing as all the rest; Burnouf Intr. 481; Wassilief B. 348; Schmidt, Ueber Das Mahāyāna, 207. Implicitly this absolute Nihilism is contained in the passage S. Nip. p. 203, already cited; cp. Majjh. N. I, 297; Bigandet II, 239. In absolute truth Paramārtha, there is neither *nirodha* nor *bhāva* : Śantideva, Zapiski IV, p. 219. In other words : there is no such thing as Nirvāṇa; it is a mere delusion : the very idea of Nirvāṇa springs from Avidyā : Beal Cat, 125.
144. This we may infer from Jāt. Intr. p. 47.
145. Hardy M. of B. 88.
146. Mhv., I, I : 46 ff. The prediction, Vyākaraṇa, of future Buddhahood, takes place in the fourth period : it is repeated by subsequent Buddhas.
147. This we may render with "Noble Being", though it looks as a veiled synonymous term for Bodhisattva. For *mahat* is synonymous with *buddhi*=*bodhi*. Other epithets in Vyu. S. 22.
148. Vyu. S. 23. where the list open with *Avalokiteśvara* : in Dharma-S. XII only eight are named, and strangely, with omission of Avalokiteśvara; see the note on l.c. for synonymous names, and

other divisions. Several Bodhisattvas are honoured by Śantideva in Bodhicary, chiefly Mañjughoṣa : Zapiski IV, pp. 158 : 161 : 225. On Lokeśvara, al, Matsyendra cp. Versl, Meded, K. Ak, of 1888. pp. 14 : 42. See further Waddell JRAS, of 1894. p. 51 : Buddh. of Tib. 356 on Avalokita.

149. The exact number is 4 Asaṅkhyeyas and 100,000 Kalpas : Saddh, S, p. : Bodhi v, p. II : less definite Mhv. I, I : "In innumerable Asaṅkhyeyas, numberless Kalpas."

150. Jāt, Intr. pp. 4ff. Hardy M, 89, ff. It should be observed that according to the theory of the Lokottaravādins the primeaval Buddha, near whom the future Śākyamunis made his vow to become a Tathāgata, is likewise named Śākyamuni : Mhv, I. I. This seems to mean that the later Śāyamuni is an Avatāra of the primeval Śākyamunis i.e. Ādibuddha or Svayaṁbhū; a tenet fully developed in the school of the Aiśvarthas, see Hodgson Ess. 46; 76. CP. Waddell Buddh. of Tib. 126; 130; 348.

151. On similar other collections see S. Oldenberg's paper "On the Buddhist Jātakas", already quoted above p. 7. note; and Iwanowski's in Zapiski VII, 289.

152. Childers Dict. p. 235. Vyu. S. 34 has likewise 10 P., but with substitution of Dhyāna, Upāya, Bala, and Jñāna for Mettī, Nekkhamma, and Upekkhā; Praṇidhana answers to the synonymous Adhiṣṭhāna. A list of 10 P. also in Dharma-S. XVII, but of 6 in XVII; see the notes there, and add Kāraṇḍa-Vy. II, 9; cp. on Kṣānti-, Vīrya-, Dhyāna, and Prajñā-Pāramitā Bodhicary. Chpp. 8-11, in Zapiski V, pp. 178 ff.

153. Childers s.v. *bodhapakkhiyo;* Lal. V. 8; 218; Dharma-S. XLIII.

154. P. Satipaṭṭhāna, a compound of *sati* and *upatthāna,* as already observedby Childers; cp. *parimukhaṇm sati upaiṭhapetvā* Aṅg. N. II, p. 38; *pratimukham smṛtim upasthāp a* Divy. 20. See further Saṃy. N. I, 180; Lal. V, 218; Dharma-S. XLIV Synonymous terms are *kāyagatānusmṛti* etc. Lal. V. 36; *kāyagatā sati, kāyānupassanā,* etc. belonging to the Kammaṭṭhānas.

155. Dharma-S. XLVII and the references; Vyu. S. 41. The four Indriyas are the same with exception of wisdom; Aṅg. N. II, p. 141.

156. Dharma-S. XLVIII; Vyu. S. 42. The four Balas are the same, except wisdom; Aṅg. N. l.c.

157. Dharma-S. XIX and note; Vyu. S 43; Majjh. N. I, p. 61; Mil. P. 83. Sometimes, only 6 Sambojjhaṅgas are mentioned, memory being excluded; Aṅg. I. p. 53; here with cp. the Yogāṅgas of the

Yoga—As to the rendering of Samādhi cp. the synonyms of Samādhāna and Duyāna in Bodhicary, Zapiski IV, p. 208.

158. To the Bodhisattvas are ascribed 10 Vaśitās, mights, Vyu. S. 27; Dharma-S. LXXIV.

159. The P. terms are : *dāna, peyyavajja* or piyavacana, atthacariyā, and *samānattatā* Aṅg. N. II, p. 32; in Dharma-S. XIX : *dāna, priyavacana, arthacaryā,* and *samānārthatā;* so too, in Lal. 39; 183; 218; but *priyavāhya* and *arthakiyā*. Slightly different in Mhv.I, 3 *āna, tathārthacaryā, priyavādya* and *samānasukha atuḥkhātā* i.e. taking part in another's joy and sorrow.—The addition of the words "appertaining to kings" in Childers, p. 447 is a mistake, as is evident from Aṅg. N. I. c. and Divy. 95.

160. I. 76 ff. The names are : Durārohā, Baddhamānā, Puspamanditā, Rucirā, Cittavistarā, Rūpavatī, Durjayā, Janmanideśa, Yauvarājya, and Abhiṣeka-bhūmi.

161. For references see Dharma-S. LXIV; cp. Daśabhūmīśvara in JRAS. of 1875, p. 4. —A list of 13 Bhūmis occurs Dharma-S. LXV.

162. Enumerated Jāt. Intr. vss. 252-258.

163. This is distinctly stated by Kṣemedra in Avad. Kalp. Nr. 59; an older reduction of this charming tale occurs, as is well-known, in Divy. 403 ff.

164. SBE. XXI, p. 307, ff.—It is a fact that the half pantheistic, half theistic views of the Mahāyānists were condemned by their opponents; Wassielief B. 263.

165. Manu II, 6.

166. Majjh. N. I, p. 310.

167. Aṅg. N. II, p. 51. An exemplary Ṛṣi was the hermit Asita Devala, notwithstanding his following heterodox rules *(bāhiraka mārga);* S. Nip. pp. 128ff. Cp. Mhv. II, 30, where the text, after due correction, runs thus : "ṛṣipravrajyām pravrajito mūlaphalapattra-bhakṣo uñchavṛttiḥ". He had exercised the 4 Dhyānas and had realized the 5 Adhijñās.

168. Brāhmaṇika-dhamma-S. in S. Nip. p. 50. The statement is the more remarkable because the same Sutta otherwise is a piece of wholesale and unscrupulous, silly slander; cp. Hardy Legends 42 ff. Though the Brāhmaṇas themselves are often calumniated, their gifts to the monks are always welcome and highly praised. Itiv. p. 111, Praise of the true Brahman S. Nip. p. 116.

169. Aṅg. N. II, p. 68.

170. Aṅg. N. I, p. 149 : "Attā te, purisa, jānāti saccaṃ vā yadi vā

nusā". The addition of *sakkhi,* O witness! proves that the whole metrical passage, clumsily joined to the prose, has been taken from some Dharmaśāstra; the lines occur in a slightly different redaction in anu VIII, 84 ff.

171. Aṅg. N. I, p. 151.
172. S. Nip. p. 153 : "Sabbattha munī anissito na piyaṃ kubbati no pi appiyaṃ".
173. Therag. v.s. 302.
174. Ud. I, S; Samy. N. I, pp. 37; 43; Aṅg. N. II, p. 80; Mil. P. p. 205.
175. In the picture of the Supreme Buddha the traits of the Arhat and the Bodhisattva heve been blended into an harmonious whole. In Vedānta phraseology, one might say, he combines the traits of the neuter *brahman* and the masculine *brahman*.
176. Cp. Taw Sein Ko in Ind. Ant. XXII, 165; Tār. 262.
177. See Childers s.v. *sīeṃ,* and his references. Cp. Yogas II, 30; 32.
178. The five precepts for the laity are more amply expounded S. Nip. p. 69.
179. Samy. N.I, p. 204; Jāt. III, 308.
180. A sabbath thus observed is termed *aṭṭhañgiko uposatho;* S. Nip. p. 70; Aṅg. N.I, p. 215; in the Gāthās ascribed to the Buddha we find the phrase : "Etam hi aṭṭhaṅgikam āhūposathaṃ. Buddhena dukkhantaguṇaṃ pakāsitam". It is curious to hear the Master speaking in the 3rd person.
181. An elaborate exposition of all this is given in Sāmaññaphala-S. and Subha-S. of the Dīgh. N. Cp. Burnouf Lot. 463 ff. Even the practice of medicine is forbidden to a Buddhist; S. Nip. p. 172. Sacrifices are totally discredited p. 190; but Aṅg. N. II, p. 43. only bloody sacrifices; it is added that unbloody sacrifices *nirārambha yañña)* are approved by the Masters, and agreeable to the gods; p. 44.
182. The metrical parts betray here and there their unbuddhistic origin; cp. above p. 69., note.
183. E.g. the *śīlavrataprāmarśa* P. *sīlabbataparāmāsa,* the abouse of moral vows or observances; Vyu. S. 104; Majjh. N. I, P. 433; Aṅg. N. I, 242; DH. Saṅg. 1005. Not all Śīlavratas are condemned, as appears from S. Nip. p. 196; Dhp. vs. 271; Bodhi-v. p. 76; only some (Mhv. I, 292), of the bad and foolish sort, like the *gavrata,* Lal. V. 259; *govratin, govauka* is an ascetic who feeds upon grass like a cow; Majjh. N.I, p. 387; M. Bhārata V. 3359; *kukkuravatika* is one who lives likes a dog, a cynic; Majjh. N. I.c.
184. Exceptions as the attack directed against the caste system in

Assalāyana-S. are comparatively rare. The Vajrasūci with its contents stolen from Śaṅkara deserves notice only as a literary curiousity.

185. Instances occur *passim* in the Vinaya; see e.g. MV. VI. CV. III. Cp. Yājñav. I, 156.

186. Text in Grimblot's "Sept Suttas Palis"; transl. by Childers in the Contemporary Review of 1876. The N. text is only partially known from a Chinese version Beal; Trip. 112.—A detailed account of the duties of laics occurs in Mlnayef; Reeherches I, 163-174, with copious references.

187. The Maṅgala-S. ed. and transl. by Childers in JRAS. IV, 2 (New s.); Udānavarga transl. from Tibetan by Rockhill. The Dhp. belongs properly to the Theravāda sect, as we may infer from Jātaka-M. p. 98, I. 24. It is intended chiefly for members of the Order.

188. The eating of fish and meat is allowed if it is pure in three respects to wit : if one has not seen, nor heard, nor suspected (that it has been procured for the purpose) : MV. VI, 31, 14; CV. VII, 3, 15; Mjjh. N. I, 368 ff. From the express prohibition of eating the flesh of men, elephants, horses, dogs, snakes, lions, tigers, bears, hyenas, we must infer that the flesh of other animals was no forbidden food; MV. VI, 23.

189. MV. VI, 31 : cp. I, 38 : Tib. Lib. 268. The Buddha is both a Kiriyavādin and an. Akiriyavādin, Aṅg. N. I, p. 62; Saṃ. N. I, p. 38 : *kammaṃ tassa (sattassa) parāyaṇaṃ* is no contradiction. He does not teach *sabbam atthi,* nor *sabbaṃ natthi;* Saṁy. N. II, p. 76 : he declares to proclaim nothing else but what the *loke paṇḍitās* teach; III, p. 138.

190. Aṅg. N. II, p. 227.

191. Majjh. N. I, p. 483—The doctrine of the Ājīvakas—according to their opponents is : *natthi kammaṃ, naṭthi kiriyaṃ;* Aṅg. N.I, p. 248; Cp. Dīgh. X. I, p. 53.

192. The circumstances that Jātakas refer the occurences to the times of the King Brahmadatta of Benares, shows that the home of these is the country near Benares, and not Magadha, where Buddhism arose.

193. Wassilief B. 124.

194. Huen Tsang qualifies them as "heretics" and accuses them of complotting against his life, Voy. I, 246.

CHAPTER-X

BUDDHIST ICONOGRAPHY

—Benoytosh Bhattacharyya

The foregoing is an account of the iconography of Buddhist gods and goddesses as reconstructed from Sanskrit texts of the Buddhist Tāntric literature. The study confines itself to the iconography of gods and goddesses only, excluding all other favourite themes of the Buddhists carved on stone or painting, such as the scenes from Buddha's life, the Jātaka stories, the Avadānas and others, representations of which, are available from Bharhut, Sāñchi, Amarāvati, Gandhāra or even the cave temples of Ajantā. This chapter does not refer to them nor makes an attempt to identify them by hunting out the original Sanskrit texts which are illustrated on stone in the form of stories. It is a practical handbook for the guidance of Museologists who have to handle large number of images of gods and goddesses with strange faces, weapons and poses. It is a work giving indications as to how such images should be studied, analyzed, and finally identified with the help of original Sanskrit texts such as are quoted in this chapter at every place. An image is nothing but a symbol, and it is the business of the students of iconography to find out how the image was made, by whom it was made, and what philosophical and cultural background was necessary for the production of such an image. In this work, therefore, problems such as these have been treated and enough information is given in order to understand a Buddhist image from different view-points. The scope of this work thus is limited, and it does not claim to unravel the mystery of all stones on which something is carved. But within the limited scope, it has enough information of the highest practical value to the students of iconography, and this value is enhanced by the inclusion of photographs of excellent sculptures, bronzes and original Nepalese drawings procured with difficulty and at high cost.

The Buddhist pantheon as such did not exist before 300 A.D. which is the approximate time of the composition of the famous Tāntric work the Guhyasamāja. The pantheon got a good start from the theory of the five Dhyāni Buddhas, the embodiment of the five cosmic forces, Rūpa, Vedanā, Saṁjñā, Saṁskāra and Vijñāna. The pantheon further got a fillip from the theory of the Kulas (families) of the Dhyāni Buddhas and their Śaktis or female counterparts. The Dhyāni Buddhas thus became the Kuleśas or progenitors or heads of families, and the families are seen multiplying until they become overwhelming in number. And along with numerical strength, the excellent and meritorious artists went on producing wonderful specimens of images which were backed by the religious inspiration of the most transcendental type. The pantheon became extremely attractive, and all, including the Hindus and Jainas, started building their pantheons and adding to their gods and goddesses. In the meantime other Buddhist countries like Tibet, China and Japan and the rest were struck by the wealth of gods and sculptures of the most bewildering variety, and started constructing their own pantheons according to their own national and cultural genius. The pantheon of the Buddhists created in India thus became world property, although Buddhism as a religion vanished from India the land of its birth long long ago.

These teachings of the Guhyasamāja remained dormant for some 300 years, and were handed down secretly from Gurus to disciples, but later, when it became popular, gradually the process of deification rapidly grew with newer and newer gods and goddesses. Each image received and absorbed cultural currents and cross-currents, and as a living organism took newer and newer forms according to time and according to space. It has now become so unwieldly and its ramifications have been so intricate and vast, that it has become a highly specialized study requiring experts to handle the gods and goddesses of Buddhism. The study is fascinating to the extreme, and the interest in the subject is bound to grow with the lapse of time and with the publication of the original MSS on the subject, such as the Vajrāvalī, Kriyāsamuccaya, the original Tantras like the Kālacakra Tantra, Heruka and Hevajra Tantras, Vajrayoginī and Vajravārāhī Tantras, vast in number and voluminous in extent. Let us hope that India will take care of these priceless original manuscripts, preserve them in good libraries, and gradually through publications, make them available to the world of Buddhists comprising a third of the population of the globe. Just at the present moment however, for unravelling the mysteries of the Buddhist images of gods and goddesses, there are only two books of outstanding value. These are the Sādhanamālā and the Niṣpannayogāvalī both published in the *Gaekwad's Oriental Series* for the first time. The Sādhanamālā was composed in A.D. 1165 since the earliest manuscript of the work bears a date in the Newari era which is equivalent to 1165 A.D. Niṣpannayogāvalī was written by the famous Buddhist author and mystic Mahāpaṇḍita Abhayākara Gupta whose time is co-eval with that of the Pāla king Rāmapāla who flourished in A.D. 1084-1130. Both these works were written at a time when the psychic phase of Buddhism reached its very zenith, before being destroyed by the sword of Islam. Both the Sādhanamālā and the Niṣpannayogāvalī therefore record faithfully the highest development of the psychic phase of Buddhism in the 12th century.

The Sādhanas in the Sādhanamālā were composed by men distinguished in the mediaeval age as great Tāntric authors. The Dhyānas contained in the Sādhanas laid down the essential features of different gods, and the sculptors and artists prepared images with the help of these general directions. The Dhyānas left much scope for the exercise of imagination on the part of the sculptors, and the products of their chisels were also very greatly influenced by the spirit of the age in which they flourished, as well as by the geographical situation in which they worked. The ornaments, dress and even facial expressions of the images reflected local conditions to a great extent, while the particular Tāntric rites in which the images were used had also a modifying influence.

It has been pointed out several times that the most important factor in the identification of images is the miniature figure of the Dhyāni Buddha is on their crowns. When, however, the parental Dhyāni Buddha is not present, other marks of identification have to be sought for. Moreover, difficulties may arise even when the Dhyāni Buddhas are present. In cases where all the Dhyāni Buddhas are present on the aureole, the Buddha right on the top of the head is to be taken as the parental Dhyāni Buddha. The standing figure of Khadiravaṇī Tārā in the Indian Museum, Calcutta or the Vikrampur figures of Parṇaśabarī are the cases in point. They are both emanations of Amoghasiddhi whose effigy appears right above the heads of the goddesses. The figures of all the other four Dhyāni Buddhas are not required either by the Sādhana or for identification. Their presence can only be explained by the fact that in all kinds of worship the five Dhyāni Buddhas are the first to be invoked. Sometimes, however, the Dhyāni Buddhas appear on the image for artistic reasons only, as for instance, in the case of the Dacca Museum image of Arapacana Mañjuśrī. The Java figure of Arapacana is surrounded by four companions, identical in appearance with himself, but in the Dacca Museum image there are four Dhyānis Buddhas in addition, on the aureole although the central position just above the head of the principal deity is occupied by one of the attendants of Arapacana. The Dhyāni Buddhas, here are not required by the Sādhana and are, therefore, more ornamental than otherwise.

But the most serious difficulty arises when instead of the Dhyāni Buddha prescribed by the Sādhana some other Dhyāni Buddha appears on the crown of any figure. For instance, the Sarnath image of Ucchuṣma Jambhala should have shown in accordance with the Sādhana the figures either of Akṣobhya or Ratnasambhava on its crown, but the effigy of Amitābha is shown instead. Again, when a reference is made to the Lucknow figure of Mārīcī, who according to the Sādhana should have shown the figure of Vairocana on her crown, shows Amitābha instead. Again the Indian Museum image of Uṣṇīṣavijayā shows the figure of her parental Dhyāni Buddha as Akṣobhya instead of her own sire Vairocana.

True reasons for these discrepancies can hardly be given at this state of our knowledge. The most reasonable suggestion seems to be that the original texts are not still known in their entirety. It must be remembered that the Sādhanamālā and the Niṣpannayogāvalī are not the only texts produced in Vajrayāna. It is quite likely that new Sādhanas will be forthcoming when further material is published. It is difficult, however, to believe that a new Sādhana for either Mārīcī or Uṣṇīṣavijayā will be available. In the Sādhanamālā itself a large number of Sādhanas is published, but nowhere there is any mention of any other parental Buddha than Vairocana. Thus the possibility of discovering further Sādhanas prescribing parental Buddhas other than Vairocana seems to be remote.

Another alternative suggestion presupposes the existence of different cults according as one or another of the Dhyāni Buddhas is believed to be the principal or the Ādi-Buddha.[1] The Buddhists of Nepal even now are divided into so many different cults, some regarding Amitābha as the Ādi-Buddha, and others acknowledging either Vairocana or Akṣobhya as the Ādi-Buddha. Now though the Sādhanas prescribe the figure of the Dhyāni Buddha Vairocana for both Mārīcī and Uṣṇīṣavijayā, the followers of the Amitābha cult are at liberty to assign them to that Buddha whom they consider to be the Ādi-Buddha. Similarly, Ucchuṣma Jambhala being regarded as the offspring of Amitābha, is made to bear an image of that Dhyāni Buddha on his crown in the Sarnath figure already alluded to. It is not necessary to multiply instances. This is the only reasonable explanation it is possible to offer at the present state of our knowledge.

In identifying Buddhist images the student of iconography should guard himself against taking unnecessary figures in the image for principal ones, or necessary figures for unnecessary ones. A full-fledged Buddhist icon shows in the first place, the principal god, an effigy of his sire on his crown, and the Dhyāni Buddhas on the aureole. The icon may further show miniature figures of the companions of the principal god, some worshippers, mythical figures and the three, seven, or sixteen jewels or sacred objects of Buddhism. The figure of Vajrasattva seems to be a favourite decoration with the artists. He appears on many Buddhist images and is perhaps conceived as a sort of general guardian of Buddhism and Buddhist worship. For purposes of identification the principal figure of the Dhyāni Buddha on the top, and the companions are the indispensable parts of the image. When, again, a reference is made to the Dacca Museum image of Arapacana Mañjuśrī in which besides the four companions there are present four Dhyāni Buddhas Vairocana, Akṣobhya, Amitābha and Ratnasambhava, two mythical figures supporting the lotus seat, and two worshippers to the extreme left of the pedestal. All these figures are redundant for the purpose of identification, and their absence in the Java figure Arapacana in no wise affects it. But if, for instance, the companions are confused with the worshippers the identification must be regarded as incorrect. The figures flanking Vajrāsana, for instance, are clearly Maitreya and Avalokiteśvara according to the Sādhana, but if they are described as worshippers, as has been done previously, the identification of the whole image becomes vitiated.

Another difficulty in identification arises when the letters of the Mantra of the god are deified and appear on the image. This is found on the case of Vajratārā who is surrounded by ten goddesses who originate from the ten syllables of the Mantra "Oṁ Tāre Tuttāre Ture Svāhā". It has also been pointed out previously how from the five letters of the name of Aracana Mañjuśrī originated the five deities Candraprabha, Jālinīprabha, Keśinī and Upakeśinī, and the principal deity Mañjuśrī. The Dacca image of Khadiravaṇī Tārā is a remarkable instance of the deification of the Tārā Mantra. The main figure in accordance with the Sādhana carries the Utpala in the left hand and shows the Varada mudrā in the right, and she is flanked on either side by Aśokakāntā and Ekajaṭā. But on the aureole there are eight female figures identical in appearance with the principal figure. They obviously represent none but the eight syllables of the Tārā Mantra "Oṁ Tāre Tuttāre Ture", the two others, Uṣṇīṣavijayā and Sumbha, being omitted.

Sometimes in the images of Buddhist gods and goddesses we notice the presence of Gaṇeśa, who is regarded by the Hindus as "Siddhidātā" or the Bestower of Perfection or success in Tāntric rites. The Buddhists as a proof of their aversion to the followers of the Brahmanical faith, made their gods trample upon Gaṇeśa. Thus in the Indian Museum images of Parṇaśabarī and Aparājitā, and in the Baroda Museum images of Vighnāntaka, etc., the deities have been represented as trampling Gaṇeśa under their feet. In the two Vikrampur image of Parṇaśabarī and in the Dacca Sahitya Parisat image of Mahāpratisarā, Gaṇeśa appears below the lotus seat lying prostrate on the ground crushed under the weight of Buddhist deities. Thus did the Buddhists manifest their animosity against the Hindu gods, Gaṇeśa, giving him the epithet of Vighna or Obstacle. Their animosity may be further illustrated by the following features of the Sādhanas. The four Hindu gods, Brahmā, Viṣṇu, Śiva and Indra have been designated uniformly as the four Māras or Wicked Beings, and several Buddhist gods have been described as trampling them under their feet. The Sādhanas of the Prasanna-Tārā, Vajrajjvālānalārka, Vidyujjvālākarālī, and the like, are instances in point. Trailokyavijaya has been represented as trampling upon the prostrate forms of Śiva and Gaurī; Nārāyaṇa has been made a Vāhana or vehicle by Harihariharivāhana. Poor Brahmā has been most severly handled by the Buddhists. The severed head of Brahmā is a trophy in the hands of Buddhist deities. According to Hindu traditions, Brahmā should be very old with grey beard, and four heads, and the Buddhist deities mercilessly hold the heads by the matted hair and flourish them in their hands. This is how the Buddhists attempted to exhibit the superiority of their gods over those of the Brahmanical faith. It is a matter of satisfaction, however, that the Hindus never disgraced any gods belonging to the alien faith in this manner. On the contrary, they placed Buddha among the ten Avatāras of Viṣṇu. In this connection it may be pointed out that in the Kālacakra Tantra a work of the 10th century A.D. there is evidence that an attempt was made by the Buddhists to unite with the Hindus under the common banner of the god Kālacakra 'The Circle of Time', against the cultural penetration of the Mlecchas. The later history showed, however, that the attempt proved futile.

A deep spiritual significance is attached to the colour, weapons, and the Āsanas of Buddhist gods who are either represented singly or in yab-yum. The conception of yab-yum images, however, is much more complicated than the single ones.

It has been stated in the Sādhanamālā that a single deity may take any colour according to the particular Tāntric rite in which he is invoked. For instance, in the Śāntikavidhi or propitiatory rite the god takes the white or yellow colour. In Pauṣṭikavidhi or protective rite the yellow colour is taken by the deity. Similarly, in Vaśyavidhi (bewitching) and Ākarṣaṇa (attraction) he may take yellow, green or red colour. In Ucāṭana (total destruction) and in Māraṇa (killing) the god is generally blue. It may be pointed out here that the word 'Kṛṣṇa' in the Sādhanamālā always signifies the blue colour, and not black. Buddhist gods are rarely black, not because there seems to have been some prejudice against using the black colour in the paintings of gods. It may further be pointed out that whenever a deity gets the blue colour his appearance becomes terrible with protruding teeth and tongue, garland of severed heads, ornaments of snakes and the garment of tiger-skin.

With regard to colour it may be remembered that their stock number is usually five corresponding to the five cosmic elements. Thus according to authoritative books, the element of Water is white in colour, Earth is yellow, Fire is red, Ether is green, and Air is blue. Of these the two colours white and yellow representing Water and Earth are benign, and the other colours red, green and blue are clearly malefic. The earthy and watery gods are peaceful, while the gods of the other three elements are fearful in character. Blue seems to be the most violent of all.

The Āsanas have likewise a spiritual significance. The Vajraparyaṅka attitude signifies meditation and introspection, the Ardhaparyaṅka shows serenity, the Ālīḍha heroism, the Pratyālīḍha destruction and disgust, and the dancing in Ardhaparyaṅka displays wrath and horror.

A reference may be made here to the yab-yum representations. The Tibetan *yab* means 'the honourable father' and *yum* likewise signifies the 'honourable mother'. Therefore, the word *yab-yum* means the honourable father in the company of the honourable mother. A yab-yum image has a deep spiritual significance. It signifies that the god, the embodiment of Śūnya is perfect, having attained Karuṇā and therefore the highest state of Nirvāṇa.

The conception of Śūnya in Vajrayāna took the concrete shape of a god and a goddess. Śūnya took the shape of Heruka when a male god, and become known as Nairātmā when a goddess. That Śūnya took the form of a deity does not seem strange in Vajrayāna, where we find conceptions, such as Saṅgha, Dharma, Prajñāpāramitā, the twelve Pāramitās, and the five Skandhas deified in the Buddhist pantheon. Thus the conception of Śūnya in the form of a god or a goddess is perferctly in keeping with the tradition of the Vajrayāna system. When the Bodhi Mind attains Nirvāṇa it merges in Śūnya and there remains in eternal bliss and happiness. And when Śūnya was made a goddess, it was easily understood, how eternal bliss and happiness was possible after the attainment of Nirvāṇa. The yab-yum figures, representing Śūnya in the form of Heruka in the embrace of Śūnya in the form of Nairātmā, were held up before the mass as ideals, and they readily attracted them and helped them in their conception of a bright and definite spiritual prospect.

Buddhists of the Vajrayāna consider Śūnya as the Ultimate Reality, and they believe that the host of gods and goddesses, including the Dhyāni Buddhas, are Śūnya in essence. The innumerable gods and goddesses of the Vajrayāna pantheon are all manifestations of Śūnya. The gods have no real existence, the images have not real existence, and therefore, it may be positively asserted that a true Vajrayānist never worshipped an image or god. Naturally, since these paintings, images, or even the deities themselves have no real or independent existence, they are merely manifestations in a variety of forms of the One, Undifferentiated Śūnya. But it cannot be denied that these images were very useful, since the forms they presented, in accordance with the Dhyānas, to the gaze of the worshippers undoubtedly helped the latter to visualise the deities with whom they were asked to identify themselves. As they had no real existence, these deities had to be attracted to the mind-sky from unknown regions in the firmament by the luminous rays of light issuing from the Bījamantras uttered by the worshipper. The Śūnya takes the form of a divinity in accordance with the germ-syllable uttered, and exists only as a positive idea in the mind of the worshipper who identifies himself with that transformation of Śūnya.

The question may be raised as to the necessity of a variety of gods and goddesses when one Śūnya would have been sufficient. In answer to this a number of things have to be considered. It may be remembered that Śūnya, which was identified with Compassion by the Vajrayānists was conceived as manifesting itself in different forms in accordance with the different functions it had to discharge. For instance, if any disease is to be cured, Śūnya takes the form of Siṁhanāda;

when it is a question of snake-bite, Śūnya becomes Jāṅgulī; when destruction of the wicked is needed, Śūnya takes the form of Mahākāla; when again, diseases and pestilences are to be prevented, Śūnya is conceived as Parṇaśabarī; for success in love-affairs, Śūnya is invoked in the form of Kurukullā; and when forcible submission is required in love-affairs, Śūnya becomes Vajrānaṅga, and when finally, Buddhahood is wanted by the worshipper, he should conceive himself as Heruka. From the above it appears that the conception of the multitude of Buddhist deities emerges from the one grand conception of Śūnya in accordance with the various functions it is supposed to discharge, as a mark of compassion towards the Buddhists.

Secondly, the number of gods and goddesses increases when Śūnya manifests in different forms the nine "Rasas" or dramatic sentiments. For instance, Śūnya will be Khadiravaṇī or Lokanātha when benign (Karuṇā), Mārīcī when Heroic (Vīra), Vighnāntaka, Heruka or Mahākāla when awe-inspiring (Bhaya), Aparājitā when wrathful (Rudra), Vajracarcikā in its moments of disgust and loathsomeness (Bībhatsa), Prajñāpāramitā when peaceful (Śānta), and so on.

Thirdly, the number of deities increases as objects such as the Three Jewels; philosophical conceptions such as the Pāramitās, Bhūmis or Pratisaṁvits; literature such as the Prajñāpāramitā, the Daśabhūmika Śāstra, the Dhāriṇīs and the like; desires such as for eating, drinking, sleeping and the rest; the directions such as the flute, the violin, and the drum; and other innumerable ideas and objects, are required to be worshipped in the forms of gods and goddesses. By these and various other ways the number of deities in the Buddhist pantheon increased phenomenally.

As all these deities centre round the one grand conception of Śūnya so also the host of weapons revolve round the one grand conception of Bodhisatta or the will to Enlightenment. As these weapons are required to discharge different functions, the Bodhicitta resolves itself into so many different forms of weapons.[2] For instance, when the darkness of ignorance is to be dispelled Bodhicitta becomes a sword by which the veil of ignorance is cut asunder. The sword is also to be used to destroy the Māra hordes who disturb the worshippers. Bodhicitta becomes the Aṅkuśa (goad) when the hearts of the wicked are to be pierced. It is conceived as a noose when the Māra hordes are to be securely bound. It becomes a needle and a thread when the eyes of the wicked have to be sewn up. Bodhicitta becomes a Kartri (knife) when the wicked have to be chopped. It is a Bhiṇḍipāla (javelin) when Māras have to be attacked from a distance, and a bow and an arrow if the distance be greater.

The Mudrās also are nothing but the manifestations of the Bodhicitta. If protection is needed, Bodhicitta is conceived as the Abhaya mudrā; if boon is desired it becomes Varada; when instruction in Buddhist Law is required it becomes Dharmacakra, and so on.

The Bodhicitta, or the Will to Enlightenment, is that state of Mind which has already acquired the potentiality of dissolving itself in Śūnya. As a matter of fact, Śūnya or Nirvāṇa would be unattainable without the help of the Bodhicitta, which like Śūnya exists only in the mind. The Bodhi mind leads the aspiring soul into the very presence, so to speak, of Śūnya; it ultimately merges and loses itself completely in Śūnya.

The gods of the Buddhist pantheon are conceived as carrying the Bodhicitta in their hands, both being of the nature of Śūnya. It is with the help of this Bodhicitta that a god is supposed to confer Buddhahood or success in Tāntric rite upon his worshipper. The yab-yum conception of deities is still more sublime. The god Heruka, the embodiment of Śūnya, carrying weapons the embodiments of Bodhicitta also of the nature of Śūnya, is embraced by Nairātmā, whose essence is Śūnya, carrying weapons also of the nature of Śūnya. Thus the Infinite with the Infinite commingless. In Involution, the Many become One. This is the highest state—the Anupādhiśeṣa-Nirvāṇa.

Kṛto vaḥ sarvasattvārthaḥ
siddhir-dattā yathānugā /
Gacchadhvaṁ Buddhaviṣayaṁ
punarāgamanāya Muḥ //

"Gods, I bid You farewell ! Ye have fulfilled the desires of all beings. Ye have conferred the desired success. Go Ye to the region of the Buddhas. Return Ye once again, Muḥ".

REFERENCES

1. The theory of Ādi-Buddha originated in the Nalanda monastery about the beginning of the 10th century and was accepted first in the Kālacakrayāna, a later form of Vajrayāna. See Csoma de Koros : *The Origin of the Theory of Ādi-Buddha* in J.A.S.B., Vol. II (1833), p. 57f. See also Bhattacharya : *Buddhist Iconography* in JOBRS, March, 1923.
2. Compare the statement in the Jñānasiddhi of Indrabhūti in the *Two Vajrayāna Work;* (GOS), pp. 80, 81.
   Bodhicittam bhaved Vajram Prajñā Ghaṇṭā vidhiyate /
   Cakram-ajñānacchedāt ca Ratnantu durlabhādapi //
   Bhavadoṣair-aliptatvāt jñānam tat Padam-ucyate /
   Khaḍgaḥ kleśārisamcchedāt Utpalam plavanāt tataḥ //

CHAPTER-XI

BUDDHISM AND SARNATH

—Kamla Rohatagi and S.P. Rohatagi

The 6th century B.C ushered in an era of intellectual upheaval and was, indeed a turning point in the religious history of mankind. The quickening pulse of humanity was felt in far reaching intellectual movements in countries far apart from one another as Greece, Israel and India, China and Persia. In spite of the vast distances and political and racial distinctions raising considerable barriers between them, there emerged a community of ideas and a kinness of spiritual striving which no political conflict could ignore or supress. The developing mind of humanity and its profound quests were evident in the vital spirit of the age. Great religious movements under great thinkers and philosophers sprang up and fairly revolutionized the old religious beliefs and practices.

In India there appeared Mahavira and Buddha who were expounding their theories of the miseries of life and their solution in the debating halls of the peoples of eastern India while Pythagoras preached the doctirne of the one in many and Heraclitus discoursed on elemental matter and the nature of the soul in the porticoes of lonian temples. In China there appeared Confucious and Lao-Tzo, and in Persia an Aryan thinker Zoroaster protested against the sacredotal corruption and formulated his militant ethics.

Contemporary India not only witnessed the culmination of considerable philosophical thought but also marked a summit which could have been reached after a considerable march and a long period of wide and deep speculations. Though Brahmanism predominated in the noth-west, it hardly affected the eastern regions. Magadha was full of wandering ascetics who appear to have upheld the boldest paradoxes, intellectual and moral. At Rajgriha and other places Buddha met many a wandering philosopher and encountered, fought and foiled the current geipping philosophies not unoften himself testing reverses at the hands of formidable adversaries. There were, however constructive elements in their doctrines, for most of them believed in the re-incarnation of soul and maintained and ascetic discipline. They belonged mostly to the warrior caste and were considerably independent. They were outside the pale of Brahmanism and a fair deal opposed to it.

By this time not only had the Brahmans become an organized intellectual force which asserted for itself the leading position even in political affairs hitherto held by the Kshatriyas (warrior caste), but they had established a monopoly in ministering to the religious needs of the Indo-Aryan community at large which brought in its train unscrupulous exactions and encouraged the grossest superstitions.

But dawn the march of post-Vedic times the tide of Brahmanism was gradually ebbing and now Brahman priesthood as a class came to depend in the first instance upon the accident of birth and high ideals of purity and altruism set forth in the laws of Manu and accepted as the guiding principle of Brahmanhood was given up in place of unscruplous or ignorant exercises of rituals and sacrifices. "Their indiscriminate slaughter of animals and their free indulgence in the intoxicating juice of the Soma plant associated with Vedic rituals involved the tacit recognition of many obscene orgies of the most uncivilized nature."

Among the Brahamans, there were, however, many sincere believers in the divine revelation of the Vedas who were, nevertheless, dissatisfied with the method of Brahmanical rituals and sacrifices, and could not be blind to the superstitions involved in them. In the course of several centuries "the sacrificial rites had grown into a fine art directly or indirectly for the personal advantage of the officiating priests and their servants, for the efficacy of the sacrifice was said to depend largely upon the liberality of the indispensable dakshina, or reward, bestowed upon them and it extended to every concern of public and private life, both wealthy and poor."

Now time was ripe for the appearance of a doctrine appealing to the deep religious conscience for removing the influences of all these vices that crept into the Brahmanical priesthood advantageous to its vested interest and also giving a fresh light to the ignorant mass from whom the Brahmans held aloof through their craft and language. And no one could have been better fitted to make such an appeal than this young Kshatriya prince Siddhārtha (Gautama Buddha) who, in search of a better conduct of life, renounced all personal ties, his dearest wife and child, wealth and estates. He began by acquiring knowledge from the most famous Brahman philosophers. He also learnt the practices of Yoga and underwent the severest penance prescribed for ascetics who sought divine knowledge through self-mortification. He mastered all the important philosophical theories current at this time. India indeed prepared to wintness great counter movements with the appearance of the mighty personality in Gautama Buddha.

Buddha was not really in sharp conflict with the fundamental principles of the Vedic religion or with the tradition to the Aryan life. He stood for the re-organisaiton of Aryan society upon a wider and more candid basis and a re-adaptaion of religious practices to the new resurgent spiritual needs of the time. His was a new interpretation rather an entire repudiation of the Vedic tradition. Revolting against the ceremonial sacredotal religion of the Brahman priesthood, he yet strongly emphasised the transcendental aspect of the Upanishads albeit an extension of the Kshatriya revolt against the Brahmanistic formalism enriched it with a wealth of ethical refinement and enforced the doctrines of Sāṅkhya and Yoga with a unique precision and clarity of thought. He was against class domination which had been a natural sequence of the Brāhmaṇas becoming intermediaries between man and God. According to him, not birth but character must deserve honour.

Buddhism was much more a social than a religious revolution. Buddha was both a philosopher and a social reformer. His rare political insight revealed itself in the method of his teachings. He was more careful to insist on the fact that what he preached and what he expected his disciples to follow was the "Aryan way." All his metaphors were taken from the life of the Aryan rural community. The church (Sangha) which he founded was based on the model of an Aryan clan. It is rightly said, "It was a select spiritual brotherhood within the larger brotherhood of the secular Aryan community." He was very paritcular that his Sangha should not be used as a means of secular obligations or of evading Aryan laws. No one was permitted to enter his Sangha to avoid payment of debts; criminals and robbers were not permitted entry. He was extremely conscious of the diverse social needs of the times He first formed two categories of his followers. Those who were the members of the Sangha were called Bhikkhus (monks) and those who followed the laws of the Buddha but were not members of the Sangha were called Upasakas (lay-adherents). Ceremonies and doctrines had hardly any place in his code during his life time. He enjoined good conduct and morality upon his lay-worshippers.

Buddha occupies a peculiar place among the greatest men of the world. It is difficult to decide whether we should place him in the category of prophets or of philosophers. In spite of long controversies both philosophy and religion continue to claim the Buddha. To many his role of a philosopher is clear than that of a prophet. He made his enquiries in order to solve the problems of life and not to search for the existence of God or to speculate on the nature of things. Similarly his quest ended with the solution of that problem and did not concern itself with either the nature of things or the existence of God. He did not talk about the soul either. It is in this sense that he completely broke away from that religious life of India which believed in innumberable gods and goddesses. It is of course true that some centuries after his death, his teachings were gradually transformed into a full-fledged religious cult and his followers placed the Buddha himself on the vacant throne of the deity, besides bringing the entire Hindu pantheon to attend on him. This was, however, a turn and course which Buddhism took but for which Buddha was not responsible.

Gautama the Buddha

Buddha's life was not written in the sense of a biography, for the idea of biography was unknown to the ancient Indian literature. In the Brahamanas and Upanishads were documented beliefs and practices of sages, the doctrines they expounded, but even rarely an outline of their lives were mentioned. A western historian justly remarked, "Whether the Hindus write about a man of religion or a philosopher, their weak historical sense and their strong feeling for the importance of their teachings lead them to neglect the figure of the teacher and present a portrait which seems to us dim and impersonal."

All his teachings and incidents of his life were committed

to writing long after his death. As the centuries rolled by, his life acquired an increasing garland of fabulous adventure and blended with numerous myths and miracles. But inspite of the centuries which separate us from him and the misty and unreal atmosphere which in later times hangs round his name, the magnetic force of this character retains his personality in a more distinct and life-like manner that of many later teachers. Though the Pali texts do not give the story of Buddha's life in a connected form, they do give us some details about his many important life events.

The Suttas which relate the close to the Buddha's life and the portion of the Vinaya which tells how he obtained enlightenment and made his first convert are of considerable length.

The Brith of Gautama

Buddha was born in the Kshatriya family and was of the Sakya clan. His father, Suddhodana, was styled a Raja, and though not a King as often discribed, he was a chief of the Sakya clan, whose principality lay along the southern Nepal. Maya, the elder wife of Raja Suddhodana, saw in her dream a snow-white elephant entering her womb. The court astrologer was summoned and he interpreted the dream as the approaching conception of the queen and predicted the birth of a wonderful child, who would either be a Buddha or universal monarch. She gave birth to a child under sal tree in the Lumbini grove while on her way to her father's house.

The child was called Siddhartha, meaning "One who had accomplished his object." His family name was Gautama. The date of his birth is still controversial but it is probable that he was born in 563 B.C At the age of sixteen he was married to his cousin Yaśodhara, a lady of an aristocratic family of the closeby Koliyas. He was reared up in princely galore and his father strove to avert from the prince all acquaintance with suffering and constrained him to remain whithin the precincts of the palace.

The Great Renunciation

In spite of his father's efforts to keep all knowledge of worldly woes from his eyes the young Prince while driving forth from the palace to the pleasure garden saw an old man, then a sickman, then a dead man, and lastly an ascetic and at the sight of each asked his charioteer the meaning of what he saw. "This comes to all men," answered the charioteer. His mind was much troubled that such was the effect of birth and in its effects comes sorrow and pain. The sight of the miseries of life wrought a change in him. Sensual pleasures and joys of marriage had now no meaning for him. The material world appeared to him an illusion to escape from which become his chief concern hereafter.

When he was contemplating over this subject, news was brought to him that his wife had been delivered of a son, who in consequence of his father's exclamation a hinderance! was named Rahula (meaning hinderance) and six days after his birth Gautama resolved to renounce all worldly ties in order to obtain freedom from the ills of life. He bade farewell to his sleeping wife and babe and in the silence of the midnight walked forth into wilderness, the spacious path of Mahabhinishkamana, the Great Renunciation. He visited first Alara Kalama, a noted philosopher of his time, and received his first philosophical lesson. He remained with him for some times, but was not satisfied with his answers. Forsaking him for that reason he visited Udraka, an another sage, but his quest remained unanswered. Then in order to acquire a deeper insight into the mysteries of the universe he learnt the practices of Yoga and for six long years practised the most rigorous austerities. He conquered fear, subdued lusts of the flesh, controlled his mind; still his heart's imperious demand remained unanswered and his long cherished wish ungratified. Then one day he realised, "Surely not through this process shall I be able to attain the state of superhuman? The path of enlightenment is different." Consequently Gautama abandoned his fruitless practices of austerities. He decided to eat again and the five ascetices who had accompanied him through his quest thus left him in disgust. Meanwhile he accepted a bowl of milk and rice from the maid, Surjata and after having bathed and eaten, seated himself in the lotus posture at the foot of a fig tree, with determination to achieve without delay the full fruits of enlightenment.

The Enlightenment

Mara, the evil one, tried to seduce him from the path of enlightenment and claimed the throne of Grass which Buddha had made for himself. The Bodhisattva (Buddha-to-be) touched the Earth, calling her to witness that the throne was his right and the Earth gave witness. Māra with his daughters and hosts fled away. Buddha remained absorbed in his sedate posture to obtain omniscience. By an inward illumination he passed in review of his former births, the cause of all rebirths and its consequent sufferings. He then rose in full consciousness through the planes and sub-planes of material existence. He linked various component parts of the self to the self and at last the profound truth fleshed upon his mind. He attained Sambodhi (Supreme Enlightenment) which means the communion of the human self with the eternal self in his inmost being, he was a manifestation on earth.

Having fully enlightened, the Buddha began to contemplate whether he should preach to the world the great truth he had realised and to whom he should first proclaim his doctrine and who would be able to understand his 'dhamma'. First he thought of addressing his former teachers Alara Kalama and Udraka, but finding that they were no more, he decided to preach his doctrine to his former five companions, who faithfully had attended him during the period of his austeries and had departed to Rishipatana when he partook of food.

Now the Blessed One rose and slowly made his way to Banaras. There on its outer-skirt lay the Deer-park of Rishipatana, where he met them and they called him by his name as well as with the appellation"friend".

At this the lord said to the five monks, "Don't, O monks, address the Tathāgata by his name or with the title of 'Friend'. Monks, I am an arhat, a Tathāgata, fully enlightened. O monks, listen, I teach you the immortal turth I have attained. I preach you the doctrine. Acting according to the teaching for the sake of which ye, youths of good family, rightly wander from out of home to a homeless life, you will in a short time, learn, realise and attain the supreme end of the truth and live in it."

At this the five said, "Even by such exercises, Friend Gautama, by those austerities and practices of self-mortification, you have not won the superhuman power and insight. How will you now living in abundance, having given up the exertions and returned to luxury, gain the superhuman power and knowledge and insight ?"

"The Tathagata does not live in abundance nor has given up exertion, he has not turned to the life of luxury" said Buddha.

Thus convinced they paid him the respect that was due to him. During the third watch of the ensuing night he preached to them his first sermon. He spoke of the two extremes of sensuality and mortification. "There are two extremes, O monks, which ought to be avoided. What are these two extremes ?

(1) "Attachment to passions and wordly enjoyments or that which is low, sensual, ignoble and useless; (2) practice of self-torture is also painful, ignoble and useless. O, monks ! by avoiding these two extremes the Tathagata has gained the knowledge of the Middle path which gives insight and wisdom and which leads to calmness, to enlightenment and to Nirvāṇa (final escape)."

"Which, O monks, is the middle path discovered by Tathagata which gives insight, leads to clamness, to wisdom, to enlightement, to Nirvāṇa? It is the noble eightfold path, namely, Right View, Right Aspirations, Right Speech, Right Conduct, Right Living, Right Effort, Right Mindfulness and Right Meditation."

"This, indeed, O monks, is the noble eight-fold path gained by the Tathāgata." "Now, four are, ye monks the noble Axịoms. And what are these four? The noble Axịom about suffering about the origin of suffering, the noble Axiom about the cessation of suffering and the noble Axiom about the way leading to the cessation of suffering." "Thus, O monks! suffering is the noble truth; birth is suffering, decay is sufffering, illness is suffering, death is suffering, association with unpleasant objects is suffering, separation from the desired object is suffering, not to obtain one's desire is suffering."

"The origin of suffering, O monks is the noble truth. Thirst (desire) which leads to re-birth is accompanied by pleasure and attachment. It is thus craving for pleasure, thirst for life and thirst for non-existence."

"This, O monks ! is the noble truth of the cessation of suffering—the complete cessation without a reminder of that craving abondonment, forsaking, release, non-attachment. Now this, O monks ! is the noble Truth of the path that leads to the cessation of suffering. This is the noble eightfold path."

Thus in the Deer-park of Sarnath, Buddha proclaimed his Dhamma, "glorious in the beginning glorious in the middle, glorious in the end.'' This Sarnath naturally become the symbol and radiating centre of light throughout the Buddhist world.

Then Buddha, set-forth the famous Anatta doctrine and according to this all the five aggregate of personal being, body, feeling perception, predispositions of mind, and consciousness alike are prone to suffering, temporary without a permanant soul. Of the nature of the soul he said nothing.

Buddha was in the habit of moving from place to place in order to propagate his teachings and it was to his missionary zeal that Buddhism acquired from the first a missionary character. Within a few days of the first sermon, he inspired his handful of converts with the famous exhortation, Go Ye forth, O Bhikkhus ! on your journey for the profit of the many, for the bliss of the many, out of compassion for the world. Go not any two together."

The Buddha himself returned to Uruvela in the district of Gaya, Bihar, where he had obtained his enlightenment to keep the rainy season and here he found a group of fire-worshippers headed by Kassapa and he preached to them his famous Fire Sermon.

"All things", said he, "are on fire ; the eye is on fire, forms are on fire, the impressions received by the eye are on fire, and whatever sensation originates in the impressions received by the eye is likewise on fire. And with what are these things on fire ? With the fires of lust, anger, illusions, with these are they on fire, and so with the other senses and so with the mind. By conceiving disgust for the things of the senses, and being divested of desire for the things of the senses, one can remove form his heart the cause of suffering." Kassapa and all his followers become his disciples.

The Buddha then set forth for Rajagriha, where his fame had preceded him. King Bimbisara came to him with a host of citizens, and on fearing his teachings was converted. He also dedicated his own pleasure garden, the Venuvana (Bamboo Grove) to the fraternity of bhikkhus with the Buddha as its head. At this time Sariputta and Moggallana, joined the Buddhist order and later on became his chief disciples.

By now Raja Suddhodana was longing to see his son, and sent him repeated messages and for the first time since the Enlightenment Buddha saw his father and wife and child. It is said, how the princess, who was the mother of Rahula sent him to the glorious figure in the yellow robe to ask for his inheritance. The boy asked for his inheritance and the Buddha, his father, turning to Sariputta said,"Receive him into the order."

Lord Buddha again returned to Rājagriha, where Anathapindika, a wealthy merchant of Śrāvastī who came to see his daughter invited Buddha to Śrāvastī (Sahet Maheh in U.P) and there presented the order with the Jetavana Monastery. The Buddha received him as his disciple.

In this way he continued his preaching since his enlightenment for nearly fortyfive years till before his Mahā Pariniravāṇa about 483 B.C. He visited many places in northeast India propagating and organizing the expansion of the order and in his life time his doctrines spread over Magadha, Kośala and Śrāvastī. Women were also admitted and Mahāprajāpati, Buddha's step mother was the first to be admitted in the order at the insistence of Ananda. On this, Buddha is reported to have said that their admission would materially shorten the life of the Buddhist order. He renounced the world at the age of twenty-nine and for fortyfive years he kept moving about preaching what he had found. Buddha breathed his last at Kusinara (Modern Kusinagara) which was one of the capitals of the Mallas, who were also an aristocratic republic like the Sakyas and Vajjians. The Bhikkhus assembled about him but Ananda stood a way off in grief. The Buddha sent for him and exclaimed, "Do not weep Ananda. It is the very nature of things most near and dear to us that we must part from them. All that is born, brought into being and put together carries within itself the necessity of dissolution. For a long time, Ananda, you have been very near to me by acts of love and beyond all measure. You have done well, Ananda. Be earnest in your efforts and you too shall be free form the evils—form the cankers of sensuality, from individuality, from delusion and from ignorance." He then sent Ananda to the nearby villages of Kusinara to inform the Mallas that the Tathagata was about to pass away. The Mallas came to the master one by one. He received all of them into the Order and no one was left in doubt regarding his Dhamma. Then again the All Enlightened one addressed the assembled Bretheren, saying, "Decay is inherent in all component things! Strive earnestly. Work out your own salvation with diligence."

Thus ended the career of a man who was undoubtedly one of the greatest toilers in the cause on humanity, one that sought found and walked the path that he laid bare and strove to better the lot of mankind through love and fair living.

Emperor Asoka and the spread of Buddhism

I have already stated that Buddha spent his major portion of life in continuous moving from place to place in order to propagate his teachings and even in his life time won great support of the ruling clans, royal princes and wealthy merchants. During the first two centuries after his demise, little is known of the actual history of Buddhism. This much is, however, certain that during his life time his doctrine spread over Magadha and Kosala (south Bihar and Oudh). For many centuries his teachings were not recorded and the record of Buddha's words was merely a recollection of what had been told. In the very beginning of Buddhism strict discipline was enjoined upon the members of the Sangha. As years rolled by, the members of the Sangha revolted against the rigidity of discipline imposed on them and disaffsection among groups were already in evidence in the Second Great Council, convoked at Vaisali in 383 B.C. when the Mahasanghikas were expelled from the orthodox church by the Elders on the ten minor points of discipline. For want of a central authority after Buddha's Nirvāṇa, Buddhism was gradually being divided into different sects, and it was but natural that. "Each school should maintain that the memory of its own scholars had transmitted the most accurate and complete account and that tradition should represent the successive councils as chiefly occupied in reciting and shifting these accounts."Owing to different collection of scripture much divergences prevailed between the different Schools. These different Schools agreed in essentials and differed only in details, for it was the outcome of the natural sequence of the gradual elucidation of the Buddhist doctrine." It has been rightly remarked that "In different epochs and countries Buddhism presents a series of surprising metamorphoses and differences between the different Schools existing in India and abroad at any given time are less profound in character and less violent in expression than the divisions of Christiantiy."

We are not here concerned with all these details. It may suffice to know that there had appeared as may as eighteen sects of Buddhism during or shortly before the reign of Asoka about the middle of the 3rd century B.C. The great landmark in the earlier history of Buddhism is the reign of Asoka

Buddhism owes as much to Asoka as Christinity does to Constantine.

Asoka came to the throne about 270 B.C. and inherited the vast kingdom of his father and grand-father. The most important documents for the chronology and history of his reign are his personal edicts inscribed on rock's surface or on free-standing columns.

From these contemporary records we learn that in the nineth year of his reign, Asoka entered upon the conquest of Kalinga, a powerful kingdom of the east coast lying between the rivers Mahanadi and the Godavari. In his Rock edict XIII it is stated that "One hundred thousand peoples were slain, one hundred and fifty thousand carried away as prisoners, and that vast numbers of non-combatants perished." He conquered and annexed Kalinga but at the expense of an enormous number of lives. However, this was the end of his military career. The horror and brutality incidental to war filled his heart with profound sorrow and awakened in him a genuine compassion for the sufferers. He declared that in his opinion the only true conquest lies in the conquest of self. We find a similar parallel to this maxim in Mahābhārata where Bhīma says, "King should first subdue himself and then seek to subdue his foes. How could a king who has not been able to conquer his own self be able to conquer his foes!" (Santi Parva)

Sometime after this event, Ashoka came under the influence of Buddhist teachers. First he became a lay-adherent of the order for some two and a half years; later on he was ordained as a member of the Buddhist Sangha. His succeeding proclaimations record the gradually increasing zeal for the propagation of the Buddhist faith.

The Buddhism he taught was practical morality. Nowhere

in his edict do we find specific injunctions to follow the four Noble Truth, the Eight-fold path,the chain of causation and the belief in Nirvāṇa. On the other hand, we find the quintessence of what is good and generally common to all religion. On some of his edicts, Asoka enumerated what he meant by true Dhamma. His Dhamma is noting but simple code of noble conduct, morality and ethics—for example obedience to parents and elders, respect for teachers, proper behaviours towards friends, proper treatment of the Brahmans and monks, charity towards fellow beings and compassion towards animals. "What he spoke, he spoke as a layman speaking to laymen, leaving the niceties of doctrine to the more learned brethern," In short he directed his full energy towards the happiness of his subject and the propagation of Dharam among them. The whole machinery of the state was directed for this purpose. He provided both material and moral support to the Buddhist Sangha. His own example and such a personal zeal for the propagation of Buddhism could not fail to attract his subject to this faith. He undertook religious tours and adorned important Buddhist sites with splendid specimens of architecture under such royal patronage, Buddhism spread like tide in India and abroad. Asoka was an ardent missionary. He sent Buddhist missions to all other parts of India as well as to Syria, Egypt, Cyrene, Mecedonia and Epirus, the five Greek states of western Asia, Egypt and eastern Europe.

According to a Sinhalese tradition the most important and successful of Asoka's missions was one headed by Asoka's son Mahindra, who had followed his example by joining the order, and there is no doubt about it that the conversion of Ceylon to Buddhism was due to Asoka's missionary efforts. With the reign of Asoka's stone and brick replaced wood.

II

A SHORT HISTRRY OF SARNATH

In the preceeding pages the readers have already taken a glimpse of the development of Buddhism up to the reign fo Emperor Asoka and now I would like to draw their attention towards the ancient site of Sarnath of which a short hitory is given below.

In ancient Buddhist texts this place is referred by the names of Isipatana or Rishipatana and Mrigadava. In Mahavastu, a Sanskrit Buddhist work we find the following account regarding its former name :

"Once there lived five hundred Rishis of Pratyeka Buddhas in a forest (where Sarnath is now situated) in the vicinity of Banaras. They once rose to the sky attained salvation. Thus the bodies of the Rishis or Paratyeka Buddhas fell on that forest it came to be known as Rishipatana, i.e. Where the Rishis fell down. "The Chinese pilgrim, Fa-Hein (A.D. 405-411) records in his itinerary that "Once there lived a Prateyka Buddha and on hearing of the appproaching Enlightenment of Gautama Buddha attained salvation." The simple meaning of the word, however, is the abode or habitat, patana, of sages, rishis.

The second name is explained by one of the Jatakas stories which is commonly known as Nigrodhamiga Jataka. Jatakas are the stories of the previous births of the Buddha as told by him on different occasions to his disciples to elucidate his moral teachings. "According to Indian ideas, every living being, whatsoever he may be, is not only sure of dying, it is no less certain that he must be born again and agian in one of the five conditions of lost soul, ghost, animal, man or god, unless he attains salvation, which is nothing else than the final escape form his frightful circle or transmigration." It is nothings but one's past deeds that fatally decides one's future, destiny and each of the ephemeral existences are regulated automatically by a moral law, the law of 'action' or of Karma.

In the second place, it is a belief no less generally admitted in India that whosoever has attained sancity possesses among other supernatural faculties, the previlege of remembering his past existences and even those of others.

Thus the synthesis of Indian religious ideas which formed the body of Buddhist doctrine contained two other cardinal beliefs common to all schools of thought and deeply rooted in a remote antiquity. The first is re-incarnation and the second is salvation. In the earlier days of the Buddhist propaganda the dogma of re-incarnation had been explained to the people, by adaptations of the village folk-lore in the tales of the Jatakas—the previous births of the Enlightened One recount the many deeds of self-sacrifice in lower planes of existence by which the Bodhisattava, or Buddha that was to-be prepared himself for the final victory over the powers of evil in the great conflict under the Bodhi-tree. The Jatakas (Birth-stories), says Christmas Humphreys, "'Many of which reappear in Aesop's and La Fontaine's Fables, are a history of the evolution of consciousness upon this earth as recorded in what, for want of a better term, may be called the "Esoteric tradition."

Sarnath was known to Buddhists as Mirgadava or Deer-park which owes its origin to the fact that herds of deer roamed there as they had been granted immunity by the king of Banaras moved to Compassion by the spirit of self-sacrifice of the Bodhisattva Nyagrodhamriga for his fellow beings.

In mediaeval inscriptions the place is referrd to as the Dharmachakra (convent of the wheel-of-the-law) or Saddharma-chakra-pravatana-vihara (convent of the turning of the wheel-of-the good law). General Cunningham suggests that the present name Sarnath has been derived from Saranganatha and means Lord of the deer. It is interesting to note that Saranganatha is also an epithat of Lord Śiva and the name is still borne by a small Mahadeva temple situated half a mile east to the ancient ruins.

The Deer-park is one of the four most sacred Buddhist sites directly connected with Buddha's life, the rest three being Lumbini, the place where he was born, Bodh-Gaya, where he attained supreme Enlightenment and Kusinara where he breathed his last. Also a relatively ancient text, the Mahaparinibbana sutta already recommends a pilgrimage to these four sacred places. It was also in the Deer-park that Buddha laid the foundation of his Sangha the order of monks.

Sarnath is situated at a very short distance from Banaras, the holiest city of the Hindu faith for it is no less important that famous Buddhist sites should generally be situated on the outskirts of some great city, as "peace and quietude on the one hand and propinquity to the haunts of men on the other, were in effect indispensable for such establishment whose inmates spent half their day begging alms among the townsfolk and other half at their religious devotions."

The preaching of the first sermon is believed to have occured in 528 B.C. For nearly three centuries after that event nothing is recorded regarding the history of Deer-park of Banaras, though it may be assumed that soon after Buddha's nirvāṇa it become a place of pilgrimage. No antiquity of that period has yet been discovered there. We may therefore suppose that such members of religious order founded by the great teacher as settled down at the Deer-park were content as were the other hermits of the time with simple huts made of bamboo and wood, the usual prevailing type on which the later stone structures were modelled.

As already stated, about a couple of centuries after the Nirvāṇa of Lord Buddha, ruled Asoka. At Sarnath he erected several monuments. A stupa which was pulled down in a A.D 1793-94 by one Jagat Singh of Banaras is supposed to have been originally built by emperor Asoka. The other monuments of Ashoka are the monolithic column, once surmounted by the magnificant Lion, Capital, and a monolithic stone-railing. An other high stupa now known as Dhamekh (Dharmakhya bearing ther name of Dharma) also seems to have had its origin in Ashoka's time.

Not much is known of Sarnath during the following century, i.e. the Sunga period. The excavations have, however, revealed some railing pillars of about the 1st centry B.C., unearthed near the Dharmarajika stupa. These may have formed part of the stone-railing as provided around that stupa, just as the stupas at Sanchi were provided with railings at this time.

"Form the first century before and after the commencement of the Christian era, the progress of Buddhism was identified with the growth of Kushan political power in the nothr-west India. This new development of Buddhism which synchronised with the foundation of the Kushan empire had the more far-reaching effect upon both eastern and western religions. The Mongolian connections of the Kushan people gave an immense impetus to Buddhist propaganda in China and at the same time the Hellenistic culture of western Asia imbibed the Buddhist idealism which so deeply impressed the ritual and folk-lore of Christinity. Their supremacy over the Indian border land and their adaptation of Buddhist culture brought law and order into that unsettled region, and formed a half-way house between India and Rome on the hand and India and China on the other."

At the time of emperor Kanishka, the Kushana held

under its suzerainty the whole of northen India as far east as Banaras, Mathura was the greatest centre of this new religious and artistic activity, and unlike that of Gandhara School, Mathura School of Art represented an outgrowth of the ancient Indian School. Along with Mathura, Sarnath also prospered and received inspiration from Mathura. At the time of the great Kushan emperor, Kanishka, Bhikshu Bala of Mathura established at Sarnath a colossel Bodhisattva image of red-sandstone together with a large parasole crowning it. It also seems that the monks of the Sarvastivadin order were prominent at that time at Sarnath and established there a few monastries.

Under the rule of the Guptas (4th century A.D. to 6th century A.D.) Sarnath witnessed and unprecedented artistic activity and a separate school appears to have them originated here. The gradual development to those indigenous iconographic and plastic peculiarities, marked a new epoch in representation and portraiture and most of the beautiful images of Sarnath were made at that time. What the Bharasiva Nagas had achieved by launching a national war against the Kushans in the field of politics much the some was accomplished by the Guptas in the domain of art when the foreign schemetic fonality was reset to form the perfect Indian pattern.

The Main shrine was erected and the Dhamekh stupa was encased with delicate and superb carvedstones. Fa-Hien, who visited Sarnath at the time of Chandragupta II found four big stupas and two monasteries here.

Though Sarnath seems to have met a setback during the Huna invasions, it soon recovered from the effects of the fury of the Hunas. The reign of Harshavardhana (A.D. 606-48) coincides with fresh religious activity and the earlier buildings at Sarnath are restored. During his reign, Yuan-Chwang, the renowned Chinese pilgrim, visited Sarnath and afforded in his itinerary a vivid account of its monuments and of the religious activity of the monks. He saw both the Dharmarajika stupa and the stone-pillar of Ashoka. He found some fifteen hundred monks residing at Sarnath who were the followers of the Sammitiya School of early Buddhism.

He also saw a lofty structure of about two hundred feet high (probably the Main shrine) and a big metal image of / Buddha in the attitude of turing the wheel enshrined into the main sanctum of this temple.

Itsing who visited India shortly after Yuan-Chwang, mentions a corridor at the Deer-park "where the Lord Buddha used to walk."

Sarnath continued to prosper during the reign of the Pala kings who proved energetic patrons of the faith and under whose rule a vast crop of exquisite bronzes and sharp featured stone sculptures were forged and formed. At the time of Mahipāla I (A.D. 992-1040), Banaras lay in his dominion. According to an inscription discoverd at Sarnath, that monarch ordered the two brothers Sthirapāla and Vasantapala to restore the main buildings at Sarnath. He also added a new shrine to existing ones.

In the eleventh century A. D. the Kalachuris seems to have held sway at Sarnath and when this establishment came to be known as Saddharma Chakra-pravartanamaha-vihara.

How long this state lasted is not known, but the inscriptions discovered at Sarnath extending to the twelfth century A.D., show that the connection of Sarnath with Buddhism was still maintained.

During the reign of king Govindchandra (1114-1154) of the Gahadavala dynasty of Kanauj, his Buddhist queen Kumara Devi built a great monastery at Sarnath and must have provided gifts to the Buddhist monks for their maintenance.

During the rise of the Islamic power in India the glories of such ancient religious places gradually faded. The condition of the excavated ruins leaves no doubt that a violent catastrophe and wilful destruction and plunder overtook the place. Time coupled with further depredations, completed the work of ruin. In course of the succeeding centuries the very name and object of the place were forgotten, when a chance discovery at the close of the 18th century drew public attention to the ruins and led to their subsequent exploration.

Exploration

As stated before, Jagat Singh of Banaras demolished the Dharmarajika stupa of Ashoka and utilized its material to build a mart at Banaras which is still named after him as Jagatganj. Its demolition led to the first recorded discovery of antiquites at Sarnath and initiated the era of archaeological exploration of the site. While digging for bricks and stones, his workmen accidently struck upon the relic chamber of that stupa and rifted it of its contents. Most of the relics seem to have been disposed of by the finders, but a green marble casket with a few charred bones, pearls, rubies and gold leaves found its way into the hands of Mr. Jonathan Duncan. Mr. Duncan has left us an account of the discovery of urns by Jagat Singh and communicated it to the Asiatic Society of Bengal, instituted only a few years before "for inquiring into the history and antiquities, the arts, sciences and literature of Asia." The bones and other articles were ignorantly consigned to the Ganges by Jagat Singh. This stupa did not vanish without revealing some of its lost history. This discovery of urns roused a wide-spread interest in the ruins of Sarnath. In 1815 Col. C. Mackenzie carried out some exploration but no account of his work has been preserved.

In 1835-36 Sir Alexander Cunningham, the great pioneer of Indian. Archaeology continued further explorations of a more scientific nature. He aimed at an examination of the three large stupas. At his own expense he excavated the Chaukhandi stupa and discoverd a few images of Buddha and Bodhisattva and some carved bas-reliefs, most of which were in the Gupta style and he assigned the original monument to the Gupta period. He also opened Dhamekh stupa and found a stone slab inscribed with the Buddhist creed. He traced out the outer stone box of the Dharmarajika stupa, referred to above, explored a monastry and a temple. His excavations yielded a large collection of images and bas-reliefs, now displayed in the Indian Museum, Calcutta.

The next reported excavation, were carried in 1851-52 by Major Kittoe. He exposed numerous stupas and shrines round the Dhamekh stupa. His work also revealed a quadrangular building to the north of the Jain temple. While clearing another monastery situated to the west of the Jain temple, he fell ill and died before he could write an account of his excavations.

Besides these known excavation, there must have been many more unauthorised and unrecorded excavation carried by curio-hunters, to whom the locality offered great temptations when there was no check on these depredations.

After an interval of half a century since Major Kittoe's excavation, came Mr. F.O. Oerted. He directed his attention towards the unemplored mound situated immediately to the north of the Dharmarajika stupa. There he unearthed the remains of a large temple, probably the main shrine of the whole establishment. He is also credited with the discovery of the Ashokan pillar and its wonderful Lion-capital at the back of the main shrine, as well as the most famous image of the preaching Buddha. Evidently he had struck the nucleus of the ancient Deer-park. His excavations revealed no less than 476 peices of sculptures and 41 inscriptions.

In 1907 the work was resumed by Sir John Marshall, Director General of Archaeology, assisted by Dr. Sten, Mr. W.H. Nicholls, Mr. D.R. Sahni and Mr. Chakravarti. His excavations covered a much larger area than any of the previous explorations and for the first time conveyed a clear idea of the general topography of the site and of relative positions of the large groups of buildings. He unearthed the northern half of the site situated on the other side of the heavy compound wall. Three monastries of the late Kushan period were discovered beneath Kumara Devi's monastery of the mediaeval period. In 1914-15 Mr. Hargreaves excavated the area to the east and the west of the main shrine. His excavation exposed an apsidal temple of the late Mauryan period and above it traces of a monastery of a later date as well as other structural remains. The numerous sculptures exposed by him range in date from the Mauryan to the Mediaeval period.

The last major excavation at Sarnath was conducted by Mr. D. R. Shani for five field-seasons. He completely opened up the area between the Dhamekh stupa and the main shrine, discovered a long covered passage to the west of the Kumāra Devī monastery and brought to views the main drainage system of the establishment.

The Monuments

The accidental discovery of Sarnath in the closing decade of the 18th century and its succeeding explorations up to the beginning of the 20th century led to the revealing archaeological remains in abundance. A brief account of the monuments is drawn here—

Chaukhandi Stupa—First of all on the left side of the road to Sarnath we notice a lofty brick structure now known as Chaukhandi stupa, crowned with an octagonal tower. This sturcture seems to be a memorial stupa and is said to have been erected on the spot where Gautama Buddha on his way to Deer-Park first met the five of the 'Blessed Band'. In 1905 Mr. Oertel exhumed three terraces about 12' high, and a portion of an octagonal plinth of the stupa with star-like points. The original fabric of the structure had disappeared but we find the remains of niches on the outer walls of the terraces, separted by brick pilasters.

The surmounting octagonal tower was constructed by Emperor Akbar to commemorate a visit by his father Humayun to that place.

Monastery V—Now on entering the site one can notice the remains of two monasteries on the right and left. On the right hand side is monastery V excavated by Major Kittoe in 1851-52. It contains an open courtyard in the centre surrounded by rows of small cells on four sides. The central room on the north was the entrance chamber and three chambers projecteted towards the north consisting of portico in the centre and two guardrooms on its either side. Fom the cells of the southern row were discovered a terracrotta sealing with Buddhist creed in the characters of 9th century A.D. and an alms bowl of fine clay containing cooked rice and other earthen vessels.

Monastery VII—On the left hand side is a smaller monastery of the mediaeval period built on the ruins of an older structure. There is the same open courtyard, 30' square, sorrounded by verandah pavements with rows of cells on the four sides and a well in the north-east corner of the courtyard. The cells have all disappeared. Of the clay-seals and sealing found there was a dia. 1½" in diameter, stamped with "Sri Sishyada" in the character of mediaeval period. The condition of the bases of the verandah columns found in situ indicates that fire was also the cause of its destruction.

Dharmarajika stupa

Moving a few yards towards north, we will see this

illfated stupa which was seriously damaged by the workmen employed by Jagat Singh. In spite of its demolition by Jagat Singh, the further operations conducted by Sir John Marshall in 1907-08 around its base revealed the history of successive additions and alterations carried out at different periods over the core of the original stupa at dfferent levels. The diameter of the innermost ring at the bottom measures 44'-3" and that of another ring 55'-3". The excavation revealed traces of six successive encasements of the original stupa at different times. Shell after shell was added to the stupa, the ground level rose and the floors of successive periods are considerably above the original floor level. The first addition appears to have been made in the Kushan period with bricks measuring 15" × 10½" × 2¼", but half bricks and bats are also noticed. The second enlargement belongs to the 5th or 6th century A.D when a circumambulatory path encircled the stupa and was encompassed by a solid outer wall of 4' 5" high, pierced by four entrances at each of the cardinal points. In the 7th century A.D. the circumambulatory path was, however, filled up and access to the stupa was provided by placing from outside four monolithic staircases. The next two additions date back to the 9th-11th century A.D. and the last encasing of the stupa took place when the Dharma Chakra—Jinavihara of Kumara Devi was built in the 12th century A.D. to the north side of the site.

Main Shrine—Some 20 yards north of the Dharmarajika stupa stands a ruined temple upto a height of 18', surrounded by a concerete pavement extending some 40' in every direction. The building 60' along each side, is square in plan and faces to the east. Form the well-preserved mouldings on all sides of the outer facings, the thick walls intended to support a massive and lofty superstructure and the description recorded in Hiuen-Tsang's account, it seems not improbable that this magnificent building was the 'Chief Fane' (Mulagandhakuti) about 200' high and surmounted by what he calls a golden amra fruit. The brick mouldings on the plinth consists of a torus and scotia with fillet between and those of the existing walls are decorated with circular niches adorned with pilasters with vase-shaped bases and bracket capitals and are of the Gupta period. The corner chapels projecting from the south, west and north sides and the portico on the east make the plan of the shrine a regular Greek cross. The original structure has undergone many changes, and in order to protect the roof from collapse brick walls within the principal chamber were added at a later date thus reducing its size to 23' 6' on each side.

Monolithic Railing

While following the foundations of the southern chapel of the main shrine, Mr. Oertel discovered the plain stone railing of Ashoka, each side 8'.4" in length and 4'.9" in height, fenced round a small brick stupa. The railing, though devoid of any ornament, displays, the high workmanship attained in the Mauryan period on account of its brilliant polish and the exquisite precision. It was carved out from a single block of Chunar sandstone. The railing originally must have formed the crowning harmika of the Dharmarajika stupa as is the case with other stupas built by Ashoka. Two inscriptions are engraved on the railing. The one on the east plinth mentions the 'Homage of the teachers of the Sarvastivadins.' [acha(rya)nam Sarvastivadinam......... parigahetavam], Dr. Sten, observes that the inscription consists of two distinct parts in different characters. The beginning belongs to the 3rd or 4th century A.D. The final portion, parigahetavam, is older by about four centuries. Therefore, it appears that the first part of the earlier inscription has been erases and a different beginning subsitiuted. The second epigraph on the central bar of the southern side records :

(a) acharyyanam Sarvvastiva.

(b) dinam parigrahe.

'Homage of the teachers of the Sarvastivadin seet.'

From the above records we may reasonably infer that the sarvastivadins scratched out the name of some other sects and substituted their own name, perhaps to assert their predominance at Sarnath.

The concrete pavement around the main shrine dates from the same age as the later brick walls inside the principal chamber. Beneath this pavement was found a succession of layers superimposed one above the other at different periods. The lowermost layer in front of the main entrance was found composed of stone taken from earlier structures. Among them are : A votive slab (ayagapata) of the Ist century B.C., bearing an ornamental wheel sorrounded by four triratna symbols and lotus buds and a fragmentary railing pillar with two dedicatery inscriptions incised on it one of about the second century B.C and the other of about the fifth century A.D., when the railing pillar was converted and rededicated as a lamppost for the main shrine, now kept in the Museum of Sarnath. Another slab representing an ornamental thunderbolt and svastika of the Ist century B.C. was also unearthed and kept in the same museum.

Ashok Columun

To the west of the main shrine were found the stump and fragments of a large round monolithic column. The inscribed stump 6'.8" high stands in situ, protruding slightly above the concrete pavement of the main shrine. Originally this column was about 50' high and was surmounted by the famous Lion-Capital which was exhumed in 1904 close to the western wall of the main shrine.

The pillar bears three set of inscriptions. The earliest is an edict of Asoka in clear-cut Brahmi character in which the emperor issued warning to the monks and nuns creating schism in the order. The second epigraph is of the Kushan period and reads as follwes—'In the fortieth year of Rajan Asvaghosa, in the first fortnight of winter on the tenth day.... It is not known who this ruler was. It is noteworthy, however, that his name with the title of Rajan also occurs on an inscribed fragmentary slab of the same period descovered some 70 ft. to the east-north-east of the main shrine. It should be noted that the spititual teacher of Kaniska was also called Asvaghosa. there are some letters at the beginning and the end of the inscription which have been intentionally rubbed off.

The third inscription is in character of the early Gupta period and reads as 'Homage of the masters of the sammitiya sect (and) of the vastiputrika school.'

Apsidal chapel

Just a few yards to west of the Ashoka column came to light an apsidal remains of the late Mauryana period and above it remains of the late Mauryana period and above it traces of a monastery of a later period and other structural remains. The apsidal type of building is very important in the early Buddhist architecture and does not survive in later Indian works. It is 82'-6" in length and 38'-10" in width with a semi-circular apse and its back towards the west. Further examination of the area revealed antiquities ranging in date from the Mauryan epoch down to the later Gupta period. The very nature of the finds indicates that the monuments of this side were wilfully destroyed.

Area North of the Main Shrine

The remains to the north-east and north-west of the Main Shrine are of different periods. About some 20 yards north-west of the steps terminating the passage, Sir John Marhsall exposed late Gupta shrine with an opening on east and west and brought to notice two-carved pilasters originally forming the jambs of a door-frame on the east and stone umbrellas from outside. The finds there included a magnificent stone lintel of Gupta period, about 16' long, decorated with figures of Jambhala, Bodrisattva, ladies with musical instruments and dancing girls. It is divided into side panels of which four panels illustrate the Kshantivadin Jataka, 'The preacher of forbearance.' On the east side of the main shrine and in front of which is a large rectangular court and further east a long passage had been added in later period on either side of which we notice rows of votive stupas and many ruined shrines of various sizes.

Dhamekh

Beyond this limit and further south-east satnds a great stupa Known as Dhamekh. The name Dhamekh seems to have been derived from a Sanskrit word Dharma chakar meaning wheel of the law. According to other it is a derivation from dharmeksha and means. 'The pondering of the law.'This stupa is a soild tower cylindrical in shape, rising to a height of 103' above the paved terrace of the Jain temple, or 143' if we include the foundation which lies burried underground. The diameter at the base is 93ft. and the structure above the foundation is of stone-work to a height of 36' and 9'. The stones in each layer were bounded by means of iron clamps. The lower portion with existing stone-work is relieved on the outside by eight projecting faces with a large niche, one on every projecting faces. Some of the niches still contain pedestals formerly meant for statues. The speical interest of this stupa lies in its scheme for the decorative treatment of the outer stone facing which includes not only ornamental elements but some singificant implications. Each projecting faces of this stupa were originally adorned with deep cut incisions of foral arabesque combined with a broad band of intricate geometrical patterns. In the south-west face one can notice a clinging human figure holding lotus in both the hands and birds playing on the foliage denote the lyrical movement of the relief, delicate curves of lines shooting out the meandering leaves and buds at the junction of the stem and finally encircling flower or group of turned-back leaves illustrate the rhythmic trend of the indigenous mind. A triple band of ornament below the niches encircle the body of the stupa. The decorative motives are remarkable for its intrinsic elegance and are superbly graceful. Each of the eight areas between the projecting niches contains a running 'fret' design, all different as each is based on a separate combination of lines, figures and angles. Here one can also dicern of that rythmic fluency as devised on a geometrical system of straight lines, parallel to each other, which is a rare and unique example of this form of treatment in the field of Inidan decorative art. From the character of the stone carving, it obvisouly dates from the Gupta period. Really with the intellectual faculties the aesthetic sensibilities of the age also found their appropriate expression in the embellishment of this remarkable stupa.

Sir Alexander Cunningham in 1834 while examining the stupa in search of a relic chameber drove a vertical shaft through its centre down to the foundations and discovered at 3 ft. below from the top an inscribed slab with the Buddhist creed in character of 6-7th century A.D. At a depth of 110 ft. from the top it was noticed by him that the stone-work gave place to brick work belonging to an earlier structure and most probably erected on the spot by Emperor Asoka.

Northern half of the Monastery area—This area is marked by a large compound wall about 760' long running from east to west. On the other side of this wall covers the northern area of the site, were laid bare several monasteries and all of them followed more or less one general plan. The entrance chamber led into a pillared verandah courtyard surrounded by cells on the four sides for habitation of monks, one cell being set spart for the statuary. The open court perhaps served as the open assembly for the monks. Access to the cells was provided by a covered walk supported on pillars around the court.

This extensive area was occupied in earlier days by several monasteries and subsequently buried under later bulidings. The most imposing structure was, however, one built by Kumara Devi, the Buddhist queen of king Govinda Chandra of Kanauj in between A.D. 1114 to 1154 A.D. This building represented an epoch of construction at Sarnath when ideas of splendour and comfort had replaced that of an austere and simple monastic life. The basement of the monastery is built of finely chiselled bricks, decorated with a variety of elegant mouldings on both its exterior and interior faces, and standing to a height of about 8 ft. The superstructure seems to have been built of carved stone and plenty of these structural remains in the forms of door jambs, lintels, pillars, caves etc., employed in this building were found lying in great heaps over the basement and in the courtyard.

The two extensive courtyards which precede the main building on the east side were furnished with handsome entrance, styled First Gateway and Second Gateway in the plan of excavations. The northern bastion of the first entrance has survived in good condition, of the second entrance only the heavy foundations of considerable depth was discovered which must have supported a lofty super-structure.

Monastery II : Beneath the western area of the Kumara Devi monastery is the Monastery II. This monastery dates back to the early Gupta period and the size of bricks applied in its constructions also confirms this date. The ground plan of the monastery confirms the same general pattern of a Buddhist monastery viz. a central courtyard, surrounded by low walls, 3'-3" thick which must have carried the verandah pillars in front of which nine cells on the west have survived. Another monastery III lies in front of the eastern entrance of the Dharmachakarjina-vihar of Kumara Devi; and a third monastery IV standing beneath the second courtyard. Some portions of this monastery is still buried under the southern boundry wall. Its verandah pillars were found intercolumned into a wall. A collosal image of Lord Siva in the attitude of killing a demon was discovered lying above the top of the existing walls of the eastern cells.

At the western most extremity of the site, a special feature of interest in a subterranean passage, about 180 ft. long with side walls 6 ft. high leading into a small mediaeval shrine. It commences 34 ft. to the west of the Kumara Devi Vihara and is provided with a flight of steps leading to the underground passage about 10 ft. below the present ground level. The steps end at a low entrance, the ceiling infornt being so low that the votary must have had to crawl here evidently as a mark of reverence to its shrine referred to above. The greater part of the passage must, however, have remained in darkness even during the day. The inner side walls of this passage have been provided here and there with little niches of corbelled tops evidently to hold earthern lamps. The main purpose of this structure would appear to have been to provide the monks with a solitary place for meditation. Its association for the observance of some secret tantric rites may also be surmised as later Buddhism confirms to such rites.

The Museum

The excavation carried on at Sarnath from time to time

described above have bequeathed us plenty of sculptures, inscription, and numerous other antiquities. These finds naturally afford sufficient scope for our purpose of study. In view of this need Sir John Marshall proposed to found a local museum amid its natural surroundings. The construction of the building took place on the opposite of the Deer-Park and was completed in 1910 A.D. The plan of the building followed the general quadrangular pattern of an ancient Buddhist monastery. The present building forms one-half of the plan of a complete monastery. The finds are arranged in the main hall, in long galleries and in the side verandahs.

Main Hall : On entering the main entrance, the first object which attracts our attention is the famous 'Lion-Capital', which once crowned the Ashok column at Sarnath. 'The Capital,' Dr. Marshall writes, 'which measures 7 ft. high, is of the persepolitan bell-shaped type, surmounted by four magnificent lions sitting back to back with a wheel between them symbolizing the law of the Buddha which was first promulgated at Sarnath. Beneath the lions is a drum ornamented with four animals in relief viz. a lion, an elephant, a bull and a horse separated each other by four wheels. The four crowning lions and the relief below are wonderfully vigorous and true to nature and are treated with that simplicity and reserve which is the keynote of all great masterpieces of plastic art. India certainly has produced no other sculpture to equal them."

The proper significance of the Sarnath Capital is still a subject of controversy. The so-called 'bell' of Dr. Marshall is not really a bell but an inverted lotus, a symbol of creative activity. The lotus-flower has been used as a religious symbol among the Hindus since the Vedic age. 'The pink petals'of the flower are the robes of the the 'Dawn Maiden', and the pericarp is the rising sun.

According to Dr. Bloch the four animals in this case symbolise the gods Indra, Siva Surya and goddess Durga, whose vehicles these animals are, indicating their subordination to the Buddha and his law. Dr..Vogal however, remarks that these animals—the four 'noble beasts'—of the Buddhists are merely decorative. It seems more probably that these symbolical animals represent the four life events of Lord Buddha. The elephant stands for the conception of the Exalted One, as his mother saw in a dream, a white elephant entering her womb. The bull represents the Zodiac sign of Taurus in which nativity of the Buddha occured. The third symbol is a galloping horse, depicts the Buddha's great Renunciation. The fourth symbol, the lion stands for the great master himself, lion of the Sakya race, 'Sakyasimha.' It has been also explained that these four animanls facing the four directions guard the four quarters as laid down in Buddhist texts in connection with the Anotatta lake. The four wheels represents likewise the intermediate regions.

Next, the top of the Capital is surmounted by four adorsed lions with gaping mouths as if in the very act of roaring and may therefore be taken as representing to proclaim the Law of Lord Buddha to the four cardinal points. The wheel which originally adorned the capital as a crowning feature consisted of 32 spokes. It represents symbolically the Great Buddha himself, as Buddha is said to have possessed 32 signs on his person i.e. 32 marks of the great superman. The exquisite beauty of the Capital and its symbol and message of peace appealed to the peace abiding people of Indian and the national govt, chose this pattern to form its own insignia on official papers and building.

The next sculpture to the left is the colossal Bodhisattva of red-sandstone, dedicated by Friar Bala in the third regnal year of emperor Kanishka. This image is a robust figure represents Bodhisattva Gautama and indicates the period between the Great renunciation and the perfect enlightenment influence of the older tradition of the indigenous school in contrast with the feeble imitation of Gandhara art. As a whole this image is an example of indigenous development.

The octagonal shaft now stands behind the statue, once carried beautifully carved stone umbrella which is exhibited near the north-east corner of the hall. To the right of Lion-capital, there is an another Bodhisattva statue of Chunar sandstone and bears a striking resembelance to the former Bodhisattva of Mathura. Here we find an attempt of the local sculptor to imitate a faithful copy of Mathura Bodhisattva.

To the north-west has been arranged a railing of twelve pillars. These originally belong to one structure and are assigned to the Ist century B.C. Of the devices sculptured upon them the most interesting are : the triratna (trident) symbol indicating the Buddha, Dharma (law) and Sangha (order) combined with dharmachakra (wheel of the law) on the top of a persepolitan pillar ; the stupa with a double railing, parasol, streamers and garlands and a hermit's hut with its covering of leaves. The bevelled copings depict a stupa worshipped by celestial beings (half human and half birds).

The show case against the west wall of this hall contains antiquities of great interest. In the top shelf are the fragments of polished capitals inscribed with Mauryan Brhami character mentioning the names of donors of Pataliputra and Ujjayini. In the second shelf there are some male heads cut in the round with Mauryan polish, some of which show a little influence of Hellenistic feature, but their head-dress are carved in Bharhut style. A begging bowl of black clay is also exhibited in this case.

In the southern half of this hall are some important Buddha images in standing and seated postures. These figures marked the gradual development of those iconographic and plastic quality which herald the dawn of that new epoch known to us as Gupta period. Here we find some innovations, such as a halo at the back of lotus and scroll pattern, beautifully curly hair in place of shaven head as was the case with early Mathura Buddha statue, serene contemplative expression on the face. Transparent drapery of the egg-shell formation clearly reveals the form, is also one of the continuation of the Sarnath school in Gupta period.

Of all the Buddha images of Sarnath, the most important and exquisite example is the seated image in the attitude of first preaching at Sarnath. It is remarkable both for its aesthetic interest as well as for certain plastic and iconographic expression found in it. In this we find Buddha seated cross-legged on a lotus seat with the body covered by transparent drapery and hem of which spreads in fanship design below the legs. His hands are held on the chest in the attitude of preaching. The half-closed eyes looking towards the tip of the nose suggest concentration which annihilates all consciousness of the moribund world. The serene smile on the face likewise suggests the acquisition of boundless happiness beyond instrumentality of senses. We notice, the poise, the gentle touch and simple beauty of modelling, the psychological pose of the hands in the preaching attitude and the beautifully carved halo around the head with two flying figures on either flank. On the pedestal has been relegated a group of discriples and in the centre is the sacred monogram, "Wheel" flanked by two deer, symbolizing the First Sermon preached by Lord Buddha at Deer-Park.

Gupta Gallery : Here are exhibited numerous anitiquities, bas-reliefs and sculptures of the Gupta period. Among them, mentioned may be made of two steles, one showing scenes of Buddha's four life-events viz (i) birth (ii) Enlightenment (iii) First Preaching and (iv) demise (Nirvāṇa). Another depicts besides four life events, four miracles namely, presentation of honey by a monkey to Buddha, Buddha taming the mad elephant Nalagiri, Buddha's descent from heaven and the great miracle of Śrāvastī when Buddha, multiplied his form a thousand fold. As Dr. V.S. Agrawala observes that "by the time of the Guptas, the Mahayana Buddhism had established a separate pantheon with several Dhyani Buddhas and Bodhisattvas meant those highly evolved beings who would attain Nirvāṇa (salvation) in one birth, but according to Mahayana school they came to signify some special beings of higher order who helped mankind to attain salvation and they did so in conjuction with their female consorts. The important Bodhisattvas exhibited here are Avalokiteśvara (embodiment of supreme wisdom), Mañjuśrī (symbolizes compassion) and Vajrasattva etc. The wall-case and the table-cases contain terracotta plaques, clay seals and sealings, carved bricks and stucoo and stone heads of th Gupta period.

Medieval Gallery : As is appearnat from the exhibits of this room, the medieval school shows a profuse elaboration and over ornamentation, and lack that innate simplicity and restraint which is the very breath of Gupta art. In this room are exhibited miscelleneous images and statues of minor deities, terracotta toys, clay sealings with the Buddhist creed and some important epigraphic records. Among the female divinities standing Tara. Marichi and Khadirvani Tara are the noteworthy. Standing Tara is remarkable for its suppleness and faminine charm. She wears a transparent silken sari and highly decked with jewelleries. Her lower half body forms three bents so as to present a dancing gesture.

Marichi is also one of principle Buddhist goddesses.

She is represented as having three faces, as if to display three kings of sentiments viz. amour heroic and joy. The seven pigs of her chariot probably indicates the seven planets. Like Surya, the sun-god, she is the Buddhist goddess of dawn.

The seals exhibited there appear to have been used as votive tablets presented by pligrims to Sarnath. Some of them on the other hand, must have been employed for sealing documents. Towards the western wall of this room stands an unfinished colossal figure of Lord Śiva in relief in the attitude of piercing demon with his trident.

II

SARNATH IN RECENT YEARS

Sarnath today is not only on epitome of the Sarnath yesterday; but after a lapse of several centuries it has been again humming with intrinsic activity as one of the prime centres of the Buddhist organization in India.

Truely speaking the great personality of Buddha is not only confined into the pages of history but it also stands as a source of inspiration and still light the path of humanity to get rid of those inherent ills associated in human nature, which hankers after material inclinations and is the root cause of self-interest, lacking depth and insight and utter lack of values.

The profound imprints still eco in the serene enviornment of Sarnath and it undoubtedly attracts tourists, savants and pilgrims from every nook and corner of the world.

Mulagandha Kuti Vihara

Efforts were made in the early 19th century to pick up the past glory of Sarnath when in Nov. 1922 the foundation stone of the **Present Mulagandha Kuti Vihara** was laid Anagarika Dharmapala, the founder of the temple dedicated himself heart and soul for the construction of this sacred edifice and in 1931 it was completed.

On Nov. 11, 1931 the inaugural function of the temple was attended by hundreds of Buddhist monk from Tibet, China, Japan, Burma, Sri Lanka and India. European and American Buddhists also participated in quite a considerable number. A huge procession, which according to Colombo Buddhist report, the history of India had never witnessed for centuries on the past, was successfully arranged the whole atmosphere saturated wih melodious sound of hymneal music, Pali, Tibetan and Chinese.

The temple contains Buddhist relics discovered from the excavations of Taxila, Mirpur has and Nagarjunkonda. Now consecrated under the pedestal of the Bodhi image, these relics were presented to the Mahā Bodhi Society by late Daya Ram Sahni first Indian Director General of Archaeology Department on behalf of the then viceroy of India, Lord Irwin.

The temple was so named because the excavators had found the words 'Mulagandha Kuti', found inscribed on a stone slab discovered in a digging near the main shrine.

The chief feature of this temple is a series of interior frescoes executed by a Japanese artist named Kosetsu Nosu. Kosetsu Nosu who worked almost singlehanded took about four years (1932-36) in order to draw the frescoes piece by piece. The theme of the frescoes comprise episodes and scenes from the life of Buddha from his birth to Mahaparinirvāṇa.

The huge bell in the corridor leading to the temple was presented by the Maha Bodhi Society of Japan.

The Jain Temple

In the immediate vicinity of Dhameka stupa there stands

a Jain temple. It is believed to mark the birth place of the eleventh Tirthankar Shreyansnath. The interior of the temple is embellished with attractive frescoes deplicting the life of Lord Mahavira.

The Deer Park

The present Deer-Park has been set up as a moments of the ancient Mrigadava. A number of deers are still preserved in this Deer-park by the State Government of Uttar Pradesh. The Park came into being on the occasion of the 2500th Mahaparinirvāṇa Day of Lord Buddha.

The Chinese Termple

Built in a typical Chinese style it was founded in 1939 by Ven. Te-Yu, a disciple of his holiness. Tao-Kai, Abbot of Peking, Fa-Yuan-Tsu, the president of the Eastern Asia Buddhist Association.

The Tibetan Temple

The Tibetan temple was constructed by Rev. Thupten Jungnes of Tibet. It was founded in 1955. Hundreds of Tibetans irrespective of their sects come every year in order to worship in this temple.

Inside the temple there are abut 150 rare Buddhist scriptures. These scriptures were translated into the Tibetan language during 7th to 9th century A.D. Another important item to the temple is a number of frescoes on colth wall hangings, a few centuries old which still retain their colour fresh.

The Burmese Monastery

Built in 1934, it is situated on the low land west of the excavated area in Sarnath. In front of the temple there is a library building known as Saddhammaranasi Library.

A few yards west of these two buildings there is another building known as Burmese Rest House which was erected in 1910 with a view to provide accommodation to foreign Buddhist pilgrims. This buildings has historical importance as it was constructed by Mahavir Singh and who was the nephew of Raja Kunwar Singh of Ara, the famous warrior of the first Indian Revolt of 1857 against the British. After the revolt was crushed the family had to leave the country and some of the members stayed in Burma in exile. Mahavir Singh also was one of them and later in his life after becoming a Buddhist monk he returned to the country towards the close of the nineteenth century.

The Sarnagnath Temple

It is the solitary Hindu temple dedicated to Lord Siva.

The images of several other 'Hindu deities have also been installed in this temple. The temple was built on a huge mound near the Railway Station of Sarnath. There is a big tank at the foot of this temple. The temple is said to have been built on the site of an ancient shrine.

REFERENCES

1. Agrawal, V. S., Sarnath, Kanpur, 1956.
2. Beal, Buddhist Records of the Western world Vol. II.
3. Bhandarkar, D.R., Ashoka, Calcutta, 1969.
4. Bhattacharya, B.C., History of Sarnath, Banaras, 1924.
5. Brown, Percy, Indian Architecture, Buddhist and Hindu Periods, Bombay, 1965.
6. Chaturvedi Sitaram, Sarnath (Hindi), Varanasi, 1968.
7. Comaraswami, A., Buddha and the Gospel of Buddhism, A.P.H., 1956.
8. Foucher, A., Begining of Buddhist Art, 1918.
9. Giles, H.A., Travels of Fa-Hien, Varanasi, 1972.
10. Humpherys Christmas, Buddhism, Penguin Books, 1951.
11. Majumdar, B., A Guide to Sarnath, Delhi, 1937.

12. Radhakrishnan, S., Indian Philoisophy, London, 1957.
13. Rhys Davids, On Buddhism, Varanasi, 1971.
14. Sahni, D.R., Caralogue of the Museum of Archaeology at Sarnath Calcutta, 1914.
15. Sivaramamurti, C. : Indian Sculpture, I.C.C.R., New Delhi, 1967.

CHAPTER-XII

THE SECOND CONTACT WITH THE WEST : THE RISE OF MAHĀYĀNA BUDDHISM

—V.K. Mathur

The break-up of the Empire of Magadha had the usual repercussions on the North-Western frontier. the control of the central power being relaxed, insurgent tribes begun once more to pour through the passes into the Punjab, and the Land of the Five Rivers again becomes the chief centre of activity. In 250 B.C., while Asoka was still reigning in Pāṭliputra, two important events occurred in the West. Almost simultaneously, Diodotus, the governor of the Greek colony at Bactra or Balh, and a chieftain named Arsaces in Parthia, south-east of the Caspian Sea, threw off the yoke of the Seleucids and set up independent kingdoms. Subsequently the Greek rulers of Bactria crossed the Indian frontier and occupied Gandhāra. At first they issued coins of a purely Greek character, some of which may be ranked among the finest specimens of the coiner's art in the ancient world. The noble portraits of Demetrius (190 B.C.) wearing his elephant-head headdress, and Eucratides (175 B.C.) in a kausia or sun-helmet of a singularly modern pattern, are especially notable. As time went on, however, they became more and more Indianised. They issued coins square in shape, and bearing on the reverse legends in Brāhmī or Kharoshthī characters. It was these bilingual coinlegends which gave Prinsep the clue to deciphering the Asoka inscriptions. The only surviving monument of the Indo-Greek dynasties is a pillar, once surmounted by a Garuḍa, a mythological bird, the vāhan or vehicle of the god Viṣṇu, which was discovered at Besnagar in he extreme south of the Gwalior State in 1909. It bears the following inscription in Brāhmī characeters:

This Garuḍa-column of Vāsudeva (Viṣṇu), the god of gods, was erected here by Heliodorus, a worshipper of Viṣṇu, the son of Dion, and an inhabitant of Taxila, who came as a Greek ambassador from the great King Antialcidas to King Kasiputra Bhagabhadra, the Saviour, then reigning prosperously in the fourteenth year of his kingship.

This inscription is full of interest; it shows that by this time the Greeks born in India had become so completely Indian that they were actually received into the fold of the Hindu religion. The greatest of the Indo-Greek kings of the Punjab was Menander and we are fortunate to know more about him than any of his contemporaries, owing to the fact that he was converted to Budddhism by the Buddhist doctor Nāgasena, and his conversion is made the subject of a famous dialogue, the questions of Milinda. From it we learn that Menander was born at the village of Kalasi, not far from Alasanda of the Yonas (Alexandria under Caucasus). His capital was at Sāgala, the modern Siālkot, which is described in glowing terms:

There is in the country of the Yonakas a great centre of trade, a city that is called Sāgala, situated in a delightful country well watered and hilly, abounding in parks, gardens grooves and lakes and tanks, a paradise of rivers and mountains and woods. Wise architects have laid it out, and its people know of no oppression, since all their enemies and adversaries have been put down. Brave is its defiance, with many and various strong towers and ramparts, with superb gates and entrance archways, and with the royal citadel in its midst, white-walled and deeply moated. Well laid out are its streets, squares, cross-roads and market-places. Well displayed are the innumerable sorts of costly merchandise with which its shops are filled. It is richly adorned with hundreds of almshalls of various kinds and splendid with hundreds of thousands of magnificent mansions, which rise aloft like the mountain-peaks of the Himalayas. Its streets are filled wit elephants, horses, carriages, and foot-passengers, and crowded by men of all sorts and conditions—Brahmins, nobles, artificers, and servants. They resound with cries of welcome to the teachers of every creed, and the city is the resort of the leading men of each of the different sects. Shops are there for the sale of Benares muslin, of Kotumbara stuffs, and of other cloths of various kinds; and sweet odours are exhaled from the bazaars, where all sorts of flowers and perfumes are tastefully set out. Jewels are therein plenty, and guilds of traders in all sorts of finery display their goods in the bazaars which face all quarters of the sky.[1]

Menander himself was a scholar as well as a soldier. As a disputant he was hard to equal, harder still to overcome; the acknowledged superior of all the founders of the various schools of thought. As in wisdom, so in strength of body, swiftness, and valour, there was found none equal to Milinda in all India. He was rich too, mighty in wealth and prosperity, and he number of his armed hosts knew no end. He was not to relieve the cares of state by holding philosohical arguments with learned Brahmins and others, of whom he invariably got the better. In the end, however, the sage Nāgasena visited the city with his disciples, lighting up the city with their yellow robes like lamps, and bringing down upon it the breezes from the heights where the sages dwell. Menander, accompanied by five hundred courtiers, went to interview Nāgasena. In the arguments which follow, the Buddhist doctrine of the impermanence of the Ego is expounded, and Menander is converted. An interesting feature of the Questions of Milinda is the Socratic method of dialectic employed by Nāgasena, which gives it the air of a Platonic dialogue.

Menander was a great warior, and made an attempt to conquer the kingdom of Magadha, now very much shrunk from its former size and greatness. The Yavana horsemen overran the Middle Country, and all but succeeded in capturing the sacred horse, which the Sunga King Pushyamitra had released to wander over the country in preparation for the horse sacrifice,[2] but the Greeks were recalled by troubles which broke out in thier own country and retired. Menander's date is probably 180-160 B.C. He issued some fine coins, one of which bears the Buddhist Wheel of the Law. According to one legend, he was regarded as an arhat or saint, and after his cremation his ashes were distributed as relics, like those of the Buddha. The Greek rulers of the Punjab were in the end ovrwhelmed by invading Saka tribes from Central Asia. These Sakas or Scythians, who had long been a menace to the Persians, pushed southwards by other tribal movements from the north-east, overflowed the greek kingdom of Bactria, and occupied the valley of the Helmand, which is still known as Scistan (Sakastan). Entering the Punjab, probably by the Bolān pass, they gradually superseded the local Greek rulers. They set up principalities at Mathurā, Taxila and other centres. The use of the Persian titles Satrap and Great King of Kings, suggests that they were fedatories of the Parthian King Mithradates the Great (123-88 B.C.) whose rule extended almost as far as the Indus. The Parthians played an important part as intermediaries between Greek and Indian culture, as the excavations of the Parthian city of Sirkap in the Taxila area clearly show. One of the Indo-Parthian or Saka princes of Taxila, known to the Greeks as Gondopharnes, is of especial interest to us because, according to the apocryphal Acs of Thomas, the Apostel Thomas came to this court to preach Christianity. There was formerly a great deal fo doubt hether Saint Thomas ever visited India, but recent researches tend to prove that the legend is founded on historical fact. Bartholomew and Thomas were sent to preach the gospel in the East. Thomas probably reached Taxila by the well-known sea-route from Alexandria to the mouth of the Indus. He was hospitably received at the court of Gondopharnes, for Taxila was a cosmopolitan centre of culture and accustomed to give a ready hearing to teachers from strange countries. His missionary labours were, however, interrupted by the Kushān invasion, and Thomas was compelled to flee. He retraced his steps to the mouth of the Indus, and thence took boat to muziris, the roman colony on the Malabar coast, touching at Socotra on the way. Here he arrived in A.D. 52 and founded the Church in Malabar. Twenty years later he tranferred his labours to the East Coast, and was martyred by the Brahmins. His relics repose in the Cathedral dedicated to him at Mylapore near Madras.[1] Gondopharnes is a corruption of the Persian Vindapharna, Bringer of Victory. In the Armenian version of the story, this becomes Gathaspar, from which is derived Gaspar, the name given to the second of the magi who visited the cradle of the infant Jesus. A powerful Saka dynasty also sprang up about this time at Ujjain. Its rulers, Rudradāman, Rudrasena, etc., were known as Great Satraps, and assumed Hindu names. Their kingdom comprised Mālwā, Kathiāwār, Kacch, and Gujarāt, and they intermarried with the Andhra rulers of the Deccan. This dynasty maintained its position until A.D. 388 when it was overthrown by the Gupta Emperor Chandragupta II. Another Saka dynasty, known as the Kshaharātās, ruled for a short time at Nāsik in the Konkan, until it was absorbed by the Āndhras.

Meanwhile a nomadic horde, known as the Yuch-chi or Tokharians, was displaced by the Huns from the territory between Kanu and the Great Wall, in 174 B.C.[1] They moved westwards, entering the territoy between the Jaxartes and the Oxus, and driving the Sakas before them. In 126 B.C. fresh tribal movements from the north compelled them to travel southwards, and they occupied Bactria. Here they settled down and lost their nomadic character. In A.D. 48, a section of the Yuch-chi, the Kushāns, finding Bactria too cramped, broke off from the main body, and under a chieftain named Kadphises or Kadapha, entered Gandhāra, and overthrew the last Greek monarch, hermaeus. The Kushāns gradually reduced to subjection the various petty Greek, Parthian and Saka kingdoms, and built up an extensive empire, including the Punjab and Sind, Northern Gujarāt and part of Central India. Kadphises tried to extend his influence northwards over the Pāmirs, the ancestral home of his clan, but an expedition sent for this purpose was disastrously defeated by the Chinese. Subsequently, the Kushāns greatly expanded their territories to the east, and it is thought that the so called Saka era of A.D. 78 commemorates the conquest of Northern India by a monarch known to historians as Kadphises II.

The greatest of the Kushān rulers, and the only one of whom we have any personal knowledge, is Kanishka. His date, like that of all the Kushān rulers, has been the subject of a lively controversy, but he probably ruled from A.D. 120 to 162. His capital was at Purushapura or Peshāwar, and soon after his accesson he sent a great military expedition which annexed Kashmir and a part of Chinese Turkestan, including Kashgar, yarkhand and Khotan,. It is said that Kanishka compelled the Chinese authorities to surrender hostages, who dwelt for some years at the Emperor's capital, where they were granted special quarters and other privileges. The Kushāns, like the Moguls, looked upon Central Asia, and not India, as their homeland. Like all Central Asian folk, they detested the heat of the Indian plains, and retired to Kashmir or Afghanistan for the hot weather.

The coins, as well as some remarkable statures dug up at Mat near Mathurā, give us a clear picture of these monarchs. They were big, burly men with long beards and prominent features: They dressed in long, padded coats and wore riding-boots and spurs.

To what extent Kanishka's empire extended eastwards is uncertain. The Saka Satraps of Ujjain were apparently his feudatories, and it must have included most of the territory west of the ganges as far south as the Narbadā river. kanishka assumes the titles of Shāonānoshāo, or King of Kings, Kaioaq, and devaputra, the last being the Chinese t'ien tzu, Son of Heave; and his coins reveal that he ruled over a veritable colluvies gentium, Indo-Greek, Zoroastrian, Buddhist and Hindu, who were settled in Gandhāra, the meeting-place of the Central Asian trade-routes. The language of the Kushāns was apparently Tokhāri, which they wrote in modified Greek characters.

The Kushāns were on excellent terms with Rome. In the first century A.D. the boundaries of the two empires were less than 600 miles apart, and the Romans were anxious to cultivate their friendship, hoping to capture the silk trade with China from their rivals, the Parthians. When Trajan became Emperor in A.D. 99 a Kushān monarch (probably Kadphises II) sent an embassy to Rome to congratulate him. The ambassadors had a flattering reception, and were given the high compliment of senators] seats in the theatre. The Kushān rulers struck gold coins in imitation of those of the Roman Emperors, of the same weight and fineness as the Roman aureus.[1] They kept up a brisk trade with the Roman colonies in Asia Minor, which went on almost uninterruptedly for the next two centuries: the goods went partly by the overland route through Balkh, and partly by sea from the port of Barygaza (Broach, at mouth of Narbadā River). From Barygaza travellers would go to the head of the Persian Gulf, up the Euphrates to Thapsacus and then across the desert to Antioch. A caravan route, running through the famous city of palmyra (Tadmor in the Wilderness) connected Antioch with the port of Berenice on the Red Sea. An

Alexandrian ascaptain who visited the India coast about A.D. 80 wrote an interesting guide-book entitled Periplus Maris Erythraei, in which he speaks of the immense volume of trade in condiments, spices, unguents and silks which left the ports of Gujarāt and Sind, in exchange for Roman aurei, Greek wines and choice girls for the royal harems. Syrian and Alexandrian travellers and merchants must have been a commonsight on the coast and at towns like Broach, Ujjain and Peshāwar. videtis gentes populosque mutasse sedes, says Seneca. Quid sibi volunt in mediis barbarorum regionibus Graecae artes? Quid inter Indos Persasque Macedonicus sermo? Atheniensis in Asia turba est.[2] Among these perhaps may be reckoned the famous miracle-mnger, Apollonius of Tyana, who is supposed to have paid a visit to Taxila, of which his biographer gives a romantic description, in the first century A.D.

The most important event of Kanishka's reign was his conversion to Buddhism. Buddhism made a stronger appeal to the chieftains from beyond the border than Hinduism, with its innumerable and vexatious caste-restrictions and, according to a well-authenticated story, Kanishka was converted by Asvaghosha, a learned Brahmin from Ayodhya, who had himself become a Buddhist convert. Asvaghosha was one of the many scholars from distant parts of India who flocked to Kanishka's court, and made Peshawar a renowend centre of Buddhist culture. He was extremely versatile, a philosopher, writer, dramatist and musician,and did much to reconcile Buddhism and Hinduism by writing on Buddhist themes in polished Sanskrit. He was the author of one of the earliest Indian dramas of which we know, a Buddhist play in nine acts dealing with the conversion of the saints Sāriputra and Maudgalyayana, two of the Buddha's earliest disciples, at Rājagriha, fragments of which were recently discovered at Turfān in Central Asia. He was also the author of the Buddha Charita, a poetical history of the Buddha containing highly ornate passages of great beauty, which are among the first examples of the Kāvya or artificial epic, and were imitated by later writers like Kālidāsa.

Kanishka was duly instructed in the mystery of his new faith by his preceptor and was puzzled by the numerous Buddhist sects and their conflicting interpretations of the scriptures. In imitation, therefore, of his predecessor Asoka, on whom he appears to have modelled himself, he determined to call a Council to settle these difficulties. This, the fourth and last General Council of the Buddhist Church, met at Kundalavana Monastery in Kashmir, and was attended by 500 monks from all parts of India, but not, however, Ceylon, under the presidency of the learned Pārsva. Other celebrated scholars, including Asvaghosha, Visvamitra and Nāgārjuna, took part in its deliberations. The Council sat for six months. Elaborate commentaries on the scripture were drawn up, and a Buddhist encyclopedia, the Mahā Vibhāsa, was compiled. Eventually, as the Chinese traveller Hiuen Tsang informs us, Kanishka rājā ordered these discourses to be engraven on sheets of red copper. He enclosed them in a stone receptacle and, having sealed them, he reaised over it a stūpa with the scriptures in the middle. Here they probably still remain, awaiting the fortunate archaeologist who has the good luck to unearth them.

Kanishka's Council at Kashmir marks the beginning of a new epoch in the history of Buddhism. This was the rise of the Mahāyāna or Northern Church, which differs as much from the primitive Buddhism of the Hinayāna, or Little Vehicle of the South, as Medieval Catholicism does from the simple creed of the Christians of the first century. The change was partly due to attempts of learned Brhamin converts like Asvaghosha to reconcile Buddhism with Hinduism. But it was due still more to the fact that in North-Western India a number of new influences—Greek, Christian, Zoroastrian and Central Asian—had crept in. When Buddhism became the religion of the foreign invaders from the northern steppes, it entirely lost its original character. Buddha ceased altogether to be a dead teacher, and became a living Saviour God, incarnate, like Rāma or Kṛṣṇa, for the salvation of the human race. The theory of Avatars or incarnations, which was being applied to Vaishnava Hinduism and Jainism, was adopted by Buddism. The historical Gautama was regarded or Primeval Spirit, and fell more and more into the background. Parallel to the human Buddhas were the Dhyāni or Spiritual Buddhas, each with his won Paradise, and the Bodhisattvas—exalted beings who have reached Buddhahood, but who deliberately decline to enter into Nirvāna in order that they may devote themselves to saving mankind. These deities are now unknown except in sculptures in the land of their birth, but have survived in China and Japan, and their scriptures have mostly come down to us in translations made by Chinese scholars. The most important of the Dhyāni Buddhas is Amitābha or Āmida, The God of Boundless Light, who has a large following in China and Japan. He dwells in a glorious Western Paradise, which is the subject of many poetical descriptions, and there he will remain until the whole humanrace has found salvation through faith in him. Salvation by faith in the religion of the Aidists takes the place f the austere doctrine of salvation by works preached by Gautāma, which is admitted to be altogether impracticable for the ordinary man of the world. The believer who takes in faith the name of Āmida will be born again in the Western Paradise, and will there under more propitious conditions reach the enlightenment unattainable on earth. Among the bodhisattvas, the most important are Avalokitesvara, the God who looks down, Manjusri and Maitreya, the coming Buddha who is yet to be born. Of the Mahāyāna Scriptures, the most noteworthy is the SaddhaRāma Pundarika or Lotus of the Good Law, of about A.D. 200. In this Buddha declares that he is repeatedly born into the world of the living, and says:

I am the Father of the world, the Self-born, the Healer, the Protector of all creatures. Knowing them to be perverted, infatuated and ignorant, I teach final rest, myself not being at rest.

To what extent Buddhism and Christianity mutually reacted upon one another in the first two centuries after Christ affords interesting matter for speculation. Reference has already been made to the intimate intercourse between India and Western Asia, and at Alexandria, the great meeting-place of eastern and Western thought, Indian scholars were a common sight. The questions of Milina talks f a voyage to Alexandria as an ordinary occurrene, especially for Buddhists, who were not bound by the caste restrictions of Hinduism. Dio Chrysostom (A.D. 100) speaks fo Bactrian, Scythian and Indian residents in Alexandria. Clement of Alexandria (A.D. 200) knows a great deal about Buddhism. There are, he says, some Indians who follow the precepts of Buddha (Bovra) whom by an exaggerated reverence they have exalted into a god. They believe in transmigration and worship a kind of pyramid (stūpa) beneath which they believe the bones of some divinity lie buried. Plotinus the Neoplatonist, and Bardesanes and Basilides the Gnostic writers, all went to the East for instruction in philosophy. The resemblances between the Gnostic doctrines and Mahāyāna Buddhism are well-know, particularly those between the Pistis Sophia and the Saddharma Pundarika. Many curious parallels between the birth-stories of Jesus Christ as related in the Gospels, and of Buddha as told in works like the Lalita vistara and the Buddha Charita, have been observed, though it is impossible to say whether these themes were carried by Buddhists to Palestine, or by christian Missionaries like St. Thomas to India.[1] The climax was reached in the 9th century A.D., when, in the famous romane of Balam and Josaphat, by John of Damascus, the Buddha figures as a Christian prince.

Kanishka's empire, enriched as it was by the trade of Europe and Asia, was wealthy and prosperous to an almost unheard of degree, and he was a liberal patron of art. His capital at Peshawar was embellished by many magnificent buildings. In particular he erected a lofty wooden tower, over six hundred feet in height, in order to enshrine certain relics of the Buddha. It consisted of fourteen storeys, and was crowned by an iron pinnacle, surmounted with a number of copper-gilt umbrellas. This tower must have represented the transitional stage between the Indian dāgaba and the Chinese pagoda. Its sides were adorned with numerous images of the Buddha, and it was many times restored. It was still standing in the 6th century A.D., and foreign visitors to India regarded it as one of the wonders of the world. The site was excavated in 1908 and in the relic-chamber was found a small copper-gilt reliquary, not quite eight inches high, of a Greek pattern. On the lid are figures of the Buddha and two Bodhisattvas, while the casket itself is decorated with figures of Kanishka, Buddha, the Sun and Moon deities, and Amorini bearing garlands. An inscription in Kharoshthi proclaims it to be the work of Agesilaos, overseer of Kanishka's vihāra. (Fig. 15) Near the tower stood a large monastery, which was munificently endowed by the emperor and was long looked upon as the leading seat of Buddhist learning in North-Western India. Remains of three separate cities have been excavated on the site of the ancient Taxila. Beneath the Bhir mound to the south was the old Hindu city visited by Alexander, where Asoka must have dwelt as viceroy. In the centre, on the spot now known as Sirkap, was the Bactrian and Parthian city, while to the north at Sisuksh was found the new capital built by the Kushāns. The site contains a Kushān palace, which appears to be of an Assyrian pattern, and on the neighbouring site of Jandial a building has been discovered which has been identified as a Zoroasrian fire-temple. It has Ionic columns and pilasters. At Chu, a stūpa has been unearthed, which is decorated with some striking Buddha figures of the gandhāra school.[1]

The Kushāns, being foreigners, felt none of the puritanical scruples of the early Buddhists against the portrayal of the Master in human form. These had already begun to vanish as Buddha came to be ragarded as a god. For the purpose of embellishing their buildings, they employed Graeco-Roman craftsmen from Asia Minor, like the Agesilaos already mentioned, who probably found their way to Gandhra through the Parthian Empire.[1] These sculptors evolved a hybrid school of art, in which the whole range of Imperial Roman imagery was used to portray events from the Buddha's life, and the Buddha himself repeated the type of an early Imperial to a statue. The most important centres of the Indo-Greek or Gandhāra School are at Jallabād, Hadda and Bamiyān in Afghanistan, the Swāt Valley, and the Peshawar district. The earlier Gandhāra School are at Jalālabād, Hadda and Bamiyān in Afghanistan, the Swāt Valley, and the Peshawar district. The earlier Gandhāra sculptures, both in relief and in the round, are usually of grey slate: These are more purely Greek in type than the later stucco examples. The Buddha, while usually retaining his essential characteristics, is stylistically Hellenic: his features are Greek rather than India, and he wears his monastic robe treated like classical drapery. Plate V, representing a Buddha from Takht-i-Bāhi, near Peshawar, circa A.D. 300, is a fine example of the later gandhāra type. In some examples, representing him before his enlightenment, he appears standing or sitting in European fashion, with a moustache and jewellery, like an earthly prince. In the bas-reliefs, Corinthian capitals are introduced as motifs, and Zeus, Apollo and other Greek gods are adapted to suit Buddhist mythology. The Gandhāra type. In some examples, representing him before his enlightenment, he appears standing or sitting in European fashion, with a moustache and jewellery, like an earthly prince. In the bas-reliefs, Corinthian capitals are introduced as motifs, and Zeus, Apollo and other Greek gods are adapted to suit Buddhist mythology. The Gandhāra school flourished, roughly speaking, between A.D. 100 and 300, the age of the Antonines, and it had many points of contact with Palmyra and other Hellenistic centres of culture in Asia Minor. The Guides's Mess at Hoti Mardān, and the museums at Lahore and many different cities of India and Europe contain numerous examples of these reliefs in the Indo-Greek manner, illustrating scenes from the life of the Buddha and other Jātaka stories. These, together with stone and plaster statues, must have been turned out in large numbers to decorate the stūpas and other religious edifices of the Kushān Kings.

The researches of the French archaeologists have established that a later school, which Sir John Marshall has named the Indo-Afghan school, distinct from Gandhāra but reviving its traditions, sprang up in Eastern Afghanistan, and reached its zenith at the time of the Han invasions in the sixth century A.D.

At the same time, a purely indigenous school of contemporary art, lineally descended from that of Bharhut and Sānchī, appears to have flourished at mathurā, Bhitā, Besnagar, and other centres. Mathurā was a place of particular importance, both religious and secular. Fa Hian, writing three centuries subsequently, says that it contianed twenty Buddhist monasteries, with upwards of three thousand inmates. Excavations have also revealed the presence of a number of Jain vihāras. It was here that the worship of Kṛṣṇa developed, and Ptolemy calls it H Moovga. It was probably a provincial capital, and at the neighbouring village of Mat stood a chapel of the Kushān Kings. Mathurā was a centre of intense artistic activity, and statues from its studios, carved in the characteristic local red sandstone, were exported to Sravastī and Sārnāth, and many other sacred sites all over northern India. It was formerly the custom to attribute to foreign influence the innovation of making representations of the Buddha, Mahāvira and the Hindu gods, but it is now generally agreed that this must be traced to the indigenous artists of Mathurā rather than to Gandhāra. The earliest known Buddha image of the Mathurā school is the colossal statue in red sandstone found at Sārnāth, dedicated by the Friar Bāla in the year 3 of Kanishka. These statues revolutionised the artistic history of Northern India, as local artists began to imitate them, and a school deriving its inspiration from Mathurā gradually grew up. The Vedic religion was, it is true, aniconic, but the lower orders, whether Hindu or Buddhist, clung to their animistic beliefs, and had no doubt continued to make rude images in clay, terracotta, wood and to other perishable materials of the godlings they worshipped—yakshas, nāgas, treespirits, the mother-goddess, the lingam and the joni—uninterruptedly since the days of the Indus valley civilisation. The Buddha figure must have been produced simultaneously, probably early in the first century A.D, in Gandhāra and Mathurā, in response to a demand created by the internal development of the Buddhism which was common ground in both ares, in each case by local craftsmen, working in the local tradition.[1] Here something may be said of the chief characteristics of the classical Buddha figure. The Buddha is represented with the signs of physical perfection which distinguished him at birth—the curling hair, long ears, the protuberance (usnisā) on the skull, the mark (urnā) between the eyes, and the lucky signs on the palms and soles of the feet. He is seated in a yogic pose (āsana) on a lotus or diamond throne, in the posture in which he received Illumination : the features are calm and expressionless. Each gesture of the hands (mudra) has a special significance. His Buddhahood is symbolised by calling the earth to witness, with the hand pointing downwards. Preaching is signified by the hands turning the Wheel of the Law; meditation by the hands folded in the lap. The Right hand is raised in the attitude of warding off fear (abhaya mudra), and the first and middle fingers are joined to denote discouse. The

Buddha wears the monastic robe of the order: in some examples the Right shoulder is bare. As time goes on, the folds of the robe became fainter and fainter, until the Buddha appears closer in transparent drapery, every contour of the figure beneath showing clearly. Another feature of later Buddhist iconography is the nimbus or aureole, which appears to be of Iranian origin. Small and plain at first, it gradually increases in size and is edged with tongues of flame.

Kanishka's long and prosperous reign of nearly half a century came to an end in about A.D. 162. A strange legend is related of his death. It is said that the people grew weary of his insatiable ambition. The king, they said, is greedy, cruel and unreasonable: his campaigns and continued conquests have wearied the mass of his servants. He knows not how to be content, but wants to rule over the four quarters. The garrisons are stationed in distant frontiers, and our relatives are far from us. Such being the situation, we must agree among ourselves and get rid of him. After that we may be happy. As he was ill, they covered him with a quilt and smothered him.

He was succeeded by his sons Vasishta and Huvishka, who had probably been provincial viceroys during their father's lifetime. Huvishka's coins exhibit the same religious eclecticism as those of Kanishka. He was a patron of Buddhism and endowed a splendid Buddhist monastery at a city bearing his name in Kashmir. The last Kushān king of whom we know anything is Vāsudeva; his Hindu name, and the fact that most of his inscriptions are found at Mathurā, suggest that he had been deprived of part of his realms by foreign conquerors, perhaps the Sassanians of Persia, who rose to power at the beginning of the third entury A.D.

The Kushān Period is one of the utmost importance in the history of Indian culture. During this period nascent Christianity met full-grown Buddhism in the academies and markets of Asia and Egypt, while both religions were exposed to the influences of surrounding paganism in many forms, and of the countless works of art which gave expression to the forms of polytheism. The ancient religion of Persia contributed to the ferment of human thought, excited by improved facilities for international communication and by the incessant clash of rival civilisations.[11] Buddhism itself was transformed from a highly individualistic philosophy of life into a world religion, and spread along the Central Asia trade routes, through Khotan, where India and China meet, to China itself. It was a time of intense artistic and literary activity. Buddha and the Hindu deities appear for the first time in human guise, and Indian art, by virtue of its contact with Hellenistic Asia, acquires a fresh impetus. new literary forms come to light: the drāma and the court epic make their appearance and classical Sanskrit is evolved. The Kushān period is a fitting prelude to the Age of the Guptas.

REFERENCES

1. Sacred Books of the east, vol. XXV, pp. 2,3. It is possible that memories of Menander and Sāgala inspired the wonderful descriptions of the royal city of Kusāvati and its king, Mahā-Sudassana, a king of kings, a Righteous man who ruled in Righteousness, an anointed Kṣatriya, in the Mahā Sudassana Sutta (Sacred Books of the East, vol. VI). Such stock descriptions of the Ideal City are, however, not uncommon in Buddhist and Jain literature.
2. For Pushyamitra, see p. 80. The horse-sacrifice was offered by a king who claimed the title of chakravartin, or universal monarch. To capture the horse was to challenge this. Pushyamitra, doubtless, revived the custom in order to celebrate the return of Magadha to orthodox Brahmānism.
3. J.N. Farquhar, The Apostle Thomas in Southern India. John Rylands Library Bulletin, 1927, p. 20.
4. P. Masson-Oursel, Ancient India and Indian Civilization (1934), p. 43.
5. The Roman aureus was current all over the East. A well-known story is related by the traveller Kosmas Indikopleustes (6th century A.D.) of a Persian and Roman who met at the court of a Sinhalese monarch.

The Persian talked volubly of the greatness of his country. The roman merely produced an aureus and bade the king compare it with a Persian drachma.

6. De consolatione ad Helviam, Ch. VI.
7. Rhys Davids, Hibbert Lectures (1881), p. 93; Max Muller, Last Essays (First Series), p. 251.
8. Sir, J.Marshall, Guide to Taxila (1921).
9. The Western Aspects of Gandhara Sculpture, by H. Buchthal, Proceedings of the British Academy, 1945.
10. Kumaraswamy, Indian Origin of the Buddha Figure (Boston, 1928), A. Foucher, Beginnigs of Buddhist Art (1917), p. 113. It is interesting to note that one of Kanishka's gold coins bears a standing figure of Buddha with the inscription *BOAAo* in Greek characters.
11. V.A Smith, *Oxford History of India* (1992), p. 134.

CHAPTER-XIII

THE BUDDHISTS OF BURMA AND CEYLON

—James Bisset Pratt

From the far northwest on the borders of Afghanistan, to Orissa and Madras in the east and south, India is covered with caves, rock-cut temples, columns, statues, carvings that come from a religion now long since perished from the land. It is over a thousand years since Buddhism died out of the country of its birth. The museum for it has been substituted for the temple, and the archeologist and Pali scholar have taken the place of the yellow-robed monk and the devout lay follower of the Blessed One. Yet so great an impression has the Buddha made upon his land and upon the minds of all students of Indian religion that the spell of his personality still hangs over those regions where he lived and taught, and most of us can visit only with a very deep and genuine reverence those few well-authenticated spots where we know his "lotus feet" once trod. Most sacred, and at the same time most well authenticated and most beautiful, of all these spots is Buddh Gaya. Its great temple, to be sure, has been rebuilt and considerably changed since ancient times by the Nepalese, and the place as a whole is in the hands of the Hindus. Yet with native reverence for all that others revere, its guardians both respect and honour the temple; and it is surrounded by a garden in which all manner of fresh flowers clamber over all manner of half-ruined statues and ancient stupas, so that the whole forms a combination of loving care and picturesque decay unsurpassed in loveliness and beauty by anything in India. And over the whole place rests the spirit of the Teacher : so that I for one was not ashamed to follow the little band of Nepalese and Thibetan pilgrims in their circumambulation of the great tower and to pause and do a little puja of my own under the Bo tree which marks the spot where illumination came to him who was to be the "Light of Asia."

In fact I am sure that if the Buddha could have returned and watched us that morning, he would have preferred my homage to that of the Himalayan pilgrims who bore his name. He who came to destroy belief in the efficacy of outer forms could have marked only with deep disappointment and sorrow the fastening of gold leaf upon the temple's stones in his name, the mumbling of mystic texts and the swinging of prayer wheels, which were the principal occupations of these pilgrims. And if he could have followed them back to their mountain homes he would probably have exclaimed that the time was ripe for a new Buddha to appear on earth, for scarcely a token of his teaching would he have found.

It was not my good fortune to follow these pilgrims any farther towards their Tibetan homes than Darjeeling; but in and around Darjeeling one can get a very good idea of Tibetan and Nepalese Buddhism. Half way down the slope between Darjeeling and the valley on the east is a Buddhist temple of the Tibetan type. On the outer wall, on each side of the entrance, is a line of five or six "prayer wheels" or prayer cylinders each about two feet high and covered with sacred texts. The recitation of these texts or mantras is supposed to keep off the evil spirits which abound wherever the Lamaistic type of Buddhism is known, and the spinning of one of these cylinders produces the same miraculous result. One can set all twelve revolving at once—and the effect on the spirit world is presumably considerable. In the porch of the temple is another prayer wheel, much larger and apparently much more important and *official* than those without. It is six feet high and bears several rows of inscribed texts. The axis of the cylinder is continued by an iron rod on which it rests, and this before reaching the floor is bent outward and then back in such a fashion that by pulling a rope attached to the bend the cylinder can be easily revolved. On the top of the cylinder is an iron projection so placed that in each revolution it will hit against two bells suspended from the ceiling directly above the cylinder. When we entered the temple—and in fact throughout our visit—a boy, seated on the floor in front of the cylinder, was occupied pulling the rope and thus revolving the wheel. Apparently he was praying for the whole community—and by the hour. Thus do the Northern Buddhists "pray without ceasing".

At the farther end of the inner room of the temple were three seated Buddhas, with a row of various kinds of offerings before them. The central one of these images represented "the great Buddha"—which is not Gautama but Gautama's heavenly essence, of which the historical Gautama was only an appearance. Gautama himself was represented by the humbler figure on the left; while to the right was Gautama's reflex or Bodhisattva. For Himalayan Buddhism has not only made the Buddha into a god; it has been unsatisfied with this and has invented some twenty-eight Buddhas, made each of these into a Trinity, and deified all the members of each. Quite consistently it has also transformed its monks into priests and endowed them with all manner of powers, and in place of simple contemplation of the Blessed One and his Doctrine, it has invented magical mantras by means of which one may avoid the hordes of dangerous devils to which reference has already been made. One may use these formulae in various ways—repeat them, write them out on a prayer wheel and revolve it, wear them in a little case and carry it suspended round the neck, swallow them, or reflect them in a mirror; wash the mirror, and drink the water it was washed in,[1] etc. The favourite of these charms is the famous "*Om! mani padmi, hum*"—which means (so far as it means anything) "Om! the Jewel of the Lotus Flower! Hum!" In all the region round Darjeeling one meets women and men wandering through village streets or along country roads, fingering their rosaries of one hundred and eight beads and murmuring, "*Om meni pemi hum!*" Little hand prayer wheels are almost as common as rosaries—brass cylinders containing texts and revolved on a stick. I watched carefully two women in the streets of Darjeeling, one of whom was revolving a prayer wheel of this description. Much of the time she was talking eagerly with her companion and when not talking she was looking into the shops that they passed; but all the time she kept the wheel going. Occasionally they would enter some shop and inquire prices and haggle over bargains with the shopkeeper; but the wheel never stopped. Finally, having completed her morning devotions, she handed the wheel to her friend, who then took here turn at it. I could see no sign of what we should call real prayer or devotion in either of them or in any of the Himalayan Buddhists whom I met. Buddhism to them (so far as I could judge on a very superficial acquaintance) seemed to be merely a way of acquiring supernatural "merit" by external mechanical devices.

Far different is the impression which one gets on his first superficial acquaintance with Burmese and Ceylonese Buddhism. And the contrast between it and the lower forms of Hinduism is quite as marked. When the traveler turns his back upon India and steams up the Rangoon River, he finds great forests and green fields about him instead of the parched and dusty plains to which he has become accustomed; and when he lands and begins to watch the Burmese people at their devotions he feels that spiritually as well as physically he is in a new land and is breathing a new atmosphere. In place of the closed temple with its mysterious inner shrine, its lingam and Ganesh, its continual wash of dirty water, and its fat priest keeping out all but Hindus and extorting unwilling money from poor pilgrims,—instead of this one finds the white or golden pagoda, open on all sides to the sky, accessible to every one (with or without shoes), and guarded by no priest; and instead of the lingam or the hideous Hanuman, the dignified image of the calm Buddha. I think that travel has few experiences to give in any part of the world more striking and memorable than one's first impression of the Shway Dagon Pagoda in Rangoon. The pagoda stands upon a lofty artificial mound, and mound and pagoda together are as high as St. Paul's in London. There are approaches to the pagoda at each of the four points of the compass,—long and gentle stairways climbing by an easy ascent from the foot to the top of the mound, between continuous lines of booths where good-natured Burmese and pretty Burmese girls, in silks of many a hue and all smoking long cheroots, stand waiting to sell you candles or gongs or incense or paper flags or flowers of varied kinds and colours for your use in paying homage to the memory of the Master to whose glory the pagoda was erected. When you emerge from this sacred bazaar at the top of the steps, you find yourself on a platform in the midst of which rises the great pagoda, quite covered with gold leaf and gleaming in the sun, and surrounded by a forest of smaller pagodas and shrines of varied forms, each containing a statue of the Buddha and a profusion of tropical flowers, while palm trees wave their stately branches overhead against the blue Burmese sky, and thousands of little tinkly bells that circle the pagoda tops quiver in endless chorus as the soft breeze touches them with its unfailing caress. In every corner of the great platform and before each shrine are worshipers—here one or two, there a family or a little group—kneeling in prayer and presenting offerings of flowers and of lighted candles before some image of the founder of their faith. No priests, no supervision, no fees, no concerted and systematized worship. Here, you feel, is the religion of the individual. And though you may miss the communion of saints and the congregational singing, you can hardly go away from the pagoda without recognizing that you have been in an unmistakably religious atmosphere.

What is true of the Shway Dagon will hold for thousands of pagodas small and large in various parts of Burma,—for the great Shway Maw Daw at Pegu, the sacred Arackan Pagoda at Mandalay, the Shway San Daw at Prome (most beautiful of all Burmese buildings), and for may a small pagoda quite unknown to fame on the upper reaches of the Irrawaddy. Everywhere the same unmistakable reverence to the memory of the Buddha, the same direct, individual expression of devotion with no mediating priest, the same obvious gain of courage and poise and peace as a result of the prayer.

When one first visits a Burmese pagoda—especially if he has been reading Fielding Hall—he is likely to see only the beauty of the worship and to come away with unmixed admiration for the Burmese and their religion. A better acquaintance with their worship, however, will make one more critical. There is a great deal of externalism in their religion. I do not agree with the missionary who told me it was *all* external; but it is quite possible that if I knew as much about the matter as she does I might agree with her. But though I believe that there is more than mere externalism in the worship of the Burmese, there can be no doubt that a large part of it is merely that. Many Buddhists themselves have told me this. The "prayers" said at the pagodas are mostly formulae learned by heart, some in Burmese, some in Pali, and the Pali ones are often quite meaningless to the worshiper. Moreover, the mental attitude of the worshiper is sometimes very close to idolatry. A Buddhist layman told me that in his opinion a large number of the ignorant people really worhipped the stone image before them; and one intelligent young man assured me that many Buddhists prayed to the pagoda itself—that he had always done so as a boy and that his mother did so still. Yet for all this, Buddhist worship in Burma never loses its simplicity and beauty, its dignity and reverence. I remember a group of a dozen nuns, kneeling before the great image in the Arackan Pagoda at Mandalay. All of them had shaven heads, some of them were old and some infirm. They had come appparently from the convent across the river to lay their little offerings of flowers before the feet of the Blessed One and to acquire what merit they might by the repetition of various verses in this most sacred shrine. They may not have understood the words they used, and for aught I know they regarded the ancient image before them as having some miraculous power of its own. Only they could tell. But there was no mistaking the devotion and reverence that was in their hearts and that shone from their faces.

The most important and commonly repeated of the "prayers" or formulae of praise used by Buddhists is the "Refuge," which, of course, is always repeated in Pali. Its meaning is as follows :—

I take refuge in the Buddha.
I take refuge in the Law.
I take refuge in the Order.
A second time I take refuge in the Buddha.
A second time I take refuge in the Law.
A second time I take refuge in the Order.

A third time I take refuge in the Buddha.
A third time I take refuge in the Law.
A third time I take refuge in the Order.

The Ten Moral Precepts are also learned by all and often recited; as are also the list of the thirty-two parts of the body,—both these in Pali. Besides these there are several other prayers which are more or less popular and are often repeated at the pagodas. One of the commonest of them is the following :—

"Awgatha, Awgatha, I worship with the body, with the mouth, and with the mind, with these three 'kans'. The first, the second, the third; once, twice, until three times. The Lord, the precious one; the Law, the precious one; the Assembly, the precious one—These three precious things. I, the worshiper, most humbly, with fervid zeal, with clasped hands, pay reverence, give offerings, and with pious gaze bow me down. Thus by this worshiping I gain merit and increase in earnestness and purity of heart, and am freed from the Four States of Punishment; from the Three Evil Things, starvation, plague, and warfare; from the Eight Chambers of Hell; and from the Five Enemies. And at the end, when the last existence has come for me, may I pass into Nirvāṇa."[2]

But is not only at the pagoda that the people worship. In almost every home there is a little shrine—a picture or an image of the Buddha, and below it a shelf on which simple offerings are daily placed. The image may be of stone and rudely carved or of solid gold and carefully executed. The pictures present favourite scenes in the life of Gautama, and may be bought at the pagodas or obtained *gratis* from the Mellin's Food Company with and advertisement thrown in. Flowers are kept before the image or picture, and in one house I remember finding on the shelf that served as a shrine two bowls of rice, two bowls of water, two saucers with two bananas on each, and two jars of preserved flowers. Fresh offerings are brought every morning, and in the more devout homes verses are recited before the Buddha morning and night.

But the Buddha has to share the Burman's worship with the "nats". The nats, in fact, would insist that this is only just, for compared with them the Buddha is a newcomer in the land. They were the gods of Burma long before Gautama attained to Buddhahood—being in fact the ancient nature spirits who with their cousins ruled all the world before the rise of the "historical" religions. The Burman loves the Buddha, but fears the nats. The Buddha he knows will never, harm him, and they may. Hence pragmatically considered the nats are quite as important as the Buddha. Mr. Scott (who knows the people as few others do) writes in his "Handbook of Burma" : "A Burmese gives alms to the monks, worships at the pagodas on the appointed days, and repeats the doxologies which he has learnt at school, but he governs his life and actions by a consideration of what the spirits of the air, the forests, the streams, the village, or the house may do if they are not propitiated ..... In his everyday life, from the day of his birth to his marriage, to his old age, even to the point of death, all the prominent rites and forms are to be traced, not to the (Buddhist) Baskets of the Law, but to the traditionary whims and fancies handed down from admittedly Shamanistic forefather. If misfortunes fall upon him he makes offerings to the evil nats, who, he thinks, have brought it upon him. When he wants to build a house, launch a boat, plow or sow his fields, start on a journey, make a purchase, marry a wife himself or marry his daughter to another, bury a relative, or even endow a religious foundation, it is the spirits he propitiates, it is the nats whom he consults. His Pali prayers and invocations, lauds and doxologies, avail him nothing then, and are not even thought of."

The nats are innumerable and are ranged in a hierarchy from Thagya Min, the King Nat (the Vedic Indra), down to the nat of the meanest house. Every village has its altar to the nats, and they are worshiped both in the homes and at the pagodas.[3] These statements, of course, hold only for the less intelligent Burmese, but in matters of superstition nearly all the laymen and the majority of the monks come under this heading. By questioning the monks on this subject one gets an interesting variety of opinions. Some believe in the nats as thoroughly as the laymen; a few deny their existence altogether; and one monk told me that the nats were of two classes: those superior to men, advanced beings on the road to Nirvāṇa; and evil spirits lower than man who do not really exist and whom only the less intelligent believe in.

It would be very misleading to give even a superficial account of the religion of the Burmese layman and say nothing of its moral teaching and influence. One of the first things one of the few things which the average Burmese boy is taught by his Buddhist instructors is the moral law of the Great Teacher the Five Precepts. These are: (I) Not to take any life; (2) not to steal; (3) to avoid sexual incontinence; (4) not to lie, deceive, or slander; (5) not to drink intoxicating liquors. There can be no doubt that these Precepts have a very real influence on the life of the Buddhists. Even the most casual visitor must be struck with the very decided admiration that all the European residents have for the Burmese. As every one knows, European residents in the East are not given to magnifying the virtues of the natives; and in most Oriental lands the foreign resident—especially the business man—sees little good in the "heathen blacks." Hence it speaks well for the Burman that almost all Europeans in the land have a good word—and usually an enthusiastic word—for him. Every one will tell you that the Burmese are reliable and hospitable and that they live up fairly well to the chief moral commands of their religion. There is little drunkenness among them and that little is vigorously opposed by the more devoted Buddhists. As a people they are peaceable and honest and very kind,—kind to each other, to the stranger, and to the whole sentient world. Cruelty to animals seems to the Burmese Buddhist peculiarly abhorrent. And little acts of mercy and thoughtfulness—such as building a booth in a village street and keeping it supplied with a jug of fresh drinking-water for the benefit of travelers—are very often met with.

To be sure these acts of kindness, while prompted largely by native goodness of heart and by the example and teachings of the Buddha, are not merely altruistic in motive. The Burman wishes well to others, but he also has his eye on his next incarnation, and he knows that these acts pile up "merit" for him in a place where moth and rust do not corrupt nor thieves break through and steal. This term "merit" means to the Buddhist the obtaining of material benefits (in this or the next life), the laying-up of a good character, and "the satisfaction of a good conscience"![4] Which of these three shall receive the most emphasis will, of course, depend upon the individual. In each case, however, merit is conceived as some thing which may be acquired (in greater or less quantity), and deposited for use in another life. The prevalence of this view is largely due to that most popular of Buddhist books, the Jatakas.

Good acts, then, are a kind of insurance premium, the policy being payable in the next life. And while good acts pay well, nothing is quite so profitable as the building or gilding of a pagoda. One who has never been in Burma can with difficulty form any conception of the extent to which pagoda building has been carried and still is carried in that surprising land. As one travels on the railway, sails up the Irrawaddy, or walks along a country road, he is ever coming upon pagodas—some enormous, some tiny, some old and crumbling, surrendering their bell-shaped form as they lapse back into the plain or lose them selves in the wild growth of the jungle, some finished but yesterday and not yet gilded. At Pagan on the Irrawaddy there are upwards of ten thousand of them—and nearly all deserted. As more merit accrues through building a new pagoda than through restoring an old one (unless the old one be peculiarly sacred), the process of filling the land with more and more pagodas continues at a starting rate. Most of the smaller pagodas are built by individuals, while the larger ones are put up—or if old are regilded—by public subscription. At present a rather unusual wave of pagoda enthusiasm is passing over Burma. Nearly all the great pagodas of the land are being regilded, and at Mandalay, the religious center, the entire hill that commands the town is being covered with statues, pagodas, and other religious buildings. One of these pagodas is being built for the reception of the ashes of the Buddha recently found by Dr. Spooner near Peshawar; and as I have said, the entire hill is being covered with pagodas of various sizes, shaded stairways and passages for the accommodation of pilgrims, rest-halls, and mammoth Buddha images. The whole work is in the hands of a rather remarkable monk named U Khanthi, and known as "the Hermit of Mandalay Hill". All the funds for the new pagoda and the adornment of the hill go into his hands and are expended at his discretion, no one for a moment doubting his honesty or questioning his good taste and ability. He is a man of forty or fifty with a fine face and a quiet and commanding manner. We went to see him while in Mandalay and found him in the great hall at the top of the hill where he receives visitors. He greeted us most cordially, and we had a short interview which was broken into by the arrival of a band of pilgrims from the Shan States on the borders of China. The hermit made his apologies to us and seated himself upon what might be called his official mat in front of a blue curtain in the center of the hall, while the Shans, in their strange costumes, squatted reverently before him. He first read to them a few lines from a sacred text and then all the pilgrims handed up to him, for his signature, certificates showing that they had visited Mandalay Hill and seen its famous hermit. Nearly all these Shans, we were told, "owned" pagodas of their own at home, and they had come here to acquire merit by the pilgrimage and by the offerings for the hermit and his pious work. The offerings were now brought forth from great bags, and were piled high on the trays, provided by the hermit's servants,—rice, fruits, candles, cheroots black and white, and other worldly and religious dainties. These were for the hermit's own consumption (or for his personal charity if he preferred to give them away), and were but the beginning of the merit-acquisition; for now followed the real business of the day. Other trays were brought out by the servants, and these the pilgrims loaded with silver coins, the total contribution aggregation several hundred rupees. This money, of course, was for the hermit to use in his buildings on the hill. The audience ended with a rain-making ceremony. A woman poured water, under the hermit's directions, into several bowls while he repeated texts. This process, two of his disciples told us, if carried out carefully by the Shans on their return home would enable them to get a shower when ever needed.

This Shan delegation was interesting to me as indicating some of the strange constituents that go to make up the Buddhism of the modern Burman. And, as the reader will have seen from the above description, the superstitious side of modern Buddhism is not confined to the laity. Most of the monks are quite as superstitious as the laymen. They have, of course, a wider knowledge of Buddhism, but their Buddhistic learning consists as a rule in committing to memory certain of the sacred texts; and they have little idea and apparently little care as to what the real meaning of these texts may be. Thus two disciples of the Mandalay hermit told me that Buddha was in Nirvāṇa and entirely uninfluenced by prayers and offerings, and immediately after added that Buddha was their God, that He heard and answered prayers, and was influenced and pleased by the offerings that were given Him. I could not make them see their inconsistency, and it was evident that they had never done any thinking on the present status of Buddha and very little on any other subject connected with their religion. I was told that there were not five monks in Rangoon who could answer the questions I asked, and I am sure that a large number of those I talked with would infallibly have "flunked" the examination I give my college students on the teachings of the Buddha. Of course not all the Buddhist monks are so ignorant. In Mandalay especially there are many very learned and intelligent *pongyis*[5] who are deep students of the Pali books and real thinkers as to their meaning. But on the whole the contrast between the Indians and the Burmese in learning and real thought are not uncommonly met with; in Burma they are very rare.

The life of the monks is, on the whole, rather pleasant. They live together, in smaller or larger groups, in monastery buildings which are always comfortable. airy, and picturesque, and sometimes very beautiful. The larger monasteries in Rangoon and especially in Mandalay are genuine works of art. They are built of teak-wood, elaborately carved, and the interior is in part painted a rich red, in part gilded. In each of these monasteries there is a number of small sleeping-rooms and one large central hall with its marble or alabaster or brass image of the Buddha, and its invariable accompaniment of candles and fresh flowers. There are also sleeping-mats for the monks, a library of printed books and manuscripts and beautifully executed lacquer texts, and many votive offerings in the form of banners and Buddhas, seated, recumbent, and standing. It is in this hall that visitors are received, the younger monks instructed by the abbot, and the morning and evening worship performed in honour of the Blessed One. The number of the monks in a monastery varies considerably. In the smaller ones there may be only two or three, while in the Masoyein Taik or group of monasteries (at Mandalay) there are altogether about three hundred and fifty pongyis and a number of novices. Nearly all Buddhist boys in Burma go for at least part of their education to the monastery school, and most of them at some period of their life become novices and put on the yellow robe for a short time. If a young man decides to become a monk and join the order permanently, he is admitted at the age of twenty, after passing an examination and going through a certain ceremony. A monk who has served for ten years has the title of pongyi and the right to preside as abbot at a monastery of his own.

On entering the order the takes, in addition to the five vows of the layman, the following five : (6) Not to eat any solid food after midday : (7) to abstain from dancing, singing, plays, and all worldly and distracting amusements; (8) to abstain from the use of ornaments and perfumes and all that tends to vanity; (9) to abandon the use of high and luxurious beds and seats and to sleep on a hard low couch; (10) to possess no money, but live always in voluntary poverty.

The monks rise in the morning about five-thirty, and after their toilet the whole monastery assembles before the image of the Buddha, where they bow and pledge afresh to keep the vows that day. The pupils and novices now sweep out the monastery, fetch water, etc., while younger monks gather flowers and offer them before the Buddha, and the older ones (the pongyis proper) meditate. After a very slight breakfast the boys repeat their lessons, and then they all start out with begging-bowls through the streets to collect the food for their one genuine meal. In every Burmese village one comes upon this line of yellow-robed figures early in the morning hours, marching silently through the streets in Indian file, a monk at the head followed by a line of diminutive boys each carrying an enormous black lacquer bowl. Arrived in front of the house of some layman whose generosity and desire for merit is well known, the line halts and silently waits until the lady of the house or a servant comes out and empties a quantity of steaming rice into the big bowl and pours some curry into one of the smaller dishes carried in the bowl above the rice. The monk meanwhile looks in the other direction and tries to appear unconscious. The donation offered, the line moves on. In some of the larger monasteries the abbot does not accompany the others in their begging expedition, but spends this hour in reading or instructing some of the older monks. By eleven the boys and the younger monks have returned from their excursion with well-filled bowls; the rice is then put together, a dish of it and the best of the curry is sent to the abbot, and they all have a solid meal—which in all conscience they need, as they are to have no more for the whole day. After this the monks wash out their bowls, intone praises to the Buddha, and all have a good nap, while the boys study their lessons. After nap time the lessons are heard and some of the monks read and meditate, and at four o'clock all are free to go to some pagoda or spend their time as they like. At six they are back again in the monastery, the boys and novices repeat what they have learned during the day, and the evening devotions begin. These consist in what may be called a "general confession", namely, the recitation of a formula which amounts to the prayer, "If I have sinned this day may I be forgiven!" Other formulae of prayers are recited before the Buddha image, the abbot preaches a short sermon, the monks bow three times before him and before the Buddha, and the day is done.

The meditation of the monks to which reference has been made above has as its aim the control of the passions and the cultivation of kindness. The monk should tell over upon his beads the thirty-two constituents of the body or the nine exits and excrements of the body, and should thereby remind himself of the transitoriness of life and the disgusting nature of bodily enjoyments.[6] He should also seek to cultivate good will to every living being that his eyes light upon. If, for instance, he sees a sick dog, he should say to himself, not "How disgusting!" but rather, "What can I do to help this poor creature?" Twice a month the monks assemble to hear read the Pati Mokha, or two hundred and twenty-seven rules of the order, after which they are supposed to confess any breach of the rules they may have committed since the last reading. In addition to these efforts for their own advance in righteousness, some of the monks endeavor to help the laymen also. If invited they will go to some home and teach; and twice a month (at new and full moon) they read the Law to any who care to hear. On the whole, the monks lead a fairly moral life. Fielding Hall, who has had thirty years' experience in Burma as a magistrate, testifies that he has known of only five criminal cases with which a monk was connected, and three of these were cases of rebellion. The laity honour them and their influence is mildly helpful, though hardly so superlatively ideal as readers of Fielding Hall might suppose.

Harmless they are; and they would injure no one willingly, not even a spider. Yet I was told that exceeding few of them would go far out of their way to save a little girl from a life of shame. That is her own lookout, they would injure no one willingly, not even a spider. Yet I was told that exceeding few of them would go far out of their way to save a little girl from a life of shame. That is her own lookout, they would say. They lead "the simple life", but hardly the "strenuous" one. I asked a particularly intelligent monk in Mandalay why he had chosen to be a pongyi and his answer was significant. "I like the life", he said. Life in the monastery is one of scholarly ease—or just ease. It may offer also an opportunity for occasional usefulness as a preacher or teacher; but the monk is exceedingly rare to whom the desire for helpfulness is the chief attraction. They *like the life.*

The Buddhism of Ceylon is very similar to that of Burma. What contrast there is between the two may be stated in general terms by saying that the Ceylonese are less devout and more learned than the Burmans. This is true of both monks and laymen. On entering Ceylon from Burma one is struck by the absence of pagodas and the almost entire lack of worshipers at the shrines except on *poya* days. In place of the pagoda, with its shrine open to all who will come, is substituted the closed *vihara* or temple with its hidden image and the *dagoba* with its buried relic. These temples and dagobas are extremely rare in comparison with the pagodas of Burma, so profusely scattered over the land. Moreover, they are to be found as a scattered over the land. Moreover, they are to be found as a rule only within monastery enclosures, and the temples are regularly locked except on poya days. These come in theory four times a month, practically but twice, namely, on the new and full moon. On these two days one sees the same sort of devotion at the temples on the part of the people that one may witness almost every day at a Burmese pagoda. There are the same recitation of sacred texts in Pali and in the vernacular, the same reverence and prostrations, the same offerings of flowers and candles. In explanation of the small number of worshipers at the public shrines in Ceylon, moreover, it must be remembered that the climate here is much more trying than in Burma, and that the devout Buddhist may perfectly well perform his devotions in the coolness of his own home. Home worship is much the same in Ceylon as in Burma and there is the same appeasement of spirits good and bad. There are, to be sure, no nats in Ceylon, but their place is taken by the devas or devatas borrowed from Hindu mythology. The most important of these are Sakara (the Vedic Indra), Brahma, Vishnu, Ishwara, and Shiva. Images of these or other devatas are to be found in the vestibules of nearly all the temples, and sometimes within the temples themselves; and they receive homage and offerings only after the Buddha. Not only do the monks believe in these devas; Colonel Olcott, in his "Catechism", which has had so great an influence in Buddhist religious education, gravely teaches that there are three kinds of devas, and that if we are very good they cannot hurt us, but if we are bad we had best watch out. Another important part of Singhalese religion is the adoration of the pipal tree (*ficus religiosa*). In a monastery at Anuradhapura still stands the famous pipal tree brought by Sanghamitta, the daughter of King Ashoka, to Ceylon about 240 B.C., a scion of the sacred "Bo tree" under which Gautama received enlightenment at Buddh Gaya. A descendant of this greatest treasure of Anuradhapura is to be found in the compound of almost every large vihara in the island, where, on poya days, it receives nearly as much homage as does the image of the Buddha himself. But it is not only these monastery trees that are held sacred. On the roadside and in other places one comes upon pipal trees, large or small, before which rude altars have been erected and offerings of flags and flowers strewn. As is the case with so many other religious customs, the theory back of this is uncertain and unimportant. Some Buddhists will tell you that the spirit of the tree is being worshiped; others that the offerings are presented merely as a sign of grateful remembrance that the pipal tree once sheltered the Lord Buddha. The truth is, of course, that the theory plays but a small part in the mind of the worshiper. One adores the Bo tree because it is the thing to do—and because one thereby acquires merit.

When one reads of the devatas in Ceylon and the nats in Burma and the tree-cult in both countries, one is inclined to say, How Buddhism has degenerated since its early days! There is no doubt that modern Buddhism, even in the South, is decidedly impure; but the truth is that the Buddhism of the people, even in the good old days of its earliest propagation, has always been impure. To see what early Buddhism was one should go, not to the Pitakas, but to the Buddhist carvings from Mathura, Bharut, Sanchi, and other ancient centers of the religion. The Mathura reliefs, from the sixth century A.D., show that at that time Buddhism was shockingly intermingled with Tantra worship : gay, not to say indecent, female figures are more prominent in the sculptures than the figure of the Buddha. The Bharut Tope (150 B.C.) makes much of Sirima Devata, the goddess of wealth, and other female figures abound. And in the carvings at Sanchi, perhaps the earliest of all, Saraswati (the wife of Brahma) is an important figure, and almost the chief object of representation is the adoration of the sacred tree. Brahma and Vishnu are common figures in Buddhist sculpture all over the northwest. And if one goes back to the Pitakas themselves he finds no such pure philosophical doctrine as Western books on

Buddhism would often have one believe. The whole drama of Buddha's life is presented on a background of Hindu mythology, and even in the teachings of Gautama the old gods are referred to as real beings, quite as a matter of course. To be sure the gods through out early Buddhism are always represented as inferior to the Buddha; but so are they also in the Buddhism of Burma and Ceylon.

Ceylon, like Burma, is inhabited, or threatened, by devils who play their usual part in the production of sickness and other human ills. In both Burma and Ceylon astrology is one of the most important and lucrative of the arts, and one frequently comes upon advertisements like the following, "Horoscopes drawn telling all future events", "Marks on the body reveal all events, good and bad." The moral teachings of Buddhism are, of course, the same in Ceylon as in Burma, but on the whole they seem to have less effect. At any rate, the Ceylonese are not so noted for their kindness to animals as are the Burmese. Yet I think they would not suffer greatly in comparison with us Westerners. And certainly their religion lends all its force to the side of kindness toward the dumb world. This in fact is carried to an extent which to us would often seem fantastic. The walls of many a monastery are frescoed (for the benefit of the lay visitor) with pictures of the sufferings in hell that await the hunter and him who kills insects. Copleston asserts that an injured man might lie by the wayside all day calling for help and no Buddhist would go out of his way to help him;[7] and many missionaries (reported in Mr. Saunders's Questionnaire) insist that most Buddhists consider lying a smaller sin than killing a flea. I feel very certain that the former of these statements is mistaken and I am inclined to think the latter exaggerated.

The better class of monks in Ceylon are, as I have said, more learned and intelligent than those in Burma. This hardly holds true, however, of the rank and file—for certainly in both countries these are ignorant enough. Twenty years ago Dr. Bowles Daly made an exhaustive investigation of the monasteries in Ceylon and reports : "There are about nine thousand monks; among them a few—very few—great scholars; the majority are illiterate, and some to avoid labour, seek a life of indolence sheltered by the yellow robes of the priesthood; many are depraved. There are, however, some examples of personal piety, devotion, and self-denial, which would be an ornament to any church."[8]

The monks in Ceylon are less active, less influential, and more reserved than those in Burma. They are much less in evidence in public, as they do but little begging, their food being taken to them in the monasteries by pious laymen. Their monasteries are often, characteristically, farther removed from the madding crowd than is usually the case in Burma—tucked away on some hillside or in the heart of the jungle. It would be hard to find more ideal retreats for the contemplative life than are, for instance, some of the monasteries near Galle, in the midst of palm groves or on a forest-covered ridge, or the famous Alut Vihara at Matale, perched on the top of its isolated rock. Fortunately for the legs of the little boys, the monasteries are not the schools of the land as they are in Burma. Most boys go to Government or private schools, and it is not the custom for them, as it is for the Burmese, to take for a time the yellow robe. Still the order as a whole is respected and a family feels honored when one of its members enters the monkhood.

An interesting combination of the monk and the layman is the *upasaka*. This word originally applied to all laymen, for all were supposed to take upon themselves at times a certain additional training which ordinarily obtained only for the monks. Not many do this today, and the word upasaka now refers to particularly devout laymen (more often laywomen) who four times a month—namely, on poya days—observe the monk's sixth, seventh, and eighth vows (given above), and go daily to the vihara or temple with offerings to the Buddha and to the devatas and gifts to the monks and the poor. These upasakas are often very admirable characters, understand and obey the spirit of helpfulness that animates their religion at its best, land give up much of their time to deeds of real mercy and kindness.

In their architecture, their costumes, their customs the Singhalese are much less picturesque than are the Burmese; and largely for this reason their type of Buddhism seems to the stranger decidedly less attractive than does the Burmese type. Their closer contact with Western civilization also has not been exclusively an advantage. And, as I have said, there is no doubt that they are less devout in their religion than the Burmese. But it would be a mistake to suppose that they are a bad people or that their religion is without influence. The Singhalese are an intelligent, moral, and attractive race, and there can be little doubt that they owe an eternal debt of gratitude to Prince Mahinda, who first brought to them the teachings of India's greatest Teacher. Unfortunately neither they nor the Burmese have kept that teaching as pure as they might have—though they have done immeasurably better in this respect than any of the Northern Buddhists. And this brings us to the means by which that teaching is handed on, the religious education of both these peoples—a subject which must be reserved to the next chapter.

1. Methods of this sort are not confined to Tibet. In southern and central Italy, including Rome, pictures of the Virgin printed on very thin tissue paper may be procured, which are useful in curing headaches and other slight ailments. The method of application

is quite Thibetan : the paper is soaked in a glass of water till it has in part gone to pieces, and then the water with the fragments of paper is swallowed. The use of these miraculous papers is not confined to the lower classes, but is to be met with in some of the best families.

2. Shway Yoe (J.G. Scott), The *Burman : His Life and Notions* (London Macmillan & Co. 1882), vol. I, p. 223.
3. A well-informed Burmese Buddhist writes of his more ignorant fellow-countrymen : "They look upon Thagyamin as the *deus ex machina* in human affairs, and in time of distress they are ready to invoke the aid of Paya (the Adi-Buddha or Supreme Buddha of Northern Buddhism) and of Thagya. The common expression used is, 'Paya-thagya-ke-ba', 'May Adi Buddha and Indra save me!' (Reported by Mr. Saunders in the *Burma Critic*, February 19, 1914).
4. Saunder's Questionnaire, in the Appendix to his *Buddhist Ideals*, (Madras, Christian Literature Society, 1912).
5. Monks who have passed ten years in the order.
6. There are of course, other common subjects of meditation. In the Auguttara Nikaya, for instance, the following list of ten is recommended : (1) The Buddha; (2) Dharma (the Law); (3) Sangha (the Order); (4) the Precepts; (5) Charity; (6) the Gods; (7) inhaled and exhaled Breath; (8) Death; (9) the Thirty-two constituents of the Body; (10) release from suffering. (Atthana Vagga, I, XVI). In the early days of Buddhism the monks carried meditation to the point of *samadhi*—a state of auto-hypnosis;

but this practice has long since been given up. This Yoga practice and many of the subjects of meditation were taken over into Buddhism directly from pre-Buddhistic India, and have no relation to Gautama's essential thought. Cf. for instance, the sixth and seventh subjects of the list just given.

7. Buddhism in Magadha and Ceylon (second edition, London, Longmans, 1908), p. 285. While this assertion seems to me to give a wrong impression, if taken as a characterization of all Singhalese Buddhists, I do not doubt that in many cases it would apply. Dr. Copleston had years of experience in Ceylon and knew of what he spoke. In this connection another quotation from him may be of interest : "If it is asked, to begin with, whether the Singhalese are evidently and unmistakably influenced in their lives by the religion which they profess, as Mohammedans for instance are, the answer must be, No; except in the matter of scrupulousness about taking the life of animals. In other matters, whether a man's conduct were good or bad, he would seldom allege religion as his motive. Religion is a matter of obtaining merit by certain offerings and attendances; not, in ordinary cases, a matter of conduct." (*Op. cit.*, p. 284).

8. Quoted by H. Hackmann in his Buddhism as a Religion (London, Probsthain, 1910), p. 118.

CHAPTER-XIV

THE DOCTRINES OF MODERN BUDDHISM

—James Bisset Pratt

The most universally accepted and the most influential of the doctrines of Buddhism is undoubtedly the belief in rebirth and Karma. This, as popularly understood, differs hardly at all from the corresponding Hindu doctrine from which it was, of course, derived. The important modifications made by the Buddha, in consequence of his having done away with a substantial self or soul, are known only to the more learned, and for the layman are almost non-existent. For him the truth is very simple : one dies, goes to heaven or hell for a shorter or longer period, until a certain amount of his merit or demerit has been consumed, and then is reborn into this world in accordance with the deeds done in his former body. In a general way this belief is borne out by the orthodox Buddhist teaching—which in fact provides not only rebirth and several heavens and hells, but also a preliminary and intermediate state which two Buddhist authorities (Professor Rhys-Davids and Mr. F.L. Woodward) translate "purgatory". There is however, no place in the orthodox philosophy for the popular belief in the reward and rebirth of the identical individual. Since for Buddhism the self is merely a collection of qualities, there is no real self or ego to be rewarded or reborn. This *anatta* doctrine of the merely phenomenal nature of the self is, as I have indicated, quite unknown to most laymen and to the less learned of the monks;

but many monks there are in both Burma and Ceylon who understand and hold it and teach it in quite the manner of Nagasena in his famous conversations with King Milinda in the classic days of Buddhism The Hermit of Mandalay Hill expounded it to me by asking; "Where, sir, is the monastery? Is this column the monastery? Is this brick the monastery? Surely there is no being known as *the monastery* here to be found. So there is no self, but only a collection of members and of characteristics—name and form". This is sound Buddhist doctrine, and however it pleases us we must admit that it is surprisingly modern in tone and thoroughly consistent with Western science and philosophy. In essentials it is the doctrine of Hume, of Friedrich Paulsen and William James, of Pragmatism and of most modern psychology.

But if there be no ego or soul, what is there to be reborn? The "Buddhist Catechism", by Subhadra Bhikshu (which as I said in the last chapter is used as a textbook in some of the Buddhist schools and is, perhaps, as authoritative a presentation of Buddhism as can be found in any modern summary) answers this question as follows :—

"It is our will-to-live and our moral character that are reborn. These form the core of our being, and create for themselves after the disintegration of our present body a new one, corresponding exactly to their nature".

The "Catechism" goes on to ask :—

"Then the being which is reborn is not the same which died?"

And the answer is :—

"It is not the same and not another. It may seem to be another to a man still in the state of ignorance, who wrongly identifies his personal ego-consciousness with his true being. He who has attained wisdom knows that his real being is his will-to-live and his moral character ["Tanha" and "Karma"];

but that the recurring ego-consciousness is only a transient phenomenon, to be compared to the torch lit by a wanderer at night to find his way. When he does not need it any more he extinguishes it, to light a new torch for a later wandering. Thus, though the ego-consciousness may change, it is in a sense by the tie of Karma always the same individuality which in one birth does the good or bad deeds and in the next reaps the fruits of these deeds, though in the absence of any substance passing from one life to the next it is not absolutely the same."[2]

But just as there are few disciples of Hume who consistently speak as if the self were merely "a bundle or collection of different perceptions", so there are few Buddhists who carry out their doctrine of the ego in all its logical implications. Possibly heaven, hell and "purgatory", for which chapter and verse in the sacred books can be cited, may be made consistent with this doctrine. But it is harder to see how on this view there is any hope for the reunion of friends on the other side of death. And yet this hope certainly is held by some in both Burma and Ceylon, and even justified as a possibility by some of the scholars of Buddhism.[3]

There is, then a practical kind of agreement between learned and ignorant on the question of heaven, hell, and rebirth. And concerning retribution and the law of Karma there is even more complete unanimity. All Buddhists believe with the Hindus that sequence of reward following upon good deeds and punishment following evil deeds is eternal and inevitable; that what we sow we reap through endless ages. Whether high or low, ignorant or learned, the Buddhist has an unshakable and unquestioning, almost a naive, confidence in the absolute justice of the universe.

There is no such unanimity between the ignorant and the learned on the question of the present condition of the

Buddha—a question of very practical importance considering his central position in Buddhist thought and worship. The more ignorant Buddhists—including some even of the monks—accept the Buddha to all practical purposes as a god. For many of them he leads a conscious and joyous existence, hears the prayers of his followers and answers them. This, of course, is not the orthodox view, and all the more intelligent monks will assure you that the Buddha is beyond hearing petitions or answering prayers. In the worlds of a monk in Kandy and of another in Galle with whom I talked and whose English was not so good as their Pali, "Buddha *finish*". A monk in Rangoon put it thus : "Buddha is not living; he is beyond consciousness and has neither consciousness nor soul. He is inactive and can do nothing for us actively. He lives only in his teachings. He is in Nirvāṇa." And a monk at Mandalay put it in much the same way : "Buddha is non-existent so far as we know, and has no consciousness of what happens here. He certainly does not hear prayer. He is in Nirvāṇa."

As the words of both these monks suggest, the question of the Buddha's present status inevitably raises in the Western mind the question of the nature of Nirvāṇa. I say "in the Western mind", for Nirvāṇa as a state after death certainly plays a much more important part in Western ideas of Buddhism than in the thoughts of Buddhists. The masses know they have so little chance at Nirvāṇa for thousands of years that they do not much trouble their heads over its nature. And the two most intelligent Buddhists I ever met assured me that the fact that I asked about Nirvāṇa showed I was going at Buddhism from the wrong—the Western—end. And, indeed, they have the authority of the Buddha himself for their words. In the Majhima-Nikaya we are told that this question of the condition of the saint after death once presented itself to the venerable Malunkyaputta, one of Gautama's favorite disciples. And he said to himself :—

"These questions which the Blessed One has left unelucidated, has set aside and rejected—whether the world is eternal, whether the world is infinite, whether the saint exists after death—these the Blessed one does not elucidate to me. And the fact that the Blessed One does not elucidate them to me does not please me. I will therefore draw near to the Blessed One and inquire of him concerning this matter."

So he arose and drew near to the Blessed One and put his questions, closing them by saying :—

"If the Blessed One knows that the world is eternal, or that the world is infinite, or that the saint exists after death, or that he does not exist after death, let the Blessed One elucidate these things to me. If the Blessed One does not know, the only upright thing for one who does not know, who has not that insight, is to sav. 'I do not know : I have not that insight'.

To this the Buddha responded :—

'Pray, Malunkyaputta, did I ever say to you, 'Come, Malunkyaputta, lead the religious life under me and I will elucidate to your whether the world is eternal or infinite and whether the saint exists or does not exist after death? Malunkyaputta, any one who should say, 'I will not lead the religious life under the Blessed One until the Blessed One shall elucidate to me these questions; that person would die, Malunkyaputta, before the Perfect One had ever elucidated them to him. It is as if a man had been wounded by an arrow thickly smeared with poison, and his friends and companions, his relatives and kinsfolk, were to procure for him a physician; and the sick man were to say, 'I will not have this arrow taken out until I have learned whether the man who wounded me belonged to the warrior caste, or the Brahmin caste, or to the agricultural caste, or to the menial caste'; or as if he were to say, 'I will not have this arrow taken out untill I learn the name of the man who wounded me and to what clan he belongs; or till I have learned whether he was black, or dusky, or of a yellow skin; or till I have learned whether the arrow was an ordinary arrow, or a claw-headed arrow, or an iron arrow, or a calf-tooth arrow.' That man would die, Malunkyaputta, without ever having learned this. In exactly the same way, Malunkyaputta, any one who should say, I will not lead the religious life under the Blessed One until he shall elucidate to me whether the world is eternal and whether the saint exists after death,—that person would die, Malunkyaputta, before the Perfect One had ever elucidated this to him.

"The religious life does not depend on the dogma that the world is eternal or infinite, or that the saint exists after death, Whether these doctrines are true or false there still remain birth, old age, death, sorrow, lamentation, misery, grief, despair, for the extinction of which in the present life I am prescribing. Accordingly, Malunkyaputta, bear always in mind what it is that I have not elucidated. And why have I not elucidated these questions? Because they profit not, they have not to do with the fundamentals of religion, therefore have I not elucidated them."[4]

The Buddha, in short, insisted—and he did it repeatedly and consistently—that he came not to teach philosophy, but to save the world. And in this he showed his wisdom. He would not allow the attention of his followers to be deflected from the main issue. He was determined that the emphasis should be put in the right place. Were he alive today he would probably point out to us how sadly religion has suffered—how sadly Christianity has suffered—by the confusion of the religious life with metaphysics; and how the union of religion with speculation lays it open to certain and unnecessary attack. The state of the saint after death—Nirvāṇa—may be conscious or it may not; but in neither case has it anything to do with "absence of passion, quiescence, and supreme wisdom."

But while it is true that the Buddha never committed himself on the question whether the saint existed or did not exist after death, and while doubtless the orthodox Buddhist should follow his example, there is still something to be gleaned from the sacred books concerning Nirvāṇa, and nearly all the monks, learned and ignorant alike, have more or less decided views on the subject. One monk, who had evidently read widely in Buddhist literature, told me that Nirvāṇa was "eternal happiness". This "happiness", he said, was a very different thing from *pleasure*. There was no pleasure in Nirvāṇa, nothing worldly; but Nirvāṇa was a state of *conscious* happiness none the less and by no means a cessation of consciousness. An upasaka who taught Buddhism in a boys' school told me practically the same thing : to use his own words, Nirvāṇa means "eternal comfort"; and the abbot of the leading Malwatta[5] monastery in Kandy agreed with him in this definition. Probably this is the view that many monks and laymen hold. On the other hand, the majority of the learned monks with whom I have talked in both Burma and Ceylon, as well as several of the laymen, insisted that Nirvāṇa is not a conscious state at all. I quoted to the monk at Galle (to whom I referred above) the definitions of Nirvāṇa as "eternal happiness" and "eternal comfort," and he asserted stoutly that these views were absolutely mistaken. In his own picturesque word again, Nirvāṇa means "finish" :—"comfort and happiness finish as well as discomfort and sorrow". Something like this was the view of most of the monks with whom I talked, and it certainly would seem to be the logical conclusion from the premises. For when Karma and the will-to-live cease to act, even the shadow of a self which Buddhism recognizes ceases to exist. As there is nothing and no one to be conscious, and no reproduction of name, form, characteristics, or "Khandas," it is hard to see how Nirvāṇa can be anything but the end of consciousness—in other words, "finish"! Such was evidently the reasoning of the monks with whom I talked. And they almost all added that they longed for Nirvāṇa because conscious life was necessarily evil. The *people,* they told me,—and I thought this significant,—did not really want Nirvāṇa. What *they* desired was heaven and a good rebirth.

One old monk, however, with whom I had a long interview through and interpreter, had a more agnostic view concerning Nirvāṇa. The boy or young man who had come with me to interpret was a very well-informed and thoughtful Buddhist. We had a long talk on our way to the monastery concerning the Buddhist and the Burmese view of life, and he had assured me that may of the Burmese, in spite of their gay exterior, were sad at heart; and that for his own part, life seemed to him a rather dreary thing. When we reached the monastery and I had asked my question about Nirvāṇa, the monk defined it as a state where there is no more birth, old age, or death. The boy then added, of his own motion, that Nirvāṇa is equivalent to being totally dead; that it is as if the death of the body ended it all—except, of course, that Nirvāṇa can be attained only after a series of lives. When the monk learned what the boy had said he corrected him, insisting that we cannot possibly know so much as this. Nirvāṇa, he added, may have a kind of consciousness, and may contain a great deal of which we are entirely ignorant and at which we cannot even guess. All we know is that it is the end of birth, old age, and death, the end of lust, ill-will and ignorance. It is like a house of which we see the outside only and not the inside. We know the way thither, but what is within we can not tell. The boy was obviously much impressed by this view and said this was the first time he had ever heard such a description of Nirvāṇa. On our walk back from the monastery he returned to the subject and dwelt upon it long and thoughtfully. The possibility that Nirvāṇa might be in any sense conscious instead of blank non-existence came to him, he said, with unhoped-for comfort. Hitherto it had seemed to him (for so he had always been taught) that conscious existence inevitably involved suffering, and life had seemed to him necessarily melancholy. He had longed for Nirvāṇa as complete cessation of existence and the only possible escape. But if conscious life was really possible without sorrow, he would welcome it eagerly. And he added, "The Lord Buddha must have known what was in Nirvāṇa; and why did he not tell us? If he only had told us it would have made everything so much easier and life so much happier!" I did not venture to suggest that possibly the Lord Buddha himself did not know. I only pointed out that the tẹaching of Christianity was in some way similar to what the monk of the fetters that bind us here. The boy responded, "Christianity is certainly very much more comforting than Buddhism and if I only could believe it true I would be glad to accept it. But the question is, *Is it true*?"

None of the Buddhists whom I questioned in either Burma or Ceylon had any hope of attaining to Nirvāṇa in the next incarnation, and none of them except Mr. Dharmapala and his brother Mr. Hewavitarna (the leaders of the Maha-Bodhi movement) made any reference to the common view of the Pitakas that Nirvāṇa may be attained in this life. Instead of adopting this orthodox Buddhist view the Burmese Buddhists put off the hour of the attainability of Nirvāṇa to the indefinite distant future, and all my Ceylonese acquaintances, with the two exceptions named above, said very definitely that no man now living could attain to Nirvāṇa before the coming of Maitreya Buddha—which some placed about twenty-five hundred years from now, and others at an indefinitely later period. Mr. Kenneth Saunders, whose knowledge of both Singhalese and Burmese Buddhism is very extensive, testifies that he never met or heard of any Buddhist who expected to attain Nirvāṇa in his next birth, and none of the respondents to his Ceylonese Questionnaire had ever heard of any. This is rather surprising considering the unmistakable teaching of the Pitakas that Nirvāṇa is attainable in this life. Subhadra's "Catechism", which adopts this latter view, makes a distinction (based on the Pitakas) between the Nirvāṇa which one may attain in this life, and the state which follows upon the death of one who has attained Nirvāṇa, a state which it distinguishes by the name "Parinirvāṇa". I shall close our discussion of this subject by three quotations from this authoritative little book :—

"Nirvāṇa is a state of mind and heart in which all desire for life or annihilation, all egoistic craving has become extinct, and with every passion, every grasping desire, every fear, all ill-will, and every sorrow. It is a state of perfect inward peace, accompanied by the imperturbable certainty of having attained deliverance, a state words cannot describe, and which the imagination of the worldling tries in vain to picture to himself. Only one who has himself experienced it knows what Nirvāṇa is."

"The individuality continues to appear in constantly recurring embodiments until perfect wisdom and moral purification, Nirvāṇa, are attained. Then after the death of the last body it becomes totally extinct in Parinirvāṇa." "Parinirvāṇa, in the sense of other religions and of scientific materialism, is indeed, total annihilation, complete dissolution of the individuality, for nothing remains in Parinirvāṇa which in any way corresponds to the *human conception of existence.* But from the point of view of one who has attained to the state of the Araha [*i.e.*, to Nirvāṇa, in this life], it is rather the world with all its phenomena which is 'nothingness', a reflected image, an iridescent bubble, a terrifying dream; and Parinirvāṇa is the entrance into real existence, into the eternal, unchangeable, imperishable, where there is no diversity, no strife, and no suffering".

"It is not possible to form any idea of Parinirvāṇa : it is beyond all knowledge, beyond all conception. It cannot be said that it is or that it is not, because no forms of existence are applicable to Parinirvāṇa. One can only say it is final emancipation, the complete extinction of individuality—eternal rest and peace. "There is, O disciples, a state where there is neither earth nor water, neither air nor light, neither infinity of space nor infinity of time, neither any form of existence nor nothingness, neither perception nor non-perception, neither this world nor that world. There is neither coming into existence nor decay, neither birth nor death, neither cause nor effect, neither change nor stability. There is, O disciples, an unborn, unoriginated, uncreated, unformed. Were there not, there would be no escape from the world of the born, originated, created, formed.' Thus sayeth the Master."[6]

Whatever this may mean, it is evident that the Buddha, who long ago passed into Parinirvāṇa, is far removed from this world of ours, out of earshot of all our prayers, out of sight of all our offerings, and can neither influence us nor be influenced by us. As the monk in Galle put it, Buddha finish. That being the case, the important and practical question arises, Of what use are worship, prayer, and offering?

Most Buddhist laymen, I suppose, have no answer to this question and no explicit theory about it. Their position is that of one of their number with whom I used to talk in Mandalay. He told me first that Buddha is in Nirvāṇa and knows nothing of our prayers and praises. Then I asked him whether he prayed to Buddha is in Nirvāṇa and knows nothing of our prayers and praises. Then I asked him whether he prayed to Buddha for definite things, such as success in business, and he answered, Yes. I asked whether he thought these prayers were answered and he said he supposed so. When, then, I asked how he could make this consistent with his view of the inaccessibility of Buddha, and how he accounted for the effectiveness of his prayers, he said he didn't know. He saw the inconsistency plainly, and said his prayers were not due to any theory on the subject, but merely to a habit which he had acquired in childhood, from his parents.

Buddhists less learned in their religion than he, of course, have no such logical difficulties to face. Those who regard the Buddha practically as a god, living in heaven and hearing prayer, naturally pray to him. And this I may call the first of three theories of prayer which one finds implicit among the Buddhists. The almost irrepressible human demand for help when human help fails forces many a Buddhist to turn in prayer to the Blessed One, even if he has learned from some monk that petition to the Buddha is vain. Fielding Hall reports such a prayer bursting from the heart of a mother for the recovery of her first born. And Sounders, in reporting the answers to his Ceylonese Questionnaire, says of the Singhalese women; "It is they who frequent the temples, coming with simple offerings of flowers and a pathetic wish or prayer, 'May I be born beautiful as these in my next life!' Or one may be seen offering strands of her hair and ejaculating, 'May I be born with hair long and lustrous!' Or again a pregnant woman will offer white or yellow flowers hoping to have a fair child."[7]

Those who accept the doctrine that petitions to the Buddha are useless are not, however, thereby deprived of the use of prayer. For the nats or devatas stand always ready, and they are easily to be influenced by petitions and promises. For this reason some of these lower beings assume in the worship of a large part of the laity a much more important position than the Buddha himself. It is the old story of the "high gods of low peoples" to which Andrew Lang and others have drawn attention. The shrine of the deva of Adams Peak is much more popular than that of the Buddha on its summit : for the deva, as every one knows, can hear and answer prayer and may be influenced by the promise of an offering, not to say a bribe; whereas the Buddha—he is in Nirvāṇa! Nor is it the ignorant layman alone who makes prayers and offerings to the lower spirits. Several of the months of my acquaintance do the same, and the learned monk I found in the Galle Vihara told me of the most approved way of doing it. One makes a request to the deva and promises that if it is granted an offering will be made to the Buddha and the merit from this offering will be handed over to the deva—for devas are in as great need of merit as we, and merit (as we shall see) is transferable. This, the monk assured me, however, was not to be regarded as *religion*, but merely as *business*. It was, he said, like making a contract with Government. Religion has to do with the Teacher.

The strictly logical Buddhist view, of course, makes petitional prayer quite useless. And this is what we may call the second theory. Gautama himself held this view, and in illustration of its once said to a Brahmin : "What would you think if this stream were swollen up to the edge and a man whose business called him to the other side came up here and shouted out : 'Come over here, O thou other shore! Come over to my side!' What would you think Would all his calling and praying and beseeching and hoping bring over to him here that other shore? Even like this man are you Brahmins when ye say : 'Indra, we call to Thee! Soma, Varuna, Brahman, we call to Thee!"[8] In similar vein a monk in the Gangarama Vihara, near Kandy, said to me : "You Christians believe in '*God*' and pray to him. That is like children crying out in a storm. You are trusting to something you know nothing about. We Buddhists do nothing of the kind—we rely on ourselves alone."

This second, and logical, Buddhist view of prayer, of course, does away only with petition: other forms of worship are regularly practiced—and consistently—by the most logical monks. They make no prayers in the sense of petitions, but they recite every day certain texts of praise to the Buddha and of consecration of themselves. With a few these praises are genuine outbursts of praise to the Great Teacher, long since passed away, who showed the Path of Escape from sorrow. But this spontaneous outburst of gratitude is probably very uncommon. The whole Buddhist training is against impulse and cultivates a colder and more reasoning action. Most of those who accept what I call the second theory of prayer perform their worship for a very definite reason. They do it (and this is an interesting point) consciously and deliberately for the sake of its good subjective effects upon themselves. A monk in Rangoon said to me, "Prayer and offering are not received by the Buddha in the sense that they have any effect upon him, nor in the sense of being means of procuring anything from him. Their value is subjective purely. A prayer for purity or peace is likely to bring about its own fulfillment, especially if accompanied by the thought of the Buddha as our ideal. But he is the ideal of what humanity might be and of what each one of us ought to be. Thus prayer for the enlightened Buddhist is not supplication, but mental discipline."[9]

In like manner the offerings which the strictly logical Buddhist makes are in part performed out of gratitude to the Master and as a mark of honor to him, just as we put flowers, year after year, on the graves of those we have loved long ago; in part the offerings like the "prayers" are made for their subjective effect upon the worshiper and upon all those who see them. This is particularly true of flowers. Flowers are used not merely for the sake of their beauty as a gift on the shrine of the Blessed One. Their fading in the shrine and the subsequent necessity of casting them out to wither and disintegrate is an integral part of the ceremony and one of the aims of the offering. For this should keep the worshiper ever in mind of the fact that as these beautiful and fragrant flowers wither, so must his body and the most beautiful human bodies die and decay, in this world where all is transitory.

But there is a third theory of prayer and offering which is a compromise between the two others, and which is interesting as being particularly Buddhistic. It is a kind of extension of the subjective view of prayer—an effort to retain the subjective view and at the same time get the advantages of the objective view by applying ethical and psychological categories to the universe. The monk in Rangoon said to me: "An intense wish, when accompanied by an offering or by merit of any kind, will tend to bring about its own satisfaction,—either in this life or in another. This is plainly true of spiritual things—as the desire for purity or peace. But it is also true of physical and worldly things. Thus, if I desire wealth and pray for it, accompanying my prayer with an offering to the Buddha (for this is a way of acquiring merit), my desire is likely to be satisfied in this life or another."

I think this theory of prayer is the one most commonly held by the intelligent monk. The Buddhist is persuaded that this is essentially a moral universe; a universe in which the law of Karma—which is a moral rather than a merely physical law—reigns supreme. A good act, he is persuaded, can never fail of its reward, nor an evil one of its punishment—except, of course, in the sense that the two may balance each other as debits and credits in the cash account of the universe. He is certain that the Buddha cannot hear or answer prayer, yet, on the other hand, he is equally sure that prayer and offering to the Buddha are infallible means of acquiring merit and will be imputed to him for righteousness, and that this righteousness can in no wise lose its reward. Hence the prayer or recitation of the sacred text must have a value and a power of its own; it must work automatically and start forces going in the universe which will in their own good time have the desired effect upon his destiny.

It may very well seen odd to the reader that, in all these pages which I have already devoted to Buddhism, not a word has been said of what undoubtedly is the very heart of the Buddha's teaching—the "Four Noble Truths" of sorrow and salvation. This omission, or rather delay, has been quite intentional; for the Four Noble Truths, though fundamental in the philosophy of Buddhism, play a less important part in the religion of Buddhism, play a less important part in the religion of the people than do prayers and offerings, hopes and moral customs. But the Four Noble Truths are of great indirect importance even to popular religion, and must be dealt with carefully before we can understand Buddhism or form a just opinion as to its value.

The First Noble Truth was expressed by Gautama himself in the following words; "Birth is suffering, old age is suffering, disease is suffering, death is suffering: painful is it to be joined to that which we do not like: painful is separation from that which we do like. In brief: all the five Aspects of Existence are suffering."[10] The repeated emphasis laid upon the fact of suffering in the discourses of the Buddha, and the fidelity with which his teaching of it has been handed on and imitated, have given Buddhism the reputation of being the most pessimistic of religions. Buddhists who read European books on their religion are becoming today very sensitive, not to say touchy, on this subject. You may criticize Buddhism to a Buddhist on other points, but it is best not to tell him that his religion is pessimistic. Buddhism, we are assured, is in truth the most *optimistic* of religions. It merely points out the undoubted facts of sorrow which every religion and every philosophy must recognize, and then it goes on the show the way of escape. I cull the following sentences from an article in the "Buddhist Review" for June, 1912, entitled "The Optimism of Buddhism" : "Buddhism recognizes sorrow, recognizes evil, but it does not say, 'Blessed are the sorrowful.' It teaches that sorrow and evil are things to be recognized, but also to be grappled with and escaped from. It does not teach that man is but a worm, that his troubles and trials are a rod sent for the purposes of chastisement and that if he would know true happiness he must kiss the rod ..... Buddhism is a religion not of passivity but of activity, and it is a continual endeavor to escape from evil. ..... Buddhism is opposed to pessimism, the gospel of feebleness and failure, at every step of the way."[11]

All this is undoubtedly true. Buddhism recognizes the evils of life only that it may arouse us to save ourselves from them. It is a religion of activity and effort and courage, not one of weakness and surrender. And yet it must be admitted that there is more ground for the common view of the pessimistic nature of Buddhism than the above quotation would imply. Buddhism is founded upon a recognition of the sorrows of life in a way that no other religion is.[12] It was not by chance, but as result of very logical thinking, that the Buddha began his first sermon—and many another sermon—with the Noble Truth of Suffering which I have quoted above. It is necessary to realize that life is very evil—much more evil than good—if you are to be converted to Buddhism. This is fundamental, for without this realization you will have no wish for the salvation which the Buddha offers. "One thing only", said he to his disciples,—"one thing only do I make known : suffering and deliverance from suffering." And a recent writer in the "Buddhist Review" adds : "The question of deliverance from suffering seems to the Buddha of such great, of such commanding importance for the welfare of all beings that, in the last analysis, he considers this problem the only one really worthy of solution."[13]

And this view of the sorrow of life is so fundamental in the Buddha's teaching that it has colored the professional Buddhist world. Nearly all the monks with whom I talked assured me that life was very dreary and existence necessarily sorrowful, and that they would like to be rid of it and enter Nirvāṇa. When it is remembered that a large proportion of these monks consider Nirvāṇa to be equivalent to absolute death, it will be seen that their view of life is hardly optimistic. The confession of the boy in Rangoon concerning his views of life and Nirvāṇa, recited a few pages back, should be recalled in this connection. Neither the Burmese nor the Singhalese are naturally a melancholy race, but the monks have learned from Buddhism that they should at least try to regard the world as bad and its pleasures worthless and cultivate a taste for Nirvāṇa. An interesting light was shed on the matter for me by one of the Mandalay monks, who, when I asked whether he really thought life so very evil and really longed for the non-existence of Nirvāṇa, replied : "Yes, I do during meditation. I then realize the evil of life and long to be free of it. But at other times,—when conversing or eating, for instance—I forget what I realized in meditation. At such times life seems good and I don't want to give it up; and so for a time I become a bad Buddhist."

Buddhism differs from other religions in its view of life, not in recognizing the presence of evil, and that therefore our changing existence is necessarily and thoroughly bad. Not only is sorrow bad in itself, but pleasure is not really good, even while it lasts, because it cannot last forever. It ends in sorrow and life ends in death. He who is a mere creature of circumstance, passing from temporary pleasure to loss and grief, tossed about at the mercy of his emotions and never the master of them, is surely a pitiful figure. Is there no refuge from sorrow that one can *count* on; no method of escape that depends not on external chance but on ourselves?

The Buddha goes at the question as no other founder of a religion ever did. His method and spirit and essentially scientific. He appeals to no supernatural power, and makes use of no blind faith. Instead of this he asks first of all, What are the symptoms of our common disease? and secondly, What are the symptoms of our common disease? and secondly, What is the cause of these symptoms? And the answer to this second question he announces in the Second Noble Truth. The cause of suffering is always *desire*. We are unhappy because we have not got—and cannot get—what we want. There is no doubt that this conclusion of his was at first an empirical judgment, and that in a very great many cases it can be tested and verified by an appeal to experience. But experience cannot verify it in all cases. How, for instance, shall I explain an inherited and painful disease as the result of desire? If, indeed, I could cease to desire to get rid of pain, pain would cease to be an evil. But even so the pain antedated the desire, hence cannot have been caused by it. Yet Gautama believed that his formula would apply to such cases as this also, and that even here desire was the ultimate cause of the pain. The disease, he said, is due to the man's desire and ignorance in a previous existence. Thus, without realizing the fact, he mingled an adopted Brahmanical belief with his own empirical discovery.

The Third Noble Truth makes the obvious application of the second—namely, that by overcoming desire we may avoid sorrow—and extends this obvious application by asserting (again in part upon the strength of the prevalent Indian doctrine of Karma) that continued rebirth may be prevented by killing out the will-to-live, which is at the basis of all our ills. The most important part of the Buddha's doctrine, however, was always that relating to this life, and based upon his own empirical discovery. "The Bhagava has well preached the Dhamma, productive of immediate results *in this life*, of immediate results that can be pointed out to any one by asking him to come and see."[14]

The method by which we may kill out desire and the will-to-live, and rid ourselves of the three great fetters of lust, anger, and spiritual blindness, is given in detail in the Fourth Noble Truth, called also the Noble Eightfold Path. This is in fact a method of mental training, a systematic manner of life which if diligently followed will gradually weed out the worldly wishes, and substitute for the hot desire after personal enjoyment the calm, self-possessed character of the man who is his own master and may laugh at Fate, just because he has learned to despise all the slings and arrows of outrageous Fortune.

This is the Buddhist method of salvation; this was the

Buddha's great discovery. He came to it, a Buddhist friend of mine suggests, by a knowledge of child psychology. For years he had been searching for peace and freedom from the power of fortune. He had tried religion with its ceremonies and prayers and faith, he had tried philosophy, and he had tried asceticism. All had failed. Then, casting his thoughts back over the course of his life, he asked himself when in the whole of it he had been really without care. And he saw that his one really free and happy time had been as a young child. Then, analyzing out of the child's mental condition that element which determined its freedom from care, he saw that this was its lack of self-consciousness and individuality. The baby does not say, "This is mine! I own that! I plan thus and so!" And hence it is at peace.

Whether the Buddha ever went through any such course of thought as my friend suggests, he certainly believed—as his orthodox followers do today—that the obstacle to real self mastery and perfect peace, as well as the source of most sorrow and most sin, is to be found in the over-emphasis upon the ego. "T is self whereby we suffer."[15] The man who has learned to deny himself, to pub aside all egoistic aims, and to look down upon all personal pleasures, is the man who may snap his fingers at Fate, because he has found a peace which the world can never give nor take away. "To understand that, after all, it is the individuality, with its wants and desires opposed to those of other individualities, which causes all suffering in the world, that therefore the striving for individual happiness is according to its very nature wrong, and that it is best to relinquish it voluntarily—that is to take a great step, yea, the greatest, on the road to true knowledge."[16] "The craving for life is the worst of all diseases," says the Dhammapada, "individuality is the greatest of all evils. He who knows this truly sees in Nirvāṇa the highest bliss." It was for this reason that the Buddha laid so much stress on what would seem a purely academic question, the non-existence of a substantial self. The self we love in self-love is only a delusion, and from this delusion, this ignorance, springs all our woe. He whose eyes have been opened to the truth sees that the so-called "self" is a mere stream of passing and perishing psycho-physical phenomena; and there being for him no more delusion of self, all selfish interests with their feverish brood of desires, disappointments, sins, and sorrows vanish away, and only the great Peace, with its new kind of joy that cannot wane, is left behind.

It will thus be evident that the salvation which the Buddha offers is different in kind from that which the followers of most other religions seek after. It is not a life of happiness in some distant heaven that we are to go to after we die; it is a new character that may be won here and now. We all know the two types of people whom the Buddha would recognize as the lost and the saved. One clings to life and its ploeasure, hot with desires, lusting and robust, perhaps, or it may be even sickly, but always desiring, greedy of good things, filled with will and self-assertion; the other quiet, seeking little or nothing, ready for anything, with no intense pains, pleasures, or longings, neither wishing for life nor fearing death. To change from the first type to the second is the Buddha's way of salvarion. And it is not merely the *way* of salvation : it is salvation itself. The new character acquired through the long course of self-training outlined in the Noble Eightfold Path means peace and freedom from care and an equipoise of mind which bid defiance to the thousand frets of ordinary life. Gautama may be said to have anticipated the "Don't worry cure" : and his message and method might come as a great boon to our hustling and neurotic age. The common expression, "Blessed be nothing," the Buddha meant quite literally. If you have nothing and want nothing you will be blessed. For sorrow comes just from having and wanting. In all literalness, it is easier for a camel to go through the eye of a needle than for a rich man to enter the Buddhist Nirvāṇa. But if you give up all your possessions and all thought of ever having any and cut all the ties that bind you to this world, there will be little left to sorrow or worry over. Don't be afraid, says the Buddha, for there is really nothing worth fearing. The only thing worthy of fear is slavery; and you may break your own bonds if you only will.

"In him who has intercourse with others affections arise, and then the pain which follows affection : considering the misery that originates in affection, let one wander alone like a rhinoceros.

"Seeing bright golden bracelets, well-wrought by the goldsmith, striking against each other when there are two on one arm, let one wander alone like a rhinoceros.

"Thus, if I join myself with another I shall swear or scold : considering this danger in future, let one wander alone like a rhinoceros.

"The sensual pleasures, indeed, which are various, sweet, charming, under their different shapes agitate the mind : seeing the misery originating in sensual pleasures, let one wander alone like a rhinoceros.

Without covetousness, without deceit, without craving, without distractions, having got rid of passion and folly, being free from desire in all the world, let one wander alone like a rhinoceros.

"Not adorning himself, not looking out for sport, amusement, and the delight of pleasure in the world, being loath of a life of dressing, speaking the truth, let one wander alone like a rhinoceros.

"Having left son and wife, father and mother, wealth and corn and relatives and the different objects of desire, let one wander alone like a rhinoceros.

"Like a lion not trembling at noises, like the wind not caught in a net, like a lotus not stained by water, let one wander alone like a rhinoceros." [17]

There is much that is fine in this ideal; and I for one can seldom write or speal of it without catching some of the Buddhist's enthusiasm. But we must be serious with it and not blink its implications. One cannot wander alone like a rhinoceros and at the same time bide at home and at as beast of burden for the world. The ties that bind man most closely and that lay him most open to the slings and arrows of outrageous fortune, are often not his country, the cause which he serves. Gautama named his only child "Rahula"—a fetter; and in the Dhammapada he is reported to have said: "The wise man does not regard chains or ropes as fetters, but riches, honor, wife and child,—all that draws him down to a worldly life. Therefore he leaves all these with their sorrows and joys and goes forth into solitude." A monk near Kandy who was very learned in his religion said to my wife: "I have a mother and father, brothers and sisters, but I leave them all to them selves so as to think only of my salvation. I have to think of my salvation only and not of other people's. You have a mother and father, brothers and sisters; Leave them all to themselves, do not think about them, but think only of your own salvation. They are ties that bind you to this world." That this was the point of view of many of the early monks comes out plainly in Mrs. Rhys-Davids's recent translation of the Theregathas. Many of the monks who composed these interesting "Psalms" glory in the fact that they have deserted their wives and childern in order to win peace for themselves. And one of them writes thus: "I have vomited forth all desires, loves, hates, and things of beauty. For no one else have I done this: it is only for myself I acted thus."[18]

I do not think that Gautama would have approved of these monks, modern and ancient; but I think their attitude is quite consistent with this part of his teaching. Give no pledges to Fortune is the essence of it. And from this it must inevitably follow that it is folly to adopt the interests of others in such fashion as ever to be in danger of sharing in their grief or caring for their loss. Desire is the cause of sorrow and deliverance from sorrow is the great aim. The wise man may be helpful to others, should be helpful, for thus he will acquire merit for himself,—but he will keep his distance and never allow his affections to become involved nor imperil his peace by sharing their interests. He will retain always the stoical attitude of mind. He may enter into various helpful activities and have various relations with his fellows, but he will do this in such fashion as always to be able to take philosophically whatever happens. He must never love in such a way as to be disturbed by the death or the misery of the loved one. He may participate in a great cause, but only on condition of retaining complete indifference to its success or failure. Indifference and detachment are his great sources of strength and his never-failing armor against sorrow. "Ascending the high tower of wisdom, the wise man gazes sorrowless upon the sorrowing crowd below; wise himself, he looks upon valley.....O joy, in joy we dwell amongst the sickly full of health. In very bliss we dwell serene amidst the careworn."[19]

There is thus something upquestionably selfish about Buddhist salvation. Against selfishness of the cruder-type Buddhism makes unending war; yet this war is prompted by another and subtler kind of selfishness. It denies the existence of the ego, yet its motive force in seeking release the world is a kind of enlightened egoism.

But if I should stop here I should do Buddhism great injustice. For Buddhism teaches a genuine unselfishness and selfforgetfulness with no *arriere pensee* of the main chance in this world or any other. And more important still, this teaching is illustrated by one of the most noble, perfect, and long-continued examples of unselfish service that history and tradition have to record. Whatever we are to think of the assertion in the sacred books that, immediately upon his enlightenment, the Evil One tempted Gautama to enter at once into Nirvāṇa taking his new-won insight with him, and that the Blessed One preferred to defer Nirvāṇa and its joys for many weary years, so that he might instead return to this sad world and give his message to mankind, certain it is that he spent the remainder of his days in loving service to all within his reach and with no thought of reward or escape from sorrow on his part. Jesus' life lasted thirty-three years and his active teaching-mission only three; but for upwards of forty-five years the Buddha was labouring at the spread of his gospel of peace, and when his hair was white and his eyes were dim and his back was bent with the weight of eighty years, he was still plodding of the Master may not be accepted in their details, but there can be no doubt that we have the very spirit of the man and the ideal which he most earnestly inculcated upon his followers in the saying that he could look back over five hundred previous births, and that in each one of them he had given up his life for the benefit of some other creature. And his teaching no less than his practice expresses this all-absorbing love. I cannot here refrain from quoting his great command to his disciples: "Go ye, O Bhikkhus," the Vinaya Pitaka reports him as saying,—"go ye and wander forth for the gain of the many, the welfare of the many, in compassion for the world, for the good, for the gain, for the welfare of gods and men. Proclaim, O Bhikkhus, the doctrine glorious, preach ye a life of holiness, perfect and pure."

How can we reconcile this teaching and this of the Buddha with his doctrine of salvation from sorrow? In truth I do not think we can. The two views are esssentially irreconcilable. And it is their innate irreconcilability and at the same time their inextricable interweaving throughout the teachings of Buddhism that make the philosophy of Buddhism so difficult to grasp. In a long discussion with a most able Buddhist thinker I once pointed out this incosistency in Buddhist doctrine and at length made him see and even admit it. And then he quoted and translated to me some Pali verses in which Gautama says of his doctrine that it is deep, hard to be understood, and not logical. There are, in fact, as it seems to me, three distinct elements in Buddhism which originated quite independently, but which have been interwoven in such fashion that it is extremely diffcult to distinguish them. One of these is the Brahmanical,—the set of beliefs which Gautama either took for granted from the common beliefs of his time, or adopted into his disciples. The great example of the former of these is the belief in rebirth and Karms, which he himself accepted and made much of. The various teachings about heaven and hell, the acquisition of merit and the value of various external acts,—these very likely appealed less to Gautama than to his followers. But in any case they were simply adopted from Brahmanism and became intertwined more or less closely with what may be called the second element in Buddhism—namely, Gautama's own original doctrine, the Four Noble Truths, based upon direct experience of sorrow, sorrow's cause, and the purely psychical way of escape. Besides these two elements there was a third, namely, Gautama's own great sympathetic heart, his unselfish devotion and desire to serve and save his fellows. The attempt is usually made to expound Buddhism as if all of it follwed the Four Noble Truths. To do this successfully is really impossible, because much that is of importance in Buddhist morality and philosophy comes from the two other sources. Thus, for example, how is the First Precept— not to kill—to be derived from the enlightened egoism of the Four Noble Truths? There is no reasom why one who has broken all the bonds, including human sympathy, should not take life with impunity. The real basis for this precept is to be found in Buddha's widereaching love for all sentient creatures, combined with the general Indian belief in future existence and the acquisition of merit.[20] Further examples of this incosistency might be given, and even instances in which the logical consequences of the Four Noble Truths are *at war* with the real desire for service which characterized not only the Buddha but many of his disciples. The first great outbreak of this smouldering inconsistency came when Northern Buddhism gave up as its ideal the Arahat who attains and enters Nirvāṇa, and substituted for him the Bodhisat who deliberately surrenders Nirvāṇa in order to be reborn endlessly and serve his fellows. The same struggle between the two inconsistent ideals within Buddhism is flaming out again to-day, the monks holding to the egoistic aim, the new movement of reform among the laymen holding up the ideal of service. The monks have the advantage of overwhelming numbers; but the reformers have the newer spirit of the age upon their side. The outcome of the struggle will be decisive for Buddhism. For no man and no religion can permanently serve two masters.

REFERENCES

1. *The Questions of King Milinda*, II, I (translated by Rhys-Davids), S.B.E., Vol. XXXIV. (Oxford, Clarendon Press, I 890).
2. Pages 36-37.
3. Cf. an article, "Death and After," by Professor E.J. Mills, in the *Buddhist Review* for October, 1912, especially p. 295. Fielding Hall has a pathetic story of a Burmese women who believed that her dead lover was reborn in the body of her baby, and who when the baby died went herself into the other world hoping to join him

there. *The Soul of a People* (London, Macmillan, 1911), pp. 306-08.

4. Translated by Warren in his *Buddhism in Translations* (published by Harvard University. 1896). pp,. 117-22. I have greatly abbreviated the passage.
5. The most important of the two subdivisions of the Siamese Order of monks in Ceylon. About fifty per cent of Buddhist monks in Ceylon belong to the so-called Siamese Order. There are two other orders, the Amarapura and Ramanya.
6. Pages 22, 61 and 37 of the *Catechism*. I add here the definition of Nirvāṇa given in Colonel Olcott's *Catechism* (p. 33): "Nirvāṇa is a condition of total cessation of changes; of perfect rest: of the absence of desire and illusion and sorrow: of the total obliteration of everything that goes to make up the physical man."
   Paul Carus's *Gospel of Buddha* does not seek, as the two *Catechisms* do, to give a systematic presentation of Buddhist doctrines, but (following the example of the evangelists rather than that of the West-minister divines) times to present the teachings of the founder in his own words or in conscientious paraphrases of them. Hence from this textbook of Buddhism we get only the general teaching of Gautama himself, that Nirvāṇa means "extinction of illusion." *etc.*, and beyond that only silence on the question whether it is a final extinction of personality.
7. *Buddhist Ideals*, Appendix, p. I 34.
8. Quoted by Dahlke, *Buddhist Essays* (London, Macmillan, 1908). p. 142.
9. In this connection it is interesting to note that the two "prayers" which all Buddhists are supposed to recite at daybreak and bed-time every day are the "Refuge" and the "Five Precepts" (See pp. 345 and 348 above.) Although these are recited in Pali, their meaning, according to Mr. Maung Tha Kin, is pretty generally understood by the common people. Hence we may suppose that the recitation, especially of the Five Precepts, exerts some real moral influence upon the life of the modern Buddhist. See. Mr. Kin's paper on "The Profession of Faith" in the *Buddhist Review* for April-June, 1915.
10. From Sutta 22 of the Digha Nikaya.
11. See also another article to the same effect by "Capatin Enriquez, F.R.G.S.," in the *Buddhist Review* for December, 1914.
12. One of the most enthusiastic of Buddhist converts, Paul Dahlke,

writes: "For the Buddhist, the highest is something quite different from what it is for the adherent of another religion. The Buddhist's goal is not heaven, union with any deity; it is freedom from pain. Only in Buddhism does the conception of freedom from pain remain purely a negative thing. Buddhism is the only one among all the religions of the world that is based upon negation, yea, is negation. Hence it has value solely for such as seek the door out of life: in fact, Buddhism is nothing else but the way to this door." (*Buddhists Essays,* pp. 47-48).

13. Nyana Tiloka, "The Quintessence of Buddhism," *Buddhist Review* for January, 1914.
14. Anguttara Nikaya, III, II, 40.
15. Cf. Rhys-Davids's admirable adaptation of Symond's lines, in *Buddhism* (American Lectures, Putnam, 1904, p. 152.
16. Subhadra Bhikshu's *Buddhist Catechism,* p. 69.
17. The Sutta Nipata (translated by Fausboll) III. S.B.E., Vol. x. (Oxford. Clarendon Press, 1881).
18. *Psalms of the Early Buddhists.* Part II, *Psalms of the Brethren.* (Oxford 1913).
19. Dhammapada, 28, 198, 199, My quotations from the Dhammapada are usually taken either from Max Muller's translation (S.B.E. vol. x) or from the translation by Wagiswara and Saunders (*The Buddha's Way of Virtue*, New York, Dutton, 1912); though sometimes I have availed myself of versions by other scholars.
20. In fact this exact precept of "ahimsa" (harmlessness) is to be found in the Brahmanical literature of Gautama's time.

CHAPTER-XV

THE VALUE OF BUDDHISM AND ITS SPRINGS OF POWER

—James Bisset Pratt

It is always very much easier for the theologian to estimate the value of a given religion than for the psychologist or historian. The problem for the former is simple: he has only to analyze the beliefs of the religion in question, compare them with the doctrines of his own authoritative and infallible creed, and so point out its grain of truth and its mass of error. The student of the history or of the psychology of religion is unable to do this, because he is not in possession of any such infallible and authoritative creed. Hence, much as he may envy and admire the theologian, he is forced to follow a humbler and more difficult method. What he must first ask himself, are the values of religion in general which a merely human science can verify? And secondly, How far does the religion in question possess these values? The writer of this book is unfortunately no theologian, and in seeking to estimate the value of Buddhism will be forced to fall back on the more complex and less ambitious method of the psychologist of religion. Hence the only results he can hope to attain will not only be forever open to correction, but even if accepted as true will possess merely secondary importance. For the questions with which this chapter is to deal have to do not with the transcendental truth of Buddhism, but only with its human and humanly verifiable values.

What, then, are the values of religion from a merely

psychological point of view? Various analyses of them might be made, but for our purposes perhaps the simplest and most useful classification may be based upon and derived from the classic division of mental powers into knowing, feeling, and willing. Religion, since (as a psychological phenomenon) it involves the whole mind and is not confined to any one division of it, must have to do with all three of these. And the value of any given religion may be judged, from the psychologist's point of view, by the question, How is it related to human knowledge, to human happiness, and to human conduct?

What, then, first of all, are the bearings of Buddhism on human knowledge, such as science and history? How far are its teachings in conformity with known truth, and what is its relation to the discovery with known truth, and what is its relation to the discovery of further truth? The question is extremely complicated, but we shall simplify it to a considerable extent if we abstract from the various modifications that the teaching of the Buddha has undergone and confine our attention tc the Buddism of the ancient sacred books—i.e., to the teachings of Gautama himself so far as they are reported.

The most obvious and most striking characteristic of Buddhism in its relation to science is the extreme openness of mind that follows necessarily from the Buddhist position. The Buddhist has no infallible authority which must be consulted before he may listen to the scientist. He has no pope who may make definitions *ex cathedra* of faith and morals, no church councils with power to decree the truth, no supernaurally inspired book that cannot err. If he remains faithful to the spirit and admonitions of the Buddha, he has but one guide, which he must always follow no matter where she leads; and this guide is his own reason. A searcher after truth, named Kesaputto, once came to the Buddha and said:

"Master, every priest and monk extols his belief as the only true one and condemns that of others as false. I am troubled by doubts. I do not know whom to believe." The Buddha answered : "Thy doubts are well founded, O Kesaputto. Listen well to my words : Do not believe anything on mere hearsay; do not believe traditions because they are old and handed down through many generations; do not believe anything on account of rumors or because people talk much about it; do not believe simply because the written testimony of some ancient sage is shown to thee; never believe anything because presumption is in its favour, or because the custom of many years leads thee to regard it as true; do not believe anything on the mere authority of thy teachers or priests. Whatever according to thine own experience and after thorough investigation agrees with thy reason, and is conducive to thine own weal and to that of all other living beings, that accept as truth and live accordingly."[1]

This absolute reliance on reason and experience, coupled with a complete disregard for mere authority, is characteristic of all Gautama's teaching. There is a modern note in his words and his attitude that comes to us through these twentyfive hundred years with something like a shock of surprise and which differentiates his religion from all others. He alone of founders and prophets turned away from all supernatural sources of knowledge and attempted to think the thing out for himself, and to recommend his doctrine to others only because it was *scientifically verifiable by an appeal to experience.*

This was possible to him in part because his teaching had nothing to say of the hypothesis of a personal Creator or a personal Problem, and he insistently refused to commit himself upon it. And this atheism, this lack of the mystical element in his religion, which has been so long used as a reproach to it, has become to-day a further recommendation in the eyes of many a modern thinker. For science is atheistic in exactly the same sense as is Buddhism. Neither of them pretends to know how the word came into being; both are agnostic and silent on this point. And both turn away from ultimate problems like this to center their attention, in positivist fashion, on the phenomenal world, the world that is verifiable in human experience and has direct and obvious bearing upon human actions and human weal and woe. If a supernatural realm exists, science cannot see it, and the Buddha (when we confine our attention to the purest form of his doctrine) will not see it. When urged by one of his followers to perform a miracle in order to convert certain non-believers, the Buddha replied: "I despise and reject the miracles of magic power and divination. I and my disciples gain adherents only by the miracle of instruction. "[2]

The parenthetical clause which I inserted above is of some importance. We may say that Buddhism makes no appeal to miraculous agencies, superstition, and mythology; but we may say this provided only we confine our attention to the purest form of Buddhist doctrine. If we take the Buddhism of the Pitakas as a whole, we shall find this pure doctrine interwoven with as large a growth of supernatural stories and fanciful science as is to be found in most other religions. And even if we take refuge in so modern and generally accepted a book as Colonel Olcott's "Catechism," we shall find most of Part V given over to a defense of the "occult" in Buddhist legend and a (successful) attempt to show that all the miracles and wonders of Buddhism are in accord with "modern science." It is needless to add that the "modern science" to which the Colonel makes appeal is of the usual Theosophical variety. Hence. here again it is extremely important to distinguish clearly the three elements of Buddhism pointed out in the last chapter. If we confine our attention to those teachings which come from the Four Noble Truths or from Buddha's love for his fellows, we shall be in no danger of getting involved in the magical and fanciful. But a large part of the teachings of the Pitakas comes from what I have called the Brahmanical source; and the most enthusiastic Buddhist apologist will be unable to deny that this contains much that is unscientific if not highly fanciful. All the supernatural part of the Pitakas is, indeed, taken only symbolically today by modern Buddhists of Western education; and it is quite probable that Gautama would thoroughly approve of their actions. These supernatural tales sprang up out of the popular soil in which Buddhism grew, and have clung about the story of the Master's birth and life quite naturally and inevitably: but they are altogether distinct and very different in tone from those teachings of the sacred books which most clearly came from him. Hence we shall be justified in abstracting from them altogether in our efforts to get at the real essence of Buddhism. But unfortunately by no means all the teachings of the Pitakas which are out of harmony with modern science can be so easily disposed of. Gautama certainly had a science of his own which he took from the Indian science of his day and wove into his system. What are we to do with this? Take, for instance, Buddhist cosmology with his many Kalpas, its long periods of degeneration and its rhythmically recurring destructions and regrowths of the world. It is evident that the Buddha believed in this or something very like it. Or, more important still, take Buddhist psychology. Every modern Buddhist will tell you (and I quote the words of one) that "Buddha was the Supreme Master of psychology."[3] Are we, then, to accept his psychology with its five "Khandas" (body, sensation, perception, discrimination, and consciousness); its list of sense organs (eye, ear, nose, tongue, body, and mind); its twele "Nidanas," and all its other details, taken over as they were from the psychology of 600B.C.[4] One must, in short, take this question seriously, It is easy to say that the Buddha is the supreme master of psychology; but if one adopts his psychology one must reject modern psychology. One cannot play fast and loose with reject modern psychology. One cannot play fast and loose with these things, and run with the hounds and with the hares at the same time.

It is possible, of course, to reject the Buddha's cosmology and his psychology, together with the supernatural references of the Pitakas; but even after this one will still find on one's hands a large part of the Buddhs's inheritance from Brahmanism of which it will not be so easy to get rid, because it is more intimately interwoven with the rest of his teaching. What, for instance, shall one say of rebirth, Karma, "Parinirvāṇa," the imperishable nature of "merit," and inevitable retribution for all deeds according to their moral quality? These beliefs, let us adimt, are on a different footing from those mentioned above. They are not inconsistent—or at least not so obviously incosistent—with modern science. It is quite possible that they are true, and they involve a faith in the moral nature of the universe which is very noble. But are they scientific and verifiable? To judge by the writings of many modern Buddhist apologists—especially Western Palischolars who have given up Christianity and like to call themselves Budddhists—one would suppose that among other advantages over Christianity, Islam, and the rest, Buddhism alone among religions possesses no metaphysical postulates, makes no appeal to blind faith, and is altogether verifiable. Paul Dahlke, for instance, writes:—

"In religions founded upon a revelation, belief in certain supernatural occurrences is indispensable for one to be able truly to call one's self an adherent of the religion. Hence if my understanding will not permit me to accept the dogmas of Christianity,—if the pains with which it threatens and the problems with which it seeks to allure are to me empty words, then, in spite of the strictest obedience of behests of morality, I am not a Christian ..... On the other hand, it is not necessary to believe in order to be a Buddhist. Here belief is dethroned and replaced by knowledge and by understanding ..... In Buddhism faith is purely the product of knowledge: it is mathematical certainty pure and simple."[5]

It would be interesting to see how the doctrine of rebirth would fare if "belief" were to be altogether "dethroned and replaced by knowledge and by undersanding"; and to learn how the absolute justice of Karma is to be demonstrated as a "mathematical certainty pure and simple". Or what shall we say of such a universally accepted Buddshist belief as the following: "The unsatisfied desire for things that it draws the being back into mundane life."[6] Is this a fact of science which has been verified? Does its acceptance demand nothing in the nature of faith?

It is, of coures, natural that born and brought up in Buddhist lands should take beliefs such as these quite for granted and should hardly think of questioning or analyzing them. But is a little odd to see Europeans, trained in Western modes of thought, renouncing Christianity for Buddhism and proclaiming that they do so because Buddhism requires no faith. As a matter of fact, they are not exchanging belief for "mathematical ceraínty"; they are giving up faith in the cosmology of the Hebrews in the first century of our era only to substitute for it a faith in the cosmology of the Hindus in the sixth century B.C.

After all this has been said, however, it must be admitted that Buddhism occupies a peculiarly favorably position in relation to modern science and the advance of thought and knowledge generally. This is due to its fundamental principles already cited, which make reason and verifiable experience supreme, and authority as such of very slight importance. The Pitakas have a very different position in Buddhism from that of the Bide in Christianity, the Vedas in Hinduism, or the Koran in Islam. The Pitakas are authoritative in the way that Euclid is authoritative; not in the sense of Moses, the Rishis, and Mohammed. The modern Buddhist regards his sacred books with great reverence and goes to them repeatedly for instruction: but he considers them true because he finds them reasonable and (to the extent of his researches) verifiable. His reason never abdicates its throne, and he could not comprehend how any one could seriously say, "*Crelo quia impossibile.*"

Hence, toward the unverifiable elements that have become interwoven with the Buddhist doctrine, the modern Buddhist may choose between two attitudes. both of which are at the same time consistent with science and consistent with the spirit and the principles of the Buddha. He may reject some of the Brahmanistic elements and retain others—such as Karma and the ultimate morality of the universe—on faith, as being not indeed verifiable, but at least not inconsistent with science. Or, if he prefers, he may give up all the Brahmanistic elements of Buddhism and take as his religion only the Four Noble Truths and the altruistic teachings of the Buddha; and these, of course, can never be inconsistent with science, and, so far as they demand verification at all, are thoroughly verifiable.

This flexibility of Buddhism certainly gives it a very great intellectual advantage over all other religions as they are commonly understood and practiced today. I do not say that they give it an advantage over the Christianity of the Gospels; but Christianity has had an historical development which has deprived it of much of that flexibility which its founder meant his teachings to possess. It is with something like a shock that one turns from the words of the Buddha to some orthodox Protestant work on the "Plan of Salvation", with its neat cosmic scheme and its anthropomorphic conceptions of the First, Second, and Third Persons of the Trinity; or to a Catholic treatise on the "Infallibility of the Pope," or the necessity of infant baptism. And if we Christians allow our Christianity to be permanently identified with dogmas like these, we must not be surprised if our missionaries have but ill success in Burma and Ceylon, and if every year a few more of our learned men announce their conversion to Buddhism and spread the tidings over the Orient that Christianity is dead.

One of the great prerequisites for a religion that is to live and to serve mankind for long is its ability to grow and to adapt itself to the changing needs and the changing intellectual environments of successive ages. And its free attitude toward authority gives Buddhism this advantage in a preeminent degree. If its leaders know how to utilize this advantage they will have reason to be very hopeful for the future of their religion. Its purified form will probably appeal only to the few. But there will always be a few to whom its appeal will be exceedingly strong. Its very atheism will be a source of strength as well as of weakness. For while the great majority of man kind will doubtless always feel the need of a personal super natural power, there will always be some who do not feel this need and to whom the mystical makes no appeal To these the other great religions have little to offer that they can accept. And it is well that for them there will always be open, as a last refuge, this religion, which, while it cannot lead them to God, can lead them to a very lofty morality, and to the Great Peace.

To what extent *can* Buddhism really lead to peace and how is this possible? What are its relations to human happiness, and what are the springs of its power? It would seem to many at first that Buddhism is more likely to disseminate sadness than joy. And indeed, as I have shown (in spite of the denials of its advocates), the result of Buddhist teaching is very often a melancholy view of life and the destruction of many of its innocent pleasures. Here I need only refer the reader to what was said on this subject in a previous chapter. Life, indeed, has many sorrows, but it also has certain real joys, such as health, success, love. But Buddhism is always trying to embitter these few sweet things with the thought of their insecurity and their impermanence. The Buddhist apologists may say what they like, but there is no denying that nearly all the experiences which we naive Christians, Jews, Parsees, and Mohammedans in our ignorance call the "good things of life", are to the Buddhist evil and to be avoided. Thus the Buddhist in his extreme fear of sorrow—a fear which seems almost an obsession—deliberately cuts himself off from a large number of the positive and solid joys of life. For fear of the pains and disappointments of ordinary social intercourse, he should wander alone like a rhinoceros.

And not only does the Buddhist's fear of sorrow deprive him of much of the happiness that others possess; his philosophy, on the other hand, deprives him of the chief defences which other religions provide against sorrow I refer, of course, to the belief in a personal God, in an immortal soul, and in an eternal life of joyful reunion with those whom one has loved, and in the presence of God. The dying Christian is pointed to Christ and reminded of his endless love; for the dying Buddhist, according to fielding Hall, the only word of comfort is, "Think of your own good deeds!"

It is therefore not surprising to find, as we have found, that the pure Buddhism of Gautama had to be mingled in the very beginning with much popular belief before it could be accepted, and ever since then has been overlaid with one incrustation after another. And it is surely a significant fact that wherever Buddhism has spread, one of the most inveterate tendencies among its converts has been to transform the Buddha himself into a god, and worship him as such. Most human beings are more conscious of their weakness than of their strength, and cry out for aid from some more than human Power which can understand and help them. In like manner, popular Buddhism, even of the Southern type, has to all practical purposes restored the substantial self which philosophical Buddhism banishes, and either substituted heaven for Nirvāṇa, made Nirvāṇa over into a state of "eternal comfort", of neglected it altogether. The truth is that the ideal of peace which the Buddhism of Gautama holds out does not appeal to the masses. If popular Buddhism is to be reformed and put in accord with the teachings of the founder, the people must be taught the unpleasant tidings that the Buddha is altogether dead and gone and there is no personal God or nat or devata to help one; that prayer in the sense of petition is vain; that the goal after which all should strive is non-existence; and that even short of Nirvāṇa, there is no real self that survives death One may wish the reformers well and yet be pardoned for questioning whether such a reformation of the popular faith would work any increase in the happiness of the people.

Buddhism, however, has its consolation in sorrow, or rather several different kinds of consolation. In fact, each of the different elements of Buddhism has its own sort of comfort—warm or cold—to offer, and he who does not like one may try another Thus, in the case of the loss of dear ones, the ignorant Buddhist may hope that the Buddha will reunite him with his beloved in the next life. He to whom Buddhism means almost exclusively the loving service of his fellows will take comfort in increased activity and the effort to live worthily of the one who is gone I met one man of this sort who had lost his father, and who apparently did not look for comfort of any sort. Whether he should ever meet his father again he had no idea, and he did not think about the question. What heaven or Nirvāṇa might be he knew not. There might be another conscious life and a happy one or there might not; but for his own part he found his happiness just in doing his duty and in serving his fellows here and now. Of course there are not many men of this type—in Buddhism or in any other religion. But what ever one may think of this sort of consolation, it speaks well for Buddhism that it can occasionally produce this kind of man For he had drawn his inspiration from the Buddha.

The Buddhist whose religion consists of the Four Noble Truths and the strictly Buddhist method of deliverance will seek his consolation for the loss of friends in still a third way. He will tell himself that death is inevitable and universal and will get what comfort he can out of that. This is evidently the sort of comfort that Gautama himself believed in, for it was thus that he comforted his disciples at the prospect of his own death. "O Ananda," he said, "have I not often declared to thee that it is in the very nature of all things, how so ever dear and beloved they may be to us, that we must divide ourselves from them, leave them, sever ourselves from them? Every thing born, brought into being, and formed, contains within itself the inherent necessity of dissolution." Further than this, for the consistent Buddhist every dear one lost marks a closer approximation to one's own perfect freedom. I asked a Buddhist once what consolation his religion had to offer a mother who had lost her child. He replied by telling me of a woman of his acquaintance whose only son had recently died. At first the woman grieved, but then she took comfort in the thought that she grieved, but then she took comfort in the thought that she had one less tie to bind her to the world.

But Buddhism has more than this negative consolation to give. It does lead—and this is a verifiable fact—to an exhilarating sense of independence, of being one's own master—a deep and abiding peace, a spiritual freedom which is very real. The Buddha said of it : "Whoever hears, sees, and welcomes with joy this methodical arrangement of the Law which is a mine of happiness and prosperity, and honors it with folded hands, shall attain ..... the happiness of perfect contemplation, that deep calm of uninterrupted bliss, with his senses in the highest perfection and illuminated by unclouded knowledge."[7] And again : "He whose appetites are stilled, who is indifferent to food. Whose goal is the freedom which comes of realizing life's emptiness and transiency, is hard to track as the flight of birds in the sky. Even the gods envy him whose senses are quiet as horses well tamed by the charioteer, who has renounces self-will, and put away all taints. No more will he be born whose patience is as the earth's, who is firm as a pillar and pious, pure as some unruffled lake. Calm is the thought, calm the words and deeds of such a one, who has by wisdom attained true freedom and self-control."[8] "O joy! We live in bliss, amongst men of hate, hating none. O joy! In bliss we dwell, healthy among the ailing. Yea, in very bliss we dwell, free from care amidst the careworn. In bliss we dwell possessing nothing; let us dwell feeding upon joy like the shining ones in their splendour. Victory breeds hatred, for the conquered sleeps in sorrow. He who has given up both victory and defeat, he the contented, is happy.[9] He who has tasted the sweetness of solitude and tranquillity is free from fear and free from sin, while he tastes the sweetness of drinking in the Law."[10]

And while we may not be willing to go all the way with the Buddhist, there is no doubt that his freedom from servitude to a world of things and of egoistic desires, and most of all from the tyranny of the self, brings a peace and a joy that the hustling Westerner, with his materialistic ambitions and his constant alternations of hot hopes and chilling fears, knows nothing about.

"Tis not in seeking,
'Tis not in endless striving
Thy quest is found :
Be still and listen,
Be still and drink the quiet
Of all around.
"Not in thy crying,
Not in thy loud beseeching,
will peace draw near :
Rest with palms folded,
Rest with thine eyelids fallen-
Lo, Peace is here."[11]

The Buddhists of Burma and Ceylon, as a matter of fact, impress one as a decidedly happy people and happy in their religion. And this is true not only of the ignorant ones who have made the Buddha into a god, but also of the monks and the better-informed laymen who know quite well that Buddha is dead and gone. Their happiness, indeed, is sedate rather than jubilant; it is a calm and steady peace. The First Noble Truth has, to be sure, thrown a very superficial touch of melancholy over their lives; but on the whole they are, I repeat, a happy people, and they seem to take real joy in their religion. To one who has come to think of the joy of religion as springing from the belief in God, and who has learned that Buddhism is atheistic, this will come with some surprise : and such a one may well ask what are the sources of happiness in Buddhism.

This question can hardly be answered if we stop with the view that Buddhism is atheistic and do not go on to analyze this atheism. It is quite true that Buddhism denies the existence of "God." But while it is atheistic theoretically, it is theistic pragmatically. It has, in fact, a very pragmatic god. And here I have in mind not the religion of the ignorant who pray to nats and devatas and regard Buddha himself as a kind of god or all-powerful being who hears and answers prayers. I refer to the Buddhism of the monks themselves. For this orthodox Buddhist religion, the universe itself, under the guidance and control of the Law of Karma, takes the place of the Christian or Mohammedan God; and as I have said, a very pragmatic god it makes. For the pragmatist every real (and not merely verbal) difference, every real being (and not merely abstract term) must *make* a difference to some one : and the meaning of the term "God" pragmatically will be summed up in those things which God is conceived of as *doing* for us human beings. If you want to know what God means to the believer, ask what things would be different to him if God should, for him, cease to exist. What are these things that God does? Are not the following the more important for the rank and file of believers? (1) God is on the side of righteousness and assures ultimate victory to the ideal. (2) In more concrete phrase, He rewards virtue and punishes sin. (3) He assures to the believer a life after the death of this body, and a life in which the virtuous shall be rewarded and the sinful punished. (4) He hears and answers prayer.

Now, the point I wish to make is that the universe, with its Law of Karma, does for the Buddhist all these things. (1) The Buddhist's universe is at the antipodes from that of the materialist. It is a world of unfailing causal action, yes; but it is a world in which physical laws play a very secondary role to moral laws. As a man sows so shall he reap, teaches the

Buddhist : but this not at all in the sense of the natural scientist, but in that of the moralist. Nature for him is supernaturally moral. The universe itself is a power not ourselves that makes for righteousness. (2) Hence it results necessarily that every virtuous act brings its inevitable reward, and every sin its inescapable punishment. (3) And in order that this may never fail, Buddhism takes a future life of retribution quite for granted. The "anatta" doctrine that there is no substantial ego makes no pragmatic difference here. In heaven, hell rebirth, or Nirvāṇa, every man (however "man" be interpreted) shall, in the course of ages, receive the full reward of all his works, (4) In a very real pragmatic sense, the universe hears and answers prayer. And here I refer to what in a previous chapter I called the third theory of prayer and the one most common among the monks. This orthodox Buddhist theory of the way in which prayer is answered is different from the Christian, but the outcome is the same. For the Christian and Mohammedan, petitional prayer is an appeal to a conscious being who hears and by an act of will grants or refuses the request. In Buddhist theory there is no conscious being to hear or to will; but the universe is such that prayer has a certain amount of power to aid in bringing about its own answer. It is, if you like, a kind of magic. In this world in which physical forces are decidedly secondary to moral ones, prayer itself is a kind of force. You set it going and *something* is bound to result. Your father is ill and you pray to Lord Buddha for his recovery; or, better still, you have certain Pali verses chanted by the monks in honor of the Blessed One, and you accompany the prayer or verses with certain offerings. The Blessed One will not hear anything that is said nor take any note of your offerings; but these prayers and ceremonies will in themselves tend to restore your father to health. They will not do so infallibly any more than the prayer of the Christian will do so, for there are a great number of other moral forces at work and each of them must act as a factor in the total result; but your prayer is sure to have some effect, and it may be just enough to tip the scale. Or, you have sinned and you pray for forgiveness or do whatever corresponds to that in the Buddhist ritual. Your prayer is not heard and no superior being takes pity and pardons you; but your prayer is itself a means of acquiring merit and of counterbalancing the evil Karma which your sin piled up. Thus in a very real sense for the Buddhist all prayer is efficient, in spite of the fact there is no god there to hear it.

The Law of Karma thus acts as a very pragmatic god. I must point out, however, that the Christian God does one thing for the Christian which Karma can never do for the Buddhist. In enumerating above the pragmatic values of the idea of God, I left out what to many will seem the most important of all. I refer to what is called the mystic sense, or the felling of God's presence. For many a religious person—for all deeply religious Christians—this sense that God is near, that He sees and knows and understands, that He actually does hear, forms the chief value of the religious life. This is something for which the Law of Karma offers no substitute. Individuals who prize this personal relation to a personal God would turn sadly away, starved and unsatisfied, if you should tell them that the universe merely acts *as if* it loved and understood. You may assure them that it will give, in this life and the next, all that any god could give, and they will still feel cheated of the best. To use an illustration of William James, the difference is that between loving a woman and loving a cunningly devised automation which acts *as if* it loved you and were conscious of your love. To the true lover there could be nothing more ghastly than the discovery that his beloved is really an unconscious machine, with no loving heart back of its deceptive smile. Better, a thousand times better, he will say, that I had laid her in her grave, and gone mourning all my days, than that I should learn that she whom I loved had really never been. And to the man with any touch of mysticism in him nothing could be more ghastly than the discovery that this universe, which he had taken for the garment of God, for the bodily manifestation of the Great Companion, had in reality no conscious and loving spirit at its heart.

It is the lack of this personal touch that makes the Buddhist Karma so inferior to the Christian God in its power over men's lives. Neither prudential considerations nor moral precepts, nor even admiration for dead heroes and their ideals, ever grip the heart of a man in the way that personal relations to personal beings always do. And this, I think, largely explains the undoubted inferiority of Buddhism to Christianity as a source of happiness, and also as an inspiration for the moral life. The relation of Buddhism to this third value of religion must now be considered.

Different aspects of Buddhism as a moral religion were necessarily dealt with in the preceding chapters, hence not a great deal need be said concerning the moral value of Buddhism here. I do, however, want to point out that the whole complicated question of the ethics of Buddhism becomes very much more comprehensible if we cease to think of Buddhism as a unitary and consistent system, and regard it instead as an amalgam of the three quite different elements into which it was analyzed at the close of the last chapter. Each of these has contributed its share, and the result is that strange combination of the negative and the positive, the puerile and the profound, the selfish and the noble, which makes the moral teachings of Buddhism so difficult to understand.

The Brahmanistic preconceptions which Gautama was forced to bring into his religion, together with various popular accretions that have been added since his time, are responsible for the "sanctions" of heaven, hell, rebirth, and Nirvāṇa, which have played the same large part in the life of Buddhists through the centuries that their counterparts have played in the life of Christians and Mohammedans. There can be no doubt that many a Buddhist is withheld from sin and propelled toward acts of virtue by the thought of Karma and the hope of accumulating a goodly store of merit. On the other hand, the modes of acquiring merit are not always intelligent or uplifting. In spite of the Buddha's insistence upon the futility of merely external works, the various ceremonies at the pagoda or in the home are thought of as having a moral value of their own—a value often greater in merit-acquiring power than that of works of real mercy and usefulness. The two monk-disciples of the Hermit of Mandalay Hill told me that the merit acquired from building a hospital was great, but far greater was that which came from building a pagoda. And this is the common view all over Burma. The Buddha, I repeat, would have been as shocked and grieved at this view of merit as any one : and yet I must point out that there is in the very concept of "acquiring merit"—a concept which the Buddha certainly held—something essentially immoral. It involves the idea—either directly or indirectly—that "merit" is something to be measured quantitatively, that it is a personal possession which may be acquired and stored up and weighed and handed about. This notion of it is carried to its extreme in the orthodox Buddhist doctrine of *reversible merit.* That one may acquire merit and hand it over to some one else who has done nothing to gain it, though obviously inconsistent with the spirit of Gautama's teaching, is not only common belief, among the laity and monks alike, but is good orthodox doctrine which may be defended by quoting chapter and verse from the Pitakas—as the learned and enthusiastic Buddhist, Mr. F.L. Woodward, has done in the "Buddhist Review" for January, 1914.

But even aside from this almost materialistic extension of "merit", the emphasis which one finds so repeatedly in Buddhist writings and Buddhist thought upon acquiring merit presents exactly the wrong view of a good act, focusing the attention necessarily on the reward that one is to get out of it. Self-forgetfulness on this plan is impossible; and the Buddhist—or the Christian—who has not yet learned that virtue must be its own reward, if it is to be virtue, is bound to be merely a more or less prudent egoist.

Of course the man who clings to the pure Buddhism of the Four Noble Truths, so far as he thinks of "acquiring merit" at all, means by it the growth of a good and desirable character; and he would be one of the last to attribute any real value to external performances of any sort. "Neither the study of holy books," said the Buddha, "nor sacrifices to the gods, nor sleeping on the ground, nor difficult and strenuous vigils, nor the repetition of prayers can bring purification to the man enmeshed in delusion. Neither gifts to the priests, nor self-castigation, nor the performance of rites and ceremonies can work purification to him who is filled with craving." The true Brahmin—the man, that is, really worthy of reverence—is not one born in a particular caste or one who performs certain particular rites; but the man who has conquered himself and who gladly follows the great Law. "Not by matted locks, nor by lineage, nor by caste is one a Brahmin : he is the Brahmin in whom are truth and righteousness, and purity. What boots your tangled hair, O fool, what avails your garment of skins? You have adorned the outer parts, within you are full of uncleanliness. Not him do I call a Brahmin who is merely born of a Brahmin mother;

men may give him salutation as a Brahmin, though he be not detached from the world : but him I call a Brahmin who has attachment to nothing. Him I call a Brahmin, indeed, who has cut all fetters, who never trembles, is independent and unshackled. Him I call a Brahmin, indeed, who, though he has committed no offense, endures reproach, bonds and stripes, who has endurance for his force, and strength for his army."[12]

It is the inner side of the act alone, the intention of the will, that counts. Few moralists have ever laid more stress on the inwardness of true morality than did Gautama. And this inevitably : for the whole of his own peculiar teaching is a psychical matter. His one aim is psychological—the proper training of the mind. Hence all external acts are simply irrelevant. Hence also no one—whether god, man, or devil—can really help or harm another. In the life of self-culture all external appeal is simply silly. The Buddha's point of view is well summarized in his last words to his disciples : "Work out your own salvation with diligence."

The great moral ideal of the Buddhism founded upon the Four Noble Truths is self-mastery. "If one man conquer in battle a thousand men", says the Dhammapada, "and if another conquer himself, he is the greatest of conquerors. One's own self conquered is better than the conquest of all other people; not even a god, a demi-god, not Mara with Brahman himself, could change into defeat the victory of a man who has vanquished himself, and always lives under restraint." And the Buddha, with his keen psychological insight, saw that self-conquest and self-control meant primarily the control of the mind, the mastery of one's thoughts. The first verse of the Dhammapada reads : "All that we are is the result of what we have thought; it is founded on our thoughts, it is made up of our thoughts. If a man speaks or acts with an evil thought, pain follows him, as the wheel follows the foot of the ox that draws the carriage. 'He abused me, he beat me, he defeated me'—in those who harbour such thoughts hatred will never cease. For hatred does not cease by hatred at any time : hatred ceases by love; this is an old rule. He who lives without looking for pleasures, his senses well controlled, moderate in his food, faithful and strong, him the Temper will certainly not over throw, any more than the wind throws down a rocky mountain." "This mind of mine went formerly wandering about as it liked; but I shall now control it thoroughly, as the rider who holds the hook controls the furious elephant. Be not careless! Watch your thoughts! Draw yourself out of the evil way, as an elephant does who is sunk in mud."[13]

The morality of self-control and self-culture has never been carried further than by this aspect of Buddhism. Yet it is a limited kind of morality; and those critics who insist that Buddhist ethics are purely negative have in mind these ethical teachings that spring from the Four Noble Truths. For, as we have seen in the preceding chapter, the strictly logical consequences of this pure but narrow Buddhist doctrine are essentially egoistic. The one virtue that it really gives birth to is prudence. Wherever it exists unmingled with the genuinely altruistic feeling which I have called the third element in the Buddha's teaching, it results in a type of character which is ever looking out for number one, with a coldly calculating rationality which knows to a hair the cash value to self of every seemingly unselfish act. Buddhism has few apologists so enthusiastically sympathetic as Paul Dahlke; who writes as follows : "That cordiality which forgets itself for other, that affection which breeds tenderness and emotion, is entirely wanting here. The whole moral scheme in Buddhism is nothing but a sum in arithmetic set down by a cold, clear egoism; as much as I give to others, so much will come again to me. Karma is the most exact arithmetician in the world."[14]

The man whose morality is described in this sentence of Dahlke's is not likely to be capable of much enthusiastic devotion to a great cause. The Buddhist monk is usually "harmless"; ahimsa, harmlessness, in fact, is one of his great virtues. But it would not be wise to good to the monasteries in search of a hero. There is something about the Buddhist's fear of sorrow that seems to the Western mind unaccountable, if not downright pathological. Is, then, sorrow such a dreadful thing? Is there nothing else so bad?

The extreme individualism of that kind of Buddhism which is founded on the Four Noble Truths, and which is represented in the quotation above from Dahlke, makes social and cooperative work among the Buddhists almost impossible. The missionaries, at any rate, of both Burma and Ceylon will tell you that the Buddhists of their acquaintance seem to be almost incapable of cooperation with each other in any common charitable work and that very few care to try. Charitable they are, extremely so at times, but only as isolated individuals. This fact, if it be a fact, as I suppose it is, would at any rate follow naturally from the individualism of the Four Noble Truths. Each man's great task is to cultivate his own character, to pile up merit for himself, to cut all ties (social as well as sinful), and to get out of this evil world into Nirvāṇa as soon as may be. The Buddhist ideals are all individualistic; there is no place in Buddhism for an endeavour to make this world a better place to lie in, to build up a new social order, to bring about the Kingdom of Heaven. There is an article in the "Buddhist Review" for July, 1910, which is interesting in this connection. It is entitled "Buddhism and Social Problems", and the author Madame Alexandar David, an enthusiastic Buddhist, does her best to show that Buddhism is not out of line with the modern ideals of social helpfulness. The best that she can say for her religion is that it might make war upon ignorance and that Gautama's own spirit of love and helpfulness is what the sad world needs. It is noticeable that she says nothing of the Four Noble Truths; and as I have so often pointed out, Gautama's altruistic spirit points directly away from the individualism which they inculcate.

But the spirit of Gautama forms after all the dominant note in Buddhist ethics. The universal love and good-will toward all sentient creatures which so filled his teachings and his life have been carried by Buddhism to the ends of the earth and characterize this religion, to some extent at least, wherever it is found. Thanks to this Buddhist ethics, on the whole, is decidedly positive rather than negative. It will vary, of course, as embodied in different individuals according to the predominance in each of what I have called the first, second, or third elements. In an individual whose Buddhism consists merely of the Four Noble Truths, combined with various Indian beliefs and superstitions, we shall find temperance, prudence, purity, long-suffering, meekness, charity, but all of them cultivated in a coldly calculating spirit with an eye on the main chance. On the other hand, wherever the loving spirit of the Buddha forms an important constituent in a man's morality we shall have a result worthy of genuine respect. And whenever this spirit is combined with the self mastery, the philosophical attitude of mind, the poise and self-reliance, the superiority over material things and worldly pleasures, the independence from fortune and the courageous outlook upon the future which come from the acceptance of the Four Noble Truths and the training they inculcate, we have a type of character which for strength and genuine nobility one will seldom find equalled.

The great springs of power for the moral life which Buddhism furnishes are, then (1) the belief in Karma and retribution; (2) clear understanding of the sources of sorrow and the ideal of the Great Peace; and (3) the altruistic teachings of the founder, and most of all the inspiration that comes from his example. It is from this letters especially that the finest flowers of Buddhist morality have sprung. Its influence is probably most obvious among the members of the new reform movement; but one meets with it also among much more simple and less learned men. The first Buddhist with whom I became acquainted in Ceylon gave me a new insight into the manner in which the spirit of Gautama might permeate many a common follower of his, and express itself in all his words and actions. The reader may not be uninterested in a short account of this man as I knew him.

It was in the Temple of the Tooth at Kandy that I made my first acquaintance in this land "where every prospect pleases and only man is vile." The temple was throned by thousands of worshipers,—for it was the evening of the full moon;—and the monks at every shrine were busy heaping up the white jasmine flowers at the feet of the Buddha and tending the hundreds of tiny flickering candles which the pilgrims had brought in token of their devotion to the Blessed One. We had seen most of the usual sights and had reached that part of the temple known as the "Great Eastern Library", where I was busy endeavoring to make an appointment with one of the monks for an interview two days later. The monk spoke only a little English, and as I was trying to make him understand me, a young Ceylonese, who had considerable command over our language, came to my assistance and helped me to make the appointment. It was evident that an interpreter would be useful at the interview, and the young man said that if he could arrange to be in town at the time he would like to help us; though he feared this would be impossible, as he was off next day for Matale (his home) to worship at the shrine there, and could hardly return for several days. He added, however, that if I wished it, he would give up his trip to Matale, and stay to act as my interpreter at the interview. Of course, I assured him that this was not necessary, and that I could doubtless find some one else. So after he had answered some questions of mine on Buddhism, and had warned me against giving to the professional beggars in the temple, he left me asking, however, that he might call at my hotel on the following Monday.

The next day the mail brought me this note : —

Sir,

I have the pleasure to inform you that I am unable to prevent my going to Matale, I who accompanied you last night to the Great Eastern Library. I hope will kindly postpone the talk with the monk concerning Buddhism till Monday. May "Triple Gem" keep sell and lady sound and healthy. I will be coming on Monday to meet you at your hotel. I will try my best to show you and lady even something about Buddhism. I remain, sir,

Yours faithfully,

V.P.H.

A few minutes later a telegram was brought me, which also was from him and to the same effect as the note. When Monday came he arrived, true to his promise, and we had our talk about his religion. He was, he told me, a upasaka, or a layman who has taken upon himself certain additional vows and duties. I asked him to tell me more in detail about them. Besides enumerating the various vows which I have mentioned in the previous chapter, he said the first duty of the upasaka was to wish well to every one,—never to think of any one without earnestly desiring for him the best things. His next duty is helpfulness to all who are in need. "If I come upon a man", he said , "who needs money, I must give it him : if I have no money I must give him my coat." The eight vows which the upasaka takes he must keep not only in the letter but in the spirit. Thus when I asked my new friend why he had both written and telegraphed to let me know that he had both written and telegraphed to let me know that he could not keep an appointment which had never been definite or really binding, he said, "Oh, that was the Fourth Precept—not to lie."

On the day following our talk, much to my surprise, my new-found friend reappeared and offered to take me to several places of interest in Kandy. "Yesterday", he said, "I came by appointment; today I come as upasaka—to help you." We spent the day visiting various monasteries and temples and talking with the monks; and on the day following he took my wife and me out to Matale to show us the famous Alut Vihara; or monastery. Matale, as I have said, was his home, and I discovered that he was a teacher of English and religion in a boys' school there, and that he had been granted two weeks' leave—which he was spending, evidently," as upasaka." The Alut Vihara is perched on a rock in the midst of the jungle. You approach it from the highway by a narrow path and after climbing a long flight of steps, you come upon the monastery gateway, in a cleft between two enormous boulders. To your left is a rock-cut temple, with a large reclining Buddha, carved many centuries age; father up is the cave in which Buddhaghosa, the famous Buddhist commentator and missionary, is said to have lived and copied out the scriptures which he had brought from India, for distribution through out Ceylon; and on the top of the highest rock, commanding a wonderful outlook over palm-grove, jungle, and mountain range, is a sacred dagoba, shining white against the sky.

It was interesting to watch my friend's bearing as we approached the monastery, and to see his reverence—of both attitude and expression—whenever we entered a shrine. "Here is our Lord Buddha," he would say in hushed tones as he prostrated himself on the ground before the image. And whenever a monk appeared, or even a little novice of ten years wearing the yellow robe; he would prostrate himself again.

Of the future of Buddhism he was quietly confident. It was, he told me, slowly and steadily growing. And when I asked him among whom it was making its converts, he answered very simply: "Among the Tamils and the Germans." Evidently the zeal of German Pali scholars is appreciated in Ceylon. But his conversation was ever returning to the intrinsic glories of his religion and to the thought of Nirvāṇa. This (in quite unorthodox fashion) he described as "eternal comfort," real and conscious joy; and he was always busy telling us of the way thither. He never said in so many words that he desired to convert us, but it was plain that this was his wish. "When you are gone from here," he said, "I will pray for you every day to the Lord Buddha and to the devatas. I will pray that you should be safe and happy; but most of all that you should come here again and stay a long time and learn more about Lord Buddha and his way to Nirvāṇa!"[15] And at another time, quite without self-consciousness or any touch of pride, he said, "Of course, if I could bring my brother to Nirvāṇa by going to hell myself, I should want to do so."

Of Christianity he knew practically nothing. The missionaries, he said, were very good people, and one of them had very recently lent him three books which he meant soon to read two chapters in one of them. He believed

Christianity was probably a very good religion. "But," he added, "I feel very sure there is no religion like that of Lord Buddha: for it leads us to Nirvāṇa."

I told him that I found many fine things in Buddhism, but that I considered the attitude of those monks who live apart from the world to save their own extremely selfish. "Yes," he said, "it *is* selfish. And not all the monks do it, though some do. But it is not the true Buddhism; it is not what the Lord Buddha did. The true Buddhist wants to help everybody, and so be like the Blessed One."

To this Buddhist, at any rate, kindness was not a matter of preaching only, but a real part of life. It beamed from his face and was unmistakable in his smile and showed itself in innumerable little acts. He never called on me without bringing some little gift for my "lady,"—a cocoanut, perhaps, or some such simple thing. When we were on our way to visit a monastery, he would stop on the road and buy some pan leaf and betel nut and fruit for the monks. And he never saw a really needy beggar in the street (and in Ceylon there are many beggars in the streets) without giving him something. In the last talk I had with him, just before we parted in the Matale railway station, he took from his pocket what was evidently a treasures, carefully unwrapped the protection paper and showed it to us. It was a small thin sheet of brass, in the form of a pipal leaf, and on it was roughly etched a seated Buddha. "This," he said, "keeps me safe from evil spirits. Two thousand Pali verses have been said over this by the monks. It is very precious and I always carry it with me. It keeps me safe." I examined the talisman closely, and when he saw my interest he hesitated some moments, apparently in thought, and then said, "If you would like this, you may keep it."

Although he had served me for several days as guide

and interpreter, he would not take anything from me payment; and the only thing he asked was that I should give him a general letter of introduction to strangers in Kandy notifying them that he would like opportunity of showing them about the city and its environs without any remuneration.

When he had seen us into our compartment for Kandy and said his last good-byes, he put his hands together and said, quite simply: "may Lord Buddha keep you! May devata keep you!"—and disappeared. In two hours more we had reached Kandy and our hotel, and a few minutes later I received a telegram. It was from our friend, and it read, " May lady and self travel healthily." It was his way of saying Bon voyage!

This was my first acquaintance in Ceylom. My last was no less interesting and no less filled with the spirit of the Buddha. He is one of the leaders of the Maha-Bodhi movement and he gives up his entire time to spreading the reform. The only reward he looks for or cares for in this life or in the other is just the doing of his duty. In our last talk together, the evening before I sailed back for Europe, we were discussing Parinirvāṇa, and when I asked him if he desired it for himself, he said: "As a fact I do not. What I should like best would be an endless succession of lives in this world so that I might use them all in helping other people."

These are examples of individuals; but, as almost all those who know the Burmese will testify, the influence of Buddhism over a whole people as a people, both for morality and for happiness, is very considerable. Its influence, of course, is not all for the good, and it has its weaknesses and its does work a certain gentleness of spirit and add a subtle charm to life which are not to be mistaken, and which are manifest not only in the individual but in the community as well. To see this at its purest one should go not to the large centers but to some isolated village on the upper reaches of the Irrawaddy, far removed from European influence, and try with sympathetic mind to inhale the spirit of the people and of their religion. It is here that one finds the actual Buddhism of the twentieth century in its living form among the lowly.

Whenever I turn my thoughts back toward the East and try to focus them upon Buddhism, the first picture that comes to my mind's eye is one of these Irrawaddy village—any one of a considerable number that the traveler passes on the Irrawaddy steamer. A crowd of quiet men, women, and children is waiting for us at the landing as the steamer turns in toward the shore, noses upstream, and makes fast. Most of the village has come down to see the big boat land, greet returning travelers, and speed those who are departing, or to carry on board the day's catch of fish or the day's product of sun-baked and hand-modeled pottery. The returning passengers walk over the gangplank and join the throng on the shore—women with babies strapped to their backs, pretty girls in their best silks, young men in equally brilliant and tasteful colors, two Buddhist monks in their yellow and orange robes—all spotlessly clean and, to all appearances, quietly and calmly happy. In mysterious fashion some scent of eternal youth seems to cling to the garments of these Burmese of the villages—even to the garments of the old men and women. Their perpetual outdoor life, their sweet neighborly relationships, the endless sunshine, and, shall we add, also the dignity and calm of their religion, have got reflected in their natures like the blue sky in the bosom of the Irrawaddy, so that the stranger, at any rate, fancies he finds in them a simplicity and serenity that make all ages of life quiet yet youthful, and that are all too rare in our hustling West, which is at so young and so very old.

The crowd is now dispersing—the little children for

their beds, the men and women to their homes, or to some shrine, the monks to their monasteries and their devotions, If you follow the through and climb the ridge above the river where the village stands, you will find first of all a group of pagodas and rest-houses, some new and many old, each with its image of the Buddha, There are more than a dozen, altogether, and the oldest ones—tokens of the piety of some long-gone generation—are now lapsing into quite ruin, the little inner chamber in which the Buddha sits filled with a wild growth of fern up to his feet, as though Nature, too, were eager to pay its reverence to him who was the Light of Asia. In the larger shrines you will find a few old women kneeling on the matting; each holding a rose or a cosmos blossom or lotus in her clasped hands, with a rosary wound round one of her fingers, as she whispers her evening prayer and alternately touches her head to the floor and then gazes upward at the calm face of the great Buddha. There are one or two men present also, and if you wait a family party may come in, father and mother and two or three small children, or a group of young men and maidens. Their gentle laughter and soft voices cease as they enter the shrine, and all knell, and holding flowers in their hands murmur their prayers, No priest or preacher here, no mediator, no spiritual authority, no cringing fear, no blood to be shed or money to be offered—just one individual soul and another reaching out toward the Determiner of Destiny in the way taught them by the words of the prayers they utter. But there can be no doubt that without understanding the words they often understand the prayers, No one who watches them can fail to see that the spirit of prayer is present—the out pouring of their hearts need, the spirit of thankfulness and of aspiration toward the great ideal of purity and peace of which the alabaster image before its prototype. Fresh flowers in a dozen vases line the lotus at its feet, and little candles, lighted by fervent worshipers, mingle with the last rays of day in the darkening shrine, just as the prayers and the praises asend to him who has long since entered into Nirvāṇa, The calm of the Buddha's face is not broken: in the Eternal Peace he notes neither worship nor neglect. One by one the worshipers depart, the sunlight dies, the flowers wilt, the candles go out. But in the darkness as well as in the light the Eternal Peace broods over the head of the great Buddha.

A scene like this makes one ask one's self how he would feel if we succeeded in converting "heathen" Burmese, broke their "idols," tore down all their shrines, and built on the high ridge where the pagodas had been a Baptist church and a Methodist church. And this question I put in all seriousness. What would be the gains and what the losses? First of all, there would be a loss in picturesqueness, certainly—and this would be a great loss to the tourist—and consequently a loss to the Irrawaddy Flotilla Company, Limited. Yet one may question whether the christianized Burmese would lose all his picturesqueness. He need not change his costume for our dull colors merely because he changes his creed. Nor need he necessarily choose as the type of his ecclesiastical architecture the brick-and-mortar edifices of our Middle West. Certainly one who doubts whether Christianity is consistent with picturesqueness of architecture and landscape has failed to travel in Italy or the Tyrol—or for that matter in England, or even New England. And, after all, is not our great concern for the picturesque a trifle selfish? Should we not ask, first, What would be the result of Christianity upon the Burmese themselves?

The answer to this question will depend wholly upon the type of Christianity proposed. I can imagine a converted Burmese village with a Baptist church at one end, a Methodist at the other, and a Presbyterian and Roman Catholic in the middle, each aspiring after the highest steeple and the biggest bell, each rent with theological controversies, casting out heretics, and predicting eternal damnation to all but themselves, each putting a premium on artificial emotion and holding experience meetings for the production of hypocritical confessions and pious cant. Or, I can picture the village street lined with fat priests who should sow superstitious fears among their converts by means of which they would extort endless contributions for masses, candles, and indulgences. And I can think that the last state of such a village would be worse than the first;—and that in spite of their acceptance of "Salvation by Faith" or of the "Blessed Trinity", they would be better off by a return to the quiet and simple adoration of him who taught the Great Peace and showed the way to it. But I can also conceive of a Burmese village in which the Buddha might still be honored and loved, but which had caught some of the spirit of a still greater Teacher, whose message was more simple than the Buddha's, whose insight into the secrets of the spirit was certainly no less deep, whose example was no less inspiring and who also taught the Great Peace and pointed out to it, as I believe, a more excellent way.

REFERENCES

1. Anguttara Nikaya, quoted in Subhadra's *Buddhist Catechism.*
2. From the Digha Nikaya, quoted on page 71 of the *Buddhist Catechism.* One should add, however, that the Buddhist books are full of miraculous happenings and picture the Buddha as believing himself and his followers to be in possession of marvelous powers.
3. *The Maha Bodhi and United Buddhist World,* for February, 1914.
4. Psychology has an unusually important place in the theory of Buddhism and permeates a large part of its literature. In some Buddhist psychology there is a good deal of insight into the life of the mind. Perhaps its chief interest for the Western psychologist is to be found in its classifications and divisions of mental phenomena, so strikingly different from our own. Buddhist psychology is very

technical, and great importance is given to exact terminology; a Buddhist psychologist will usually refuse to discuss psychological questions with you at all unless you adopt his terms and categories. But in spite of their careful distinctions Buddhists never seem able to distinguish sharply between psychology, metaphysics, and ethics, the two latter being usually mixed up in all their treatments of mental phenomena. The reader will find a good deal of psychology in nearly all their sacred books and in the treatises of their scholars. A handy little work on the subject is Mrs. Rhys-Davids's *Buddhist Psychology* (London, Bell & Sons, 1914).

5. *Op.cit.*, pp. 44-45.
6. Colonel Olcott's *Buddhist Catechism.*
7. Quoted by Dudley Wright in the *Buddhist Review* for April, 1912 (p. 122).
8. Dhammapada, 93-96.
9. Buddhism is thoroughly opposed to war. For a scholarly discussion of its position and its influence on war see "Buddhism and War", by W.L. Hare, in the *Buddhist Review* for January-March, 1915. (pp. 4-17).
10. *Ibid.*, 197-201, 205.
11. Edward Rowland Sill.
12. Dhammapada, 393-99.
13. Dhammapada, 1, 3, 5, 8, 326, 327
14. *Op.cit.*, p. 32
15. In a letter written by my friend some months after we left India (for we still correspond), this same wish for our salvation reappears. He writes : "I will not forget you, gentleman and lady, and that affection will I hope not efface until the last moment, and I pray Sakkiya Muni and meditate to take the said affection till I, we, attain Nirvāṇa, with my soul. I hope according to Buddha's teachings that we might meet to the same place and attain Nirvāṇa—the everlasting comfort. Many a letters reach my hand—more the affection arises in my mind".

BIBLIOGRAPHY

Barth, A., The Religions of India, translated by Wood, J., London, 1882.

——, Inscriptions sanscrites du Cambodge, Paris, 1885.

Beal, Samuel, A Catena of Buddhist Scriptures from the Chinese, London, 1871.

——, Romantic Legend of Sakya Buddha, London, 1875.

——, The Buddhist Tripiṭaka as it is known in China and Japan, London, 1876.

Bigandet, P., The Life or Legend of Gautama the Buddha of the Burmese, London, 1880.

Bühler, G., Aphorismson the Sacred Law of the Hindus, Bombay, 1868, 1871.

Burgess, Jas, Archaeological Survey.

Burnouf, E., Introduction a l'histoire du Buddhisme indien, Paris, 1844.

——, Let lotus de la bonne Loi, traduit du Sanscrit, Paris, 1852.

Childers, R.C., A Dictionary of the Pāli Language, London, 1872-1875.

Colebrooke, H.T., Essays on the Religion and Philosophy of the Hindus, London, 1858.

Cowell, E.B., (ed.), The Buddha Carita of Aśvaghoṣa, Oxford, 1893.

——, (ed.), Divyavadāna, Cambridge, 1886.

Cunningham, A., Archaeological Survey of India (A Report).

D'ol Denburg, S., Extracts from the Bhadrakalpāvadāna, Zapiski, 1894.

Feer, L., Avadāna-Śataka, cent légendes (bouddhiques) traduties du sanscrit par, Annals Mus. Cuimet XVIII, Paris, 1891.

——, (ed.), Saṃyutta-Nilkāya, London, 1884.

Fergusson, History of Indian and Eastern Architecture, London, 1876.

Frankfurter, O., Handbook of Pāli, London, 1883.

Gooneratne, E.R., (ed.), Dhātukathā Prakaraṇa and its Commentary, London, 1892.

——, (ed.), Vimāna-Vatthu, London, 1886.

Hardy, Spence, A Manual of Buddhism, London, 1860.

——, The Legends and Theories of Buddhists,London, 1866.

Hodgson, Essays on the Languages, Literature and Religion of Nepāl and Tibet. London, 1874.

Jaeschkes, H.A., A Tibetan-English Dictionary, London, 1881.

Jīvānanda Vidyāsāgara, Pātañjala-darśanam Calcutta, 1874.

Koeppen, C.F., Die Religion des Buddha und ihre Entstehung, und die Lamaishe Hierarchie und Kirch, Berlin, 1857.

Kṣemendra, Avadāna-Kalpalatā, ed. Bibl. Ind. Calcutta.

Lassen, C., Indische Alterterthumuskunde, Binn, 1847.

Legge, J., A Record of Biddhis Kingdoms; being an Account by the Chinese monk Fā-Hien of his Travels in India and Ceylon (A.D. 399-414), Oxford, 1886.

Max Müller, F., Dharma-Saṃgraha, prepared for publication by Kenjiu Kasawara, Oxford, 1885.

——, (ed.), Dhamma-Saṅgaṇi, London, 1885.

——, (ed.), Ancient Inscriptions in Ceylon, London, 1883.

——, India what can it teach us, London, 1883.

——, (ed.), Paramattha Dīpanī, Part V. Commentary on the Therīgāthā, London, 1893.

——, (ed.), Sacred Book of the East (translated by various Oriental scholars), Oxford.

Minayef, J., (ed.), Kathāvatthu-ppakaraṇa-Aṭṭhakathā, JPTS, 1889.

Morris, R., (ed.), Aṅguttara-Nikāya I-IV, London, 1885-1888.

——, (ed.), Buddhavaṃsa, London, 1882.

——, (ed.), Cariyā-Piṭaka, London, 1882.

Nademale Saddhamanda, (ed.), Saddamma-Saṃgaha, London, 1890.

Oldenberg, H., (ed.), Dīpavaṁsa, London, 1879.

——, Buddha, His Life, His Doctrine, His Order; Translated from the German, London, 1888.

——, (ed.), Sutta-Vibhaṅga, (Vinaya Piṭaka III, IV), London, 1881-82.

Rhys Davids, T.W., Buddhism; Being a Sketch of the Life and Teachings of Gautama, the Buddha, London, 1878.

Rockhill, W.W., The Life of the Buddha and the Early History of his Order, London, 1884.

Schiefner, A., Tāranātha's Gesehichte des Buddhismus in indien, aus dem Tibetischen übersetzt von, St. Petersberg, 1869.

Smither, J.G., Architectural Remains, Anurādhapura, Ceylon.

Trenckner, V., (ed.), Majjhima-Nikāya, London, 1887.

——, (ed.), Milinda-Pañho, London, 1880.

Stenzler, A.F., (ed.), Yājñavalkya-Dharmaśāstram, Berlin, 1849.

Vidyānanda Vidyāsāgara, (ed.), Manu-Saṃhitā with the Commentary of Kullūka, Calcutta, 1874.

Waddell, L.A., The Buddhism of Tibetan Lamaism, London, 1895.

Windisch, E., Māra und Buddha, Leipzig, 1895.

Wright, D., A History of Nepāl, Cambridge, 1877.

Journals

Journal of the Asiatic Society of Bengal.

Journal of the Bombay Branch of the Royal Asiatic Society.

Journal of the Pali Text Society.

Journal of the Royal Asiatic Society of Great Britain and Ireland